THE RECORD COLLECTOR'S INTERNATIONAL DIRECTORY

The RECORD COLLECTOR'S INTERNATIONAL DIRECTORY

by Gary S. Felton

CROWN PUBLISHERS, INC.

NEW YORK

Inquiries should be addressed to Crown Publishers, Inc., One Park Avenue, New York, New York 10016

Printed in the United States of America

Published simultaneously in Canada by General Publishing Company Limited

Library of Congress Cataloging in Publication Data
Felton, Gary S.
    The record collector's international directory.
    Includes Index.
    1. Sound recordings—Collectors and collecting—
Directories. I. Title.
ML12.F44   338.4'7789912'025   79-27163
ISBN: 0-517-540010 (cloth)
0-517-540029 (paper)

10 9 8 7 6 5 4 3 2 1
First Edition

This book is dedicated to the millions of record
collectors everywhere in the hope that their searches
may be made easier.

CONTENTS

PART I
RECORD DEALERS—COMPLETE INFORMATION

PART II
RECORD DEALERS—ADDITIONAL NAMES AND ADDRESSES ONLY

PART III
PUBLICATIONS OF SPECIAL INTEREST

INDEXES

ACKNOWLEDGMENTS

I wish to especially thank my wife, Lynn, and my children, Colin and Megan, for all of their patience, which has made it much easier for me to run in and out of record stores throughout the world. I also wish to thank the hundreds of record dealers who contributed to the contents of this book and about whose services this writing speaks.

Contents

PREFACE

It has long been held true (courtesy of William Wycherley) that necessity is the mother of invention. Lately I have been reflecting on this time-tested maxim because it reflects the origins of this book. As an avid collector of records for more than twenty-five years I generally searched in my own local territory for records I wanted. Then, as I began to explore the domains of British folk and jazz music and Brazilian music, and as my demands for rare records grew, my difficulties began. I realized that I had run out of record stores and dealers and that those I had been frequenting had reached the limits of their own local and distant resources. Magazine auctions and direct sales as well as private dealers' listings were fine, but I wanted to be able to go anywhere in the world and find that certain record I was seeking.

At that point it occurred to me that other collectors like me might appreciate a comprehensive directory of the names, addresses, et cetera of dealers and stores throughout the English-speaking world, carrying such pressings. A volume of this sort could allow the active record-collecting enthusiast immediate access to all such outlets, and let the collector know exactly where to go for what, whether by mail order, telephone, or personal contact. And thus began the work of compiling this book.

INTRODUCTION

The material in this book is derived from several origins. One major source has been the standard commercial yellow pages of the telephone directories (both urban and suburban) of the nation's 160 largest cities. This figure represents cities of population 100,000 or greater. I have read each listing under "Records—Retail" (or comparable headings) in each of these directories and have extracted the names of outlets which refer to their records as "rare," "deleted," "discontinued," "hard-to-find," "out-of-print," "old," "hard-to-get," "oldies," "cut-out," "scarce," "hard-to-obtain," or "oldies-but-goodies." In the same manner, I have researched the telephone directories of the largest cities (even if the population is less than 100,000) in other English-speaking countries such as Australia, Canada, England, Ireland, New Zealand, Scotland, and Wales.

A second major source of names has been individual record dealers, fellow collectors, record promoters, record collectors' clubs and publications, and distributors or wholesalers throughout the world. A third major source of information has been the advertising and classified sections of the record and music industries' trade publications and commercial publications, as well as various popular music and record magazines, record dealers' auction and set-sale listings, and journals.

Careful tallying from these resources yielded more than 1,206 major record outlets that feature or specialize in rare records. In each case, a three-page questionnaire was forwarded to the dealer for completion. If people did not respond to the first mailing, a questionnaire was sent again two months later. Every effort has been made, through personal visiting and/or personal interview, to ensure the legitimacy and accuracy of the inclusions in this first edition of the book. I have painstakingly tried to eliminate the names of dealers who really do not stock rare records or who are shoddy. That is one reason why only 521 of the original 1,206 dealers' names appear here in complete form. In this regard, should you ever experience difficulty of any sort with a dealer whose name is listed here, or if you believe that any dealer listed here is misrepresenting him/herself, I invite you to write me so that I can eliminate difficulties for future readers of this book.

Since the record business is so large, and different kinds of rare records are available, I have organized the book according to information received from dealers, by dividing the rare-record outlets into two major kinds.

First are record dealers who carry true "rare" records. Although such pressings may be known as rare, deleted, cut-out, discontinued, et cetera records, I have lumped them all into the category called rare records. These records, whether 33⅓, 45, or 78 records or Edison discs, may be anywhere from one to over eighty years old and may range in value from $2.25 to $5,000. They may vary from limited edition Toscanini to early Bee Gees. Their rarity is defined by original number produced, current availability, and by collectors' demand, as well as pricing and exchange value. They are the truly rare records. Dealers in such records, to be referred to as Category I dealers, maintain sizable stock of these rare records and continually add to existing volume.

I have attempted to differentiate the above collectors' havens from other record outlets that carry a large stock within which may be nestled small amounts of recent cut-out or discontinued pressings. The latter dealerships, to be referred to as Category II dealers, are certainly of no small value to the record collector; they just happen to have rare records in limited quantities and most often carry only more recent recordings.

Thus, each dealer's name will be followed by a designation of *I* or *II,* to aid you in your reading.

This book does *not* focus on dealers who carry ordinary used records, in the sense that the records have been owned previously and have been traded in. Although many record dealers throughout the world maintain such stock, they are not the domain of this book unless they are rare-record dealerships that coincidentally carry used records.

As a convenience, the main contents of the book are presented geographically (and alphabetically) by, and then within, states of the United States, and geographically (and alphabetically) by, and then within, foreign countries. For further convenience, the indexes include a section listing dealers by the categories of recording they carry and a section alphabetically listing every dealer in the book.

Most dealers listed are open for walk-in and for mail-order business, as a retail store outlet. In some cases, dealers are exclusively a mail-order service open by appointment only, and in other cases dealers do not provide mail-order service. For both walk-in and mail-order services, relevant information has been given to aid the record hunter. Where only mail-order service is available, additional information may be obtained through direct correspondence or telephone contact with the specific dealer. With regard to inquiries you may wish to make by mail, it is always a good idea to enclose a self-addressed stamped envelope with your correspondence, since most dealers prefer or require it if you want a reply. It is also always better to contact dealers first before sending anything.

A few outlets exist that in addition to selling records, serve as record libraries or lending services. The term "record library" refers to a service whereby you may have a tape made of a record in the library. In these cases, usually records are not available directly for purchase, since they must remain in the library. Lending libraries do occasionally appear and here you can usually arrange for the borrowing of one or more of their records. In dealing with either a record library or lending service, it is wise to clarify their function before going there.

A number of dealers provide ancillary services. For example, many outlets maintain what is called a "search service." Here, you send the dealer the name of the record you seek or your "want" list, and an active search for the record(s) is made. Other outlets maintain your want list and, although no active search is undertaken, they will notify you when your requested record comes across the counter. In either case, when the dealer is able to obtain one or more of your requests, you are notified immediately of the finding, and then can make arrangements to obtain it. Information about the availability of this service is provided with each listing in this book.

A second service available through many dealers is the publishing of a direct-sale catalog or auction list of available records, usually including cost or minimum bid, as well as graded condition of the record and record jacket, and postage charges. The continuation of this service is sometimes irregular, so information about catalog availability has been included in this book for those dealers who indicated that they regularly maintain and provide such publications. Many dealers advertise regularly in major record magazines and do not publish separate catalogs and/or auction lists. In any direct mail correspondence with other dealers it is usually to your advantage to inquire about such material. There is generally either a nominal charge or no charge for such printings, particularly auction lists.

In most cases, dealers gave an approximation of the number of records stocked in each size. Sometimes the information given was a percent of the total volume of *rare* records carried rather than actual numbers of records. Occasionally, dealers indicated that they had no idea as to the number of records in stock. In the latter case, and where information was not provided by the dealer, the letters I.N.A. (Information Not Available) have been used.

Part II of this book is a listing of nearly five hundred names of dealers who are either *known* to be rare-record carriers or who are strongly *believed* to be rare-record carriers. For varying reasons, these people did not return a completed questionnaire.

One final word. When visiting rare-record dealers, always inquire about additional records. Many such dealers have only a fraction of their stock visible.

Any effort or undertaking of this size can be expected to be incomplete. Although I have taken all care in producing as comprehensive a listing here as possible, some rare-record dealers' names will be missing. Where this has happened, it is either because I had no way of knowing of the dealer's existence or because the dealer chose not to be included. To those of you who are dealers to whom this applies, I extend an invitation to include yourself in the next edition of this book. If, as a reader, you find rare-record dealers whom you know are missing, I invite your correspondence also, so that all known dealers may eventually be included. As with any other correspondence, information regarding inclusion in the book can be obtained by writing me in care of the publisher: Crown Publishers, Inc., One Park Avenue, New York, New York 10016.

PART I

**RECORD
DEALERS**

COMPLETE INFORMATION

HOW TO USE THIS DIRECTORY

Here is an example of a record dealer's entry with an item by item breakdown as to what each part of the entry means.

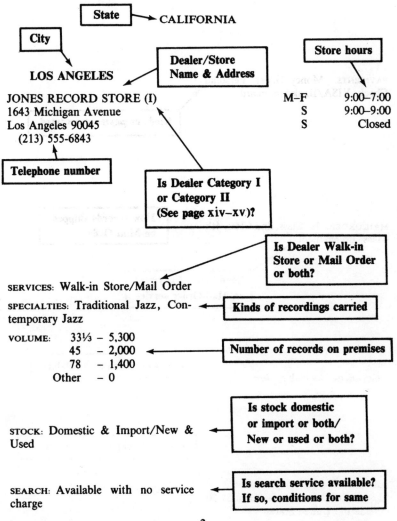

State → CALIFORNIA

City

LOS ANGELES

Dealer/Store Name & Address

Store hours

JONES RECORD STORE (I)
1643 Michigan Avenue
Los Angeles 90045
  (213) 555-6843

M–F   9:00–7:00
S   9:00–9:00
S   Closed

Telephone number

Is Dealer Category I or Category II (See page xiv–xv)?

Is Dealer Walk-in Store or Mail Order or both?

SERVICES: Walk-in Store/Mail Order

SPECIALTIES: Traditional Jazz, Contemporary Jazz

Kinds of recordings carried

VOLUME: 33⅓ – 5,300
          45 – 2,000
          78 – 1,400
   Other – 0

Number of records on premises

STOCK: Domestic & Import/New & Used

Is stock domestic or import or both/ New or used or both?

SEARCH: Available with no service charge

Is search service available? If so, conditions for same

3

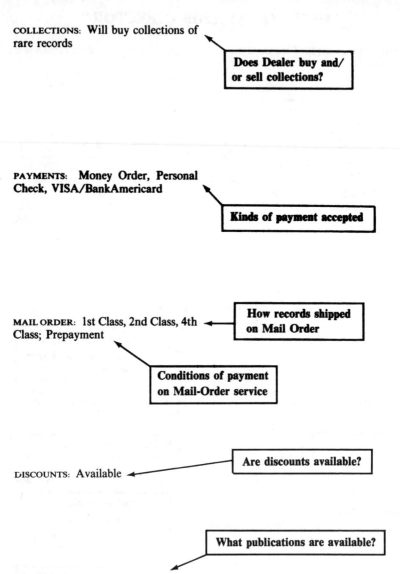

COLLECTIONS: Will buy collections of rare records

Does Dealer buy and/ or sell collections?

PAYMENTS: Money Order, Personal Check, VISA/BankAmericard

Kinds of payment accepted

MAIL ORDER: 1st Class, 2nd Class, 4th Class; Prepayment

How records shipped on Mail Order

Conditions of payment on Mail-Order service

DISCOUNTS: Available

Are discounts available?

What publications are available?

PUBLICATIONS: Catalog available at $1.00 in the United States and at $1.50 outside the United States

NAME AND ADDRESS

This information is just what it indicates. In a few instances you may notice two different names of dealers with the same address. This information has been verified as correct in each case. Some dealers actually have two different businesses operating out of the same location.

TELEPHONE

In several instances dealers requested that their phone number not be published. Such requests are to be interpreted merely as indicating that that particular dealer prefers direct mail contact and not that there is anything questionable about the legitimacy of the dealer.

BUSINESS HOURS

This section generally indicates when the dealer is open for walk-in business. Sometimes, however, it is necessary to arrange for an appointment during these specified hours. This is particularly true for mail-order-only dealers who allow customers to view their stock. When an appointment is necessary, such information will be provided in the "services" section.

SERVICES

Three different designations are used in this section, namely walk-in store, mail order, and library. Walk-in store generally refers to a retail, commercial business, although it also applies in some cases to private dealers who do business out of their residence. In the latter case, usually it is wise to contact the dealer first and make an appointment. Some dealers are listed as walk-in store but show only a post office box number as their address. This situation always means call for an appointment. Also, even with dealers listed as mail order only, it is often possible to make appointments for a visit.

Library means that the dealer has a library of records that are available for reproducing on tape. In one or two cases, such libraries are set up on a lending basis.

SPECIALTIES

Generally the listings in this section are rated and rank-ordered by each dealer as to the top ten categories/specialties carried by that dealer. In some instances, dealers did not rank the categories in the questionnaire sent so they have been listed alphabetically. Where such listings are alphabetical, it is possible, therefore, that the last-listed specialty for a given dealer is in fact that dealer's number-one specialty. In some cases where dealers did not specify categories by rank order and either checked twenty or thirty categories or every category, the designation "all major categories" has been used. One thing to keep in mind is that although many dealers ranked only their top ten specialties, they in fact have many more categories of recordings available in their stock and indeed might just have what you seek.

VOLUME

In each case, the numbers given are the dealers' report of actual volume of rare records/discs available in stock. Occasionally a percentage is given. This figure is the percent of rare records in stock and not the percent of total volume of all records. Thus, if a dealer's entry reads 33⅓–85%, 45–15%, 78–0%, that means that 85% of that dealer's stock of rare records is 33⅓. Extended-play records are included under the designation 45 r.p.m. The "other" designation is used for Edison cylinders/discs, for picture discs, for colored vinyl/wax records, and for transcriptions.

STOCK

Two bits of information are included in this section, namely origin of records carried (domestic and/or import) and general types of records carried (new and/or used). Domestic always refers to records that are produced and manufactured in the same country as the location of the dealer. Import always refers to records that are produced and manufactured outside the country of the dealer's location.

The term "new" means that records are sealed or are unsealed and guaranteed unplayed. "Used" means unsealed and played. Obviously, some used copies may only have been played one time and thus, except for the purist, can be considered to be new. Such records are still listed here as "used."

SEARCH

Dealers were asked to report whether they do or do not provide an active search service and if so, whether there is a service charge for same. Additionally, they were asked if they maintain requests for records or want lists and subsequently notify the sender if the sought-after record(s) become available across the counter. This section reports such information.

COLLECTIONS

In this section, dealers reported whether they do or do not purchase rare record collections and whether they do or do not sell collections of rare records.

PAYMENTS

Other than the obvious that all dealers will accept cash, this section spells out what forms of payment the dealer will accept. Listings here are alphabetical and do not show preference. On international orders it is usually best, unless arranged otherwise, to stick with international money orders, international postal money orders, bank drafts, or international (postal) reply coupons, all of which are guaranteed exchangeable internationally. Payments should always be made only after direct arrangements have been made with specific dealers. It is never advisable to send payment prior to such arrangements. It should be noted that the designation Master Charge is in the process of being changed to Master Card.

MAIL ORDER

This section includes two bits of information. First is listed the available choices of mail order, i.e., 1st class, 4th class, air mail. Following this information is indicated whether the dealer prefers prepayment only or either prepayment or C.O.D. on an order. With mail-order arrangements it is usually best to inquire if you are at all uncertain about how records will be shipped to you or if you want special handling of some kind. Most dealers are familiar with overseas mailing, so there are usually no problems with this, but always state what form of mail you want, just to be sure. Insurance arrangements and possibilities are sometimes difficult from or to certain countries, so rather than provide information in this book that does not apply universally, such information about insurance arrangements has been left out. If you wish packages to be insured you need to state it, since many dealers only insure when requested to do so. In addition, check when sending to, or ordering from, countries outside your own, since some countries will not insure air-mail delivery, for example. Generally, nobody ships C.O.D. overseas.

DISCOUNTS

This section is a straightforward yes or no to whether discounts are available. In some cases the discount may actually be there in the price quoted and in other cases discounts are given only on volume purchases or to dealers/wholesalers only. It is usually best to inquire about discounts if you are uncertain.

PUBLICATIONS

Listed in this section you will find information about any relevant publications, primarily in the form of catalogs, auction lists, or trade lists. If there are charges, such information has been provided. If the publications are free, that information has been provided. Increasingly, dealers are asking a small charge for publications, so it probably is wise, when requesting that you be put on mailing lists, to include in your correspondence a stamped, self-addressed envelope to facilitate and speed up replies, just in case the publications you want are no longer sent free.

MISSING INFORMATION

In any section where the dealer did not provide information, the letters I.N.A. (Information Not Available) have been used.

AMERICAN RECORD DEALERS
ALABAMA

BIRMINGHAM

KING BEE RECORDS (I)
1472 Tomahawk Road
Birmingham 35214
  (205) 798-0609 or 674-7007

M–S   10:00–6:00

SERVICES: Walk-in Store/Mail Order

SPECIALTIES: All Major Categories

VOLUME: 33⅓ – 1,500
           45 – 15,000
           78 – 500
           Other – 0

STOCK: Domestic & Import/New & Used

SEARCH: Want lists maintained and requester notified when record comes in

COLLECTIONS: Will buy collections of rare records

PAYMENTS: Money Order, Personal Check

MAIL ORDER: 4th Class; Prepayment

DISCOUNTS: Available

PUBLICATIONS I.N.A.

BIRMINGHAM

RECORD STATION (I)
2320 Stonewood Drive
Birmingham 35215
  (205) 854-4699

SERVICES: Mail Order Only

SPECIALTIES: Rock & Roll, Rhythm & Blues, Rock, Rockabilly, Promotional, Country & Western, Nostalgia, Novelty, Beatles, Elvis

VOLUME: 33⅓ – 1,000
           45 – 25,000
           78 – 300
           Other – 0

STOCK: Domestic/New & Used

SEARCH: Want lists maintained and requester notified when record comes in

COLLECTIONS: Will buy collections of rare records

PAYMENTS: Money Order, Personal Check

MAIL ORDER: 4th Class, Whatever shipment method requested; Prepayment

DISCOUNTS: Available

PUBLICATIONS: Free semiannual auction list

9

ARIZONA

FLAGSTAFF

CIRCLES (I)   M–S 10:00 A.M.–mid.
1515 South Milton Road
Flagstaff 86001
 (602) 779-4101

SERVICES: Walk-in Store/Mail Order

SPECIALTIES: All Major Categories

VOLUME: 33⅓ – 1,500
             45   – 0
             78   – 0
            Other – 0

STOCK: Domestic & Import/New &
Used

SEARCH: Available with no service
charge; Want lists maintained and requester notified when record comes in

COLLECTIONS: Will buy collections of
rare records

PAYMENTS: Master Charge, Personal
Check, VISA/BankAmericard

MAIL ORDER: 4th Class; Prepayment

DISCOUNTS: Available

PUBLICATIONS: I.N.A.

PHOENIX

CIRCLES (I)   M–S 10:00 A.M.–mid.
800 North Central Avenue
Phoenix 85004
 (602) 254-4765

SERVICES: Walk-in Store/Mail Order

SPECIALTIES: All Major Categories

VOLUME: 33⅓ – 3,000
             45   – 0
             78   – 0
            Other – 0

STOCK: Domestic & Import/New

SEARCH: Available with no service
charge

COLLECTIONS: Will buy collections of
rare records

PAYMENTS: Master Charge, Personal
Check, VISA/BankAmericard

MAIL ORDER: 4th Class; Prepayment

DISCOUNTS: Available

PUBLICATIONS: I.N.A.

PHOENIX

WORLD RECORDS, INCORPORATED (II)
1632 East Camelback Road
Phoenix 85016
  (602) 277-2659

M–S 9:00 A.M.–mid.
S   Noon–mid.

SERVICES: Walk-in Store/Occasional Mail Order

SPECIALTIES: All Major Categories

VOLUME: 33⅓ – 100%
           45 – 0
           78 – 0
      Other – 0

STOCK: Domestic & Import/New & Used

SEARCH: Available (occasionally) with no service charge

COLLECTIONS: Will buy collections of rare records

PAYMENTS: Master Charge, Personal Check, VISA/BankAmericard

MAIL ORDER: 4th Class; Prepayment or C.O.D.

DISCOUNTS: Not available

PUBLICATIONS: I.N.A.

PRESCOTT

RECORD DIGEST (I)
Groom Creek Route
Prescott 86301
  (602) 445-7015

SERVICES: Mail Order Only

SPECIALTIES: (Alphabetical) Blues, Country & Western, Easy Listening, Rhythm & Blues, Rock, Rock & Roll

VOLUME: 33⅓ – 45%
           45 – 45%
           78 – 10%
      Other – 0

STOCK: Domestic & Import/New & Used

SEARCH: Not available

COLLECTIONS: I.N.A.

PAYMENTS: Master Charge, Money Order, Personal Charge Account, Personal Check, VISA/Bankamericard

MAIL ORDER: Air Mail, 1st Class, 3rd Class, 4th Class, U.P.S.; Prepayment or C.O.D.

DISCOUNTS: Available

PUBLICATIONS: I.N.A.

SCOTTSDALE

WORLD RECORDS, INCORPORATED (II)
1402 North Scottsdale Road
Scottsdale 85257
(602) 946-6584

M–S   9:00 A.M.–mid.
S   Noon–mid.

SERVICES: Walk-in Store/Occasional Mail Order

SPECIALTIES: All Major Categories

VOLUME: 33⅓ – 100%
                   45   – 0
                   78   – 0
              Other – 0

STOCK: Domestic & Import/New & Used

SEARCH: Available (occasionally) with no service charge

COLLECTIONS: Will buy collections of rare records

PAYMENTS: Master Charge, Personal Check, VISA/BankAmericard

MAIL ORDER: 4th Class; Prepayment or C.O.D.

DISCOUNTS: Not available

PUBLICATIONS: I.N.A.

TEMPE

TOWER RECORDS (II)
821 Mill Avenue
Tempe 95218
(602) 968-7774

M–S   9:00 A.M.–mid.

SERVICES: Walk-in Store/Mail Order (Limited)

SPECIALTIES: All Major Categories

VOLUME: 33⅓ – 100%
                   45   – 0
                   78   – 0
              Other – 0

STOCK: Domestic & Import/New

SEARCH: Not available

COLLECTIONS: Will not buy collections of rare records

PAYMENTS: Master Charge, Money Order, Personal Charge Account, VISA/BankAmericard

MAIL ORDER: 4th Class, U.P.S.; Prepayment

DISCOUNTS: Available

PUBLICATIONS: Not available

TUCSON

JEFF'S CLASSICAL RECORD SHOPPE (I)   M–S   10:00–9:00
1734 East Speedway Boulevard   S   Closed
Tucson 85719
   (602) 327-0555

SERVICES: Walk-in Store/Mail Order

SPECIALTIES: Classical, Opera, Film Scores, Broadway Shows, Nostalgia, Sound Tracks, Television Shows, Comedy, British Musical Shows, Children's

VOLUME: 33⅓ – 2,000
             45 – 250
             78 – 2,000
          Other – 0

STOCK: Domestic & Import/New & Used

SEARCH: Available with no service charge; Want lists maintained and requester notified when record comes in

COLLECTIONS: Available for purchase; Will buy collections of rare records

PAYMENTS: Master Charge, Money Order, Personal Charge Account, Personal Check, VISA/BankAmericard

MAIL ORDER: U.P.S.; Prepayment or C.O.D.

DISCOUNTS: Available

PUBLICATIONS: Free bimonthly auction list

TUCSON

MAD DADDY RECORDS (I)
373 North Wilmot
Suite 901
Tucson 85711
   (602) 745-5609

SERVICES: Mail Order Only

SPECIALTIES: Rock & Roll, Country & Western, Rhythm & Blues, Nostalgia, Children's, Novelty, Old-time Country, Blues, Comedy, Rock

VOLUME: 33⅓ – 3,000
             45 – 50,000
             78 – 0
          Other – 0

STOCK: Domestic/New & Used

SEARCH: Want lists maintained and requester notified when record comes in ($5.00 deposit)

COLLECTIONS: Will buy collections of rare records

PAYMENTS: Master Charge, Money Order, Personal Check, VISA/BankAmericard

MAIL ORDER: U.P.S.; Prepayment

DISCOUNTS: Not available

PUBLICATIONS: Quarterly auction list available for $1.00

14 AMERICAN RECORD DEALERS

TUCSON

MAD HATTER BOOKS AND RECORDS (II)
1904 East Broadway
Tucson 85719
(602) 623-0171

M–F	10:00–7:00
S	10:00–6:00
S	Closed

SERVICES: Walk-in Store/Mail Order
SPECIALTIES: All Major Categories

VOLUME: 33⅓ – 500
45 – 0
78 – 0
Other – 0

STOCK: Domestic & Import/New & Used

SEARCH: Want lists maintained and requester notified when record comes in

COLLECTIONS: Will buy collections of rare records

PAYMENTS: Money Order, Personal Check

MAIL ORDER: Air Mail, 4th Class; Prepayment

DISCOUNTS: Available

PUBLICATIONS: I.N.A.

TUCSON

MODERN TIMES BOOKS AND RECORDS (II)
920 East Speedway
Tucson 85719
(602) 623-6511

M–F	10:00–7:30
S	10:00–6:00
S	Closed

SERVICES: Walk-in Store/Mail Order
SPECIALTIES: (Alphabetical) Bluegrass, Blues, Contemporary Jazz, Ethnic, Hillbilly, Religious, Rhythm & Blues, Traditional Jazz

VOLUME: 33⅓ – 100
45 – 150
78 – 0
Other – 0

STOCK: Domestic & Import/New & Used

SEARCH: Available with no service charge

COLLECTIONS: Will buy collections of rare records

PAYMENTS: Master Charge, Money Order, Personal Check, VISA/BankAmericard

MAIL ORDER: Air Mail, U.P.S.; Prepayment

DISCOUNTS: Available

PUBLICATIONS I.N.A.

ARKANSAS

EL DORADO

CRAIG RECORDING (I)   M–F   9:00–5:00
P.O. Box 943   S–S   Closed
700 West Main
El Dorado 71730
  (501) 862-5480

SERVICES: Walk-in Store/Mail Order   SEARCH: I.N.A.

SPECIALTIES: Big Band, Bop Jazz,   COLLECTIONS: Will buy collections of
Dixieland, Traditional Jazz, Sinatra, rare records
Rhythm & Blues
                                      PAYMENTS: Personal Check
VOLUME: 33⅓ – 98%
           45 – 2%   MAIL ORDER: 4th Class; Prepayment
           78 – 0   DISCOUNTS: Not available
           Other – 0
                                      PUBLICATIONS: Free quarterly cata-
STOCK: Domestic & Import/New &   log; Free quarterly auction list
Used

CALIFORNIA

ANAHEIM

BEGGAR'S BANQUET RECORDS (I)   M–S   11:00–7:00
1215 South Beach Boulevard
Anaheim 92804
  (714) 761-4712

SERVICES: Walk-in Store Only   SEARCH: Available with no service
                                      charge; Want lists maintained and re-
SPECIALTIES: Rock, Rock & Roll,   quester notified when record comes in
Punk Rock/New Wave, Rhythm &
Blues, Beatles, Blues, Surfing, Sound COLLECTIONS: Will buy collections of
Tracks, Soul, Comedy   rare records

VOLUME: 33⅓ – 400   PAYMENTS: Money Order, Personal
           45 – 1,500   Check
           78 – 0
           Other – 0   MAIL ORDER: Not available

STOCK: Domestic & Import/New &   DISCOUNTS: Available
Used   PUBLICATIONS: Not available

ANAHEIM

TOWER RECORDS (II)   M–S   9:00 A.M.–mid.
306 North Beach Boulevard
Anaheim 92801
(714) 995-6600

SERVICES: Walk-in Store/Mail Order   COLLECTIONS: Will not buy collec-
(Limited)   tions of rare records

SPECIALTIES: All Major Categories   PAYMENTS: Master Charge, Money
                                            Order, Personal Charge Account,
VOLUME: 33⅓ – 100%   VISA/BankAmericard
              45   – 0
              78   – 0   MAIL ORDER: 4th Class, U.P.S.; Pre-
            Other – 0   payment

STOCK: Domestic & Import/New   DISCOUNTS: Available

SEARCH: Not available   PUBLICATIONS: Not available

BALDWIN PARK

MR. WEB RARE RECORDS (I)   M–S   10:00–6:00
14527 Garvey   S   Noon–6:00
Baldwin Park 91706
(213) 338-4444

SERVICES: Walk-in Store/Mail Order   SEARCH: Available with no service
                                            charge
SPECIALTIES: (Alphabetical)   Broad-
way Shows, Classical, Comedy, Easy   COLLECTIONS: Available for purchase
Listening, Film Scores, Opera, Sound   PAYMENTS: Master Charge, Personal
Tracks, Television Shows   Check, VISA/BankAmericard

VOLUME: 33⅓ – 10,000   MAIL ORDER: U.P.S.; Whatever ship-
              45   – 0   ment method requested; Prepayment
              78   – 0
            Other – 0   DISCOUNTS: Not available

STOCK: Domestic & Import/New &   PUBLICATIONS: Not available
Used

BERKELEY

RATHER RIPPED RECORDS (I)   M–S   Noon–9:00
1878 Euclid
Berkeley 94709
   (415) 848-6493

SERVICES: Walk-in Store

SPECIALTIES: Rock & Roll, Space/
Meditation/Electronic, Folk, Rhythm
& Blues, Rockabilly, Blues, Easy Lis-
tening, Vocal, Soul, Sound Tracks

VOLUME: 33⅓ – 20,000
            45 – 3,500
            78 – 0
            Other – 0

STOCK: Domestic & Import/New &
Used

SEARCH: See following entry

COLLECTIONS: Available for purchase;
Will buy collections of rare records

PAYMENTS: Master Charge, Money
Order, Personal Check, VISA/Bank-
Americard

MAIL ORDER: Air Mail, 4th Class,
U.P.S.; Prepayment

DISCOUNTS: Available

PUBLICATIONS: Free bimonthly catalog; Free periodic set-sale list

BERKELEY

RATHER RIPPED RECORDS SEARCH   M–F   9:00–6:00
SERVICE (I)   S–S   Closed
1878 Euclid
Berkeley 94709
   (415) 848-6493

SERVICES: Mail Order

SPECIALTIES: Rock & Roll, Space/
Meditation/Electronic, Folk, Rhythm
& Blues, Rockabilly, Blues, Easy Lis-
tening, Vocal, Soul, Sound Tracks

VOLUME: 33⅓ – 20,000
            45 – 3,500
            78 – 0
            Other – 0

STOCK: Domestic & Import/New &
Used

SEARCH: Primary business is search
service

COLLECTIONS: Available for purchase;
Will buy collections of rare records

PAYMENTS: Master Charge, Money
Order, Personal Check, VISA/Bank-
Americard

MAIL ORDER: Air Mail, 4th Class,
U.P.S.; Prepayment

DISCOUNTS: Available

PUBLICATIONS: Free bimonthly catalog; Free periodic set-sale list

BERKELEY

TOWER RECORDS (II)   M–S   9:00 A.M.–mid.
2510 Durant Street
Berkeley 94704
  (415) 841-0101 or 0250

SERVICES: Walk-in Store/Mail Order   COLLECTIONS: Will not buy collec-
(Limited)   tions of rare records

SPECIALTIES: All Major Categories   PAYMENTS: Master Charge, Money
VOLUME: 33⅓ – 100%   Order, Personal Charge Account,
             45 – 0   VISA/BankAmericard
             78 – 0   MAIL ORDER: 4th Class, U.P.S.; Pre-
           Other – 0   payment

STOCK: Domestic & Import/New   DISCOUNTS: Available

SEARCH: Not available   PUBLICATIONS: Not available

BEVERLY HILLS

THEODORE FRONT MUSICAL LITERATURE   M–S   9:00–6:00
  (II)   S   Closed
155 North San Vicente Boulevard
Beverly Hills 90211
  (213) 658-8770

SERVICES: Walk-in Store/Mail Order   PAYMENTS: Master Charge, Money
                                         Order, Personal Check, VISA/Bank-
SPECIALTIES: Classical, Opera   Americard
VOLUME: 33⅓ – I.N.A.   MAIL ORDER: Air Mail, U.P.S.; Pre-
             45 – I.N.A.   payment
             78 – I.N.A.
           Other – I.N.A.   DISCOUNTS: Not available

STOCK: Domestic & Import/New   PUBLICATIONS: I.N.A.

SEARCH: Not available

COLLECTIONS: Will not buy collections of rare records

BURBANK

DISCONTINUED RECORDS (I)
444 South Victory Boulevard
Burbank 91502
(213) 846-9192 or 849-4791

M–F 9:30–6:00
S–S Closed

SERVICES: Walk-in Store/Mail Order/ Library

SPECIALTIES: All Categories Except Classical

VOLUME: 33⅓ – 500,000
45 – 500,000
78 – 0
Other – 0

STOCK: Domestic & Import/New & Used

SEARCH: Not available

COLLECTIONS: Will buy collections of rare records

PAYMENTS: Money Order, Personal Charge Account, Personal Check

MAIL ORDER: Air Mail, 1st Class, 4th Class; Prepayment

DISCOUNTS: Not available

PUBLICATIONS: Not available

CAMPBELL

TOWER RECORDS (II)
1900 South Bascom Avenue
Campbell 95008
(408) 371-5400 or 377-6441

M–S 9:00 A.M.–mid.

SERVICES: Walk-in Store/Mail Order (Limited)

SPECIALTIES: All Major Categories

VOLUME: 33⅓ – 100%
45 – 0
78 – 0
Other – 0

STOCK Domestic & Import/New

SEARCH: Not available

COLLECTIONS: Will not buy collections of rare records

PAYMENTS: Master Charge, Money Order, Personal Charge Account, VISA/BankAmericard

MAIL ORDER: 4th Class, U.P.S.; Prepayment

DISCOUNTS: Available

PUBLICATIONS: Not available

CARSON

NEWMANS PHOTO AND SOUND (II)	M–T	9:30–6:00
172 East Carson Street	F	9:30–7:00
Carson 90744	S	10:00–5:30
(213) 830-5958	S	Closed

SERVICES: Walk-in Store/Mail Order

SPECIALTIES: (Alphabetical) Country & Western, Disco, Easy Listening, Folk, Rhythm & Blues, Rock, Rock & Roll

VOLUME:
    33⅓ – 5,000
    45 – 9,000
    78 – 0
    Other – 0

STOCK: Domestic/New

SEARCH: Available with service charge

COLLECTIONS: Will not buy collections of rare records

PAYMENTS: Master Charge, Money Order, Personal Check, VISA/Bank-Americard

MAIL ORDER: U.P.S.; Prepayment

DISCOUNTS: Available

PUBLICATIONS: I.N.A.

CHICO

TOWER RECORDS (II)	M–S 9:00 A.M.–mid.
215 Main Street	
Chico 95926	
(916) 345-8582 or 2114	

SERVICES: Walk-in Store/Mail Order (Limited)

SPECIALTIES: All Major Categories

VOLUME:
    33⅓ – 100%
    45 – 0
    78 – 0
    Other – 0

STOCK: Domestic & Import/New

SEARCH: Not available

COLLECTIONS: Will not buy collections of rare records

PAYMENTS: Master Charge, Money Order, Personal Charge Account, VISA/BankAmericard

MAIL ORDER: 4th Class, U.P.S.; Prepayment

DISCOUNTS: Available

PUBLICATIONS: Not available

CITRUS HEIGHTS

TOWER RECORDS (II)
5419 Sunrise Boulevard
Citrus Heights 95610
  (916) 961-7171 or 7446

M–S   9:00 A.M.–mid.

SERVICES: Walk-in Store/Mail Order (Limited)

SPECIALTIES: All Major Categories

VOLUME: 33⅓ – 100%
          45   – 0
          78   – 0
      Other – 0

STOCK: Domestic & Import/New

SEARCH: Not available

COLLECTIONS: Will not buy collections of rare records

PAYMENTS: Master Charge, Money Order, Personal Charge Account, VISA/BankAmericard

MAIL ORDER: 4th Class, U.P.S.; Prepayment

DISCOUNTS: Available

PUBLICATIONS: Not available

CLAREMONT

RHINO RECORDS (I)
225 Yale Avenue
Claremont 91711
  (714) 626-7774

M   Closed
T–S   11:00–6:00
S   Closed

SERVICES: Walk-in Store Only

SPECIALTIES: All Major Categories

VOLUME: 33⅓ – 99%
          45   – 1%
          78   – 0
      Other – 0

STOCK: Domestic & Import/New & Used

SEARCH: Not available

COLLECTIONS: Will not buy collections of rare records

PAYMENTS: Master Charge, Money Order, Personal Check, VISA/BankAmericard

MAIL ORDER: Not available

DISCOUNTS: Not available

PUBLICATIONS: I.N.A.

CONCORD

BOB BERTRAM STUDIOS (I)
1069–D Shary Circle
Concord 94518
(415) 689-7371

SERVICES: Mail Order Only

SPECIALTIES: (Alphabetical) Blues, Classical, Country & Western, Easy Listening, Ethnic, Folk, Folk-Rock, Religious, Rhythm & Blues, Rock, Rock & Roll, Soul

VOLUME:　33⅓ – 1,200
　　　　　45　– 36,000
　　　　　78　– 1,200
　　　　Other　– 0

STOCK: Domestic/New & Used

SEARCH: Want lists maintained and requester notified when record comes in

COLLECTIONS: Will buy collections of rare records

PAYMENTS: Money Order, Personal Check

MAIL ORDER: 1st Class; Prepayment or C.O.D.

DISCOUNTS: Available

PUBLICATIONS: I.N.A.

CONCORD

RIP LAY RECORDS (I)
P.O. Box 342
Concord 94522
(415) 676-1650

M–S　　11:00–6:00
S　　　　　Closed

SERVICES: Mail Order Only (Above Times for Telephone)

SPECIALTIES: Rock & Roll, Rhythm & Blues, Blues, Rock, Surfing, Soul, Instrumental, Country & Western, Elvis, Punk Rock/New Wave

VOLUME:　33⅓ – I.N.A.
　　　　　45　– I.N.A.
　　　　　78　– I.N.A.
　　　　Other　– I.N.A.

STOCK: Domestic & Import/New & Used

SEARCH: Want lists maintained and requester notified when record comes in

COLLECTIONS: Will buy collections of rare records

PAYMENTS: Money Order, Personal Check

MAIL ORDER: 4th Class, Whatever shipment method requested; Prepayment or C.O.D.

DISCOUNTS: Not available

PUBLICATIONS: Periodic set-sale catalog at $3.00 per issue

CONCORD

TOWER RECORDS (II)   M–S   9:00 A.M.–mid.
1280 # E Willow Pass Road
Concord 94520
   (415) 827-2900

SERVICES: Walk-in Store/Mail Order   COLLECTIONS: Will not buy collec-
(Limited)   tions of rare records

SPECIALTIES: All Major Categories   PAYMENTS: Master Charge, Money
                                      Order, Personal Charge Account,
VOLUME: 33⅓ – 100%   VISA/BankAmericard
          45 – 0
          78 – 0   MAIL ORDER: 4th Class, U.P.S.; Pre-
       Other – 0   payment

STOCK: Domestic & Import/New   DISCOUNTS: Available

SEARCH: Not available   PUBLICATIONS: Not available

COSTA MESA

RTS/MUSIC GAZETTE (I)   M–T   Noon–4:00
P.O. Box 687   W   Closed
Costa Mesa 92627   T–F   Noon–4:00
   (714) 631-3023   S–S   Closed

SERVICES: Walk-in Store (By Ap-   PAYMENTS: Master Charge, Money
pointment)/Mail Order   Order, Personal Check, VISA/Bank-
                                      Americard
SPECIALTIES: Sound Tracks, Broad-
way Shows, Nostalgia, British Musical MAIL ORDER: 4th Class, Whatever
Shows, Film Scores   shipment method requested; Prepay-
                                      ment
VOLUME: 33⅓ – 300,000
          45 – 1,000   DISCOUNTS: Not available
          78 – 200
       Other – 0   PUBLICATIONS: Monthly catalog
                                      available for $6.00 per year; Monthly
STOCK: Domestic & Import/New &   auction list available for $6.00 per
Used   year; Monthly newsletter available for
                                      $9.00 per year
SEARCH: Available with no service
charge

COLLECTIONS: Will buy collections of
rare records

DOWNEY

WENZEL'S MUSIC TOWN (I)
13117 Lakewood Boulevard
Downey 90242
(213) 634-2928

M	10:00–6:00
T	Closed
W–S	10:00–6:00
S	Noon–5:00

SERVICES: Walk-in Store/Limited Mail Order

SPECIALTIES: Rock & Roll, Country & Western, Elvis, Rhythm & Blues, Instrumental, Beatles, Comedy, Surfing, Sound Tracks, Rockabilly

VOLUME: 33⅓ – 800
            45   – 75,000
            78   – 300
            Other – 0

STOCK: Domestic/New & Used

SEARCH: Not available

COLLECTIONS: Will buy collections of rare records

PAYMENTS: Master Charge, Money Order, Personal Check, VISA/BankAmericard

MAIL ORDER: 4th Class, Whatever shipment method requested; Prepayment

DISCOUNTS: Available

PUBLICATIONS: Free biannual catalog

EL CAJON

BLUE MEANNIE RECORDS,
   INCORPORATED (I)
1207 North 2nd Street
El Cajon 92021
(714) 442-2212

M–F	11:00–9:00
S	10:00–6:00
S	Noon–6:00

SERVICES: Walk-in Store/Mail Order

SPECIALTIES: Beatles, Rock & Roll, Rock, Punk Rock/New Wave, Elvis

VOLUME: 33⅓ – 6,000
            45   – 15,000
            78   – 0
            Other – 0

STOCK: Domestic & Import/New & Used

SEARCH: Want lists maintained and requester notified when record comes in

COLLECTIONS: Will buy collections of rare records

PAYMENTS: Master Charge, Money Order, Personal Check, VISA/BankAmericard

MAIL ORDER: Air Mail, 4th Class, Whatever shipment method requested; Prepayment

DISCOUNTS: I.N.A.

PUBLICATIONS: Free bimonthly catalog; Free bimonthly auction list

EL CAJON

TOWER RECORDS (II)   M–S   9:00 A.M.–mid.
796 Fletcher Parkway
El Cajon 92020
(714) 579-9701

SERVICES: Walk-in Store/Mail Order   COLLECTIONS: Will not buy collec-
(Limited)   tions of rare records

SPECIALTIES: All Major Categories   PAYMENTS: Master Charge, Money
VOLUME: 33⅓ – 100%   Order, Personal Charge Account,
           45 – 0   VISA/BankAmericard
           78 – 0   MAIL ORDER: 4th Class, U.P.S.; Pre-
        Other – 0   payment
STOCK: Domestic & Import/New   DISCOUNTS: Available
SEARCH: Not available   PUBLICATIONS: Not available

EL CERRITO

DOWN HOME MUSIC, INCORPORATED (I)   M–T   Closed
10341 San Pablo Avenue   W–S   Noon–7:00
El Cerrito 94530
(415) 525-1494

SERVICES: Walk-in Store/Mail Order   COLLECTIONS: Will buy collections of
                                      rare records
SPECIALTIES: Blues, Rockabilly, Blue-
grass, British Folk, Folk, Old-Time   PAYMENTS: Master Charge, Money
Country, Traditional Jazz, French   Order, Personal Check, VISA/Bank-
Folk, Cajun, Country & Western, Eth- Americard
nic, Hillbilly   MAIL ORDER: Air Mail, 4th Class,
VOLUME: 33⅓ – 20,000   U.P.S.; Prepayment or C.O.D.
           45 – 500   DISCOUNTS: Not available
           78 – 0
        Other – 0   PUBLICATIONS: Periodic catalog avail-
                                      able at $1.00; Free bimonthly newslet-
STOCK: Domestic & Import/New &   ter
Used
SEARCH: Not available

EL TORO

TOWER RECORDS (II)   M–S   9:00 A.M.–mid.
23811 El Toro Road
El Toro 92630
  (714) 770-6242 or 6316

SERVICES: Walk-in Store/Mail Order   COLLECTIONS: Will not buy collec-
(Limited)   tions of rare records

SPECIALTIES: All Major Categories   PAYMENTS: Master Charge, Money
VOLUME: 33⅓ – 100%   Order, Personal Charge Account,
             45 – 0   VISA/BankAmericard
             78 – 0   MAIL ORDER: 4th Class, U.P.S.; Pre-
          Other – 0   payment

STOCK: Domestic & Import/New   DISCOUNTS: Available

SEARCH: Not available   PUBLICATIONS: Not available

FRESNO

TOWER RECORDS (II)   M–S   9:00 A.M.–mid.
5301 North Blackstone Avenue
Fresno 93701
  (209) 431-4700 or 5722

SERVICES: Walk-in Store/Mail Order   COLLECTIONS: Will not buy collec-
(Limited)   tions of rare records

SPECIALTIES: All Major Categories   PAYMENTS: Master Charge, Money
VOLUME: 33⅓ – 100%   Order, Personal Charge Account,
             45 – 0   VISA/BankAmericard
             78 – 0   MAIL ORDER: 4th Class, U.P.S.; Pre-
          Other – 0   payment

STOCK: Domestic & Import/New   DISCOUNTS: Available

SEARCH: Not available   PUBLICATIONS: Not available

FULLERTON

RECORD RACK (I)
729 North Harbor Boulevard
Fullerton 92632
(714) 871-3724

M–S	10:00–5:30
S	1:00–5:00

SERVICES: Walk-in Store/Mail Order

SPECIALTIES: All Major Categories

VOLUME:
33⅓	–	35,000
45	–	100
78	–	1,000
Other	–	0

STOCK: Domestic & Import/New & Used

SEARCH: Available with no service charge; Want lists maintained and requester notified when record comes in

COLLECTIONS: Will buy collections of rare records

PAYMENTS: Master Charge, Personal Check, VISA/BankAmericard

MAIL ORDER: Air Mail, 4th Class; Prepayment or C.O.D.

DISCOUNTS: Not available

PUBLICATIONS: I.N.A.

GLENDALE

RAY AVERY'S RARE RECORDS (I)
417 West Broadway
Glendale 91209
(213) 245-1101 or 0379

M–T	9:30–8:00
F	9:30–9:00
S	9:30–8:00
S	Noon–6:00

SERVICES: Walk-In Store/Mail Order

SPECIALTIES: Big Band, Traditional Jazz, Bop Jazz, Blues, Broadway Shows, Contemporary Jazz, Film Scores, Nostalgia, Rock, Country & Western

VOLUME:
33⅓	–	15,000
45	–	150,000
78	–	200,000
Other	–	16" Transcriptions—3,000

STOCK: Domestic & Import/New & Used

SEARCH: Want lists maintained and requester notified when record comes in

COLLECTIONS: Will buy collections of rare records

PAYMENTS: Master Charge, Money Order, Personal Check, VISA/Bank-Americard

MAIL ORDER: 4th Class, U.P.S.; Prepayment

DISCOUNTS: Available

PUBLICATIONS: Free quarterly catalog; Free quarterly auction list

GOLETA

RECORDS INTERNATIONAL (I)　　　　M–F　　10:00–6:00
P.O. Box 1140　　　　　　　　　　　　　S–S　　　　Closed
Goleta 93017
　(805) 687-0327

SERVICES: Walk-in Store (By Appointment & Wholesale Only)/Mail Order

SPECIALTIES: Symphonic, Chamber, Instrumental, Opera

VOLUME:　　33⅓ – 6,000
　　　　　　45　– 0
　　　　　　78　– 0
　　　　Other　– 0

STOCK: Domestic & Import/New

SEARCH: Available with no service charge

COLLECTIONS: I.N.A.

PAYMENTS: Money Order, Personal Check

MAIL ORDER: Air Mail, 4th Class, U.P.S.; Prepayment

DISCOUNTS: Not available

PUBLICATIONS: Free monthly catalog

GRANADA HILLS

TEMPO RECORDS (II)　　　　　　　M–T　　11:00–7:00
17643 Chatsworth Street　　　　　　　F　　11:00–9:00
Granada Hills 91344　　　　　　　　　S　　11:00–7:00
　(213) 368-1312　　　　　　　　　　S　　Noon–5:00

SERVICES: Walk-in Store/Mail Order

SPECIALTIES: (Alphabetical) Blues, Classical, Contemporary Jazz, Country & Western, Easy Listening, Ethnic, Folk, Rock, Rock & Roll, Soul

VOLUME:　　33⅓ – 10,000
　　　　　　45　– 0
　　　　　　78　– 0
　　　　Other　– 0

STOCK: Domestic & Import/New & Used

SEARCH: Not available; Want lists maintained and requester notified when record comes in

COLLECTIONS: Will buy collections of rare records

PAYMENTS: Master Charge, Money Order, Personal Check, VISA/BankAmericard

MAIL ORDER: 4th Class; Prepayment

DISCOUNTS: Available

PUBLICATIONS: I.N.A.

HAYWARD

FLY'S RECORDS (I)
24036 Hesperian Boulevard
Hayward 94545
(415) 783-4270

M–F	10:00–9:00
S	10:00–6:00
S	Noon–6:00

SERVICES: Walk-in Store/Mail Order

SPECIALTIES: All Major Categories

VOLUME: 33⅓ – 5,000
             45 – 0
             78 – 0
     Other – 0

STOCK: Domestic & Import/New & Used

SEARCH: Available with no service charge; Want lists maintained and requester notified when record comes in

COLLECTIONS: Will buy collections of rare records

PAYMENTS: Money Order, Personal Charge Account, Personal Check

MAIL ORDER: Air Mail, 3rd Class, U.P.S.; Prepayment

DISCOUNTS: Available

PUBLICATIONS: I.N.A.

HOLLYWOOD

PEACHES RECORDS AND TAPES INCORPO-
RATED (II)
6666 Hollywood Boulevard
Hollywood 90028
(213) 466-7276

M–T	10:00–11:00
F–S 10:00 A.M.–1:00 A.M.	
S	Noon–10:00

SERVICES: Walk-in Store Only

SPECIALTIES: All Major Categories

VOLUME: 33⅓ – 1,200
             45 – 0
             78 – 0
     Other – 0

STOCK: Domestic & Import/New

SEARCH: Not available

COLLECTIONS: Will not buy collections of rare records

PAYMENTS: American Express, Master Charge, Personal Check, VISA/BankAmericard

MAIL ORDER: Not available

DISCOUNTS: Available

PUBLICATIONS: I.N.A.

HOLLYWOOD

RECORDS-RECORDS (I)
1019 North Cole Avenue
Unit 6
Hollywood 90038
   (213) 467-7983

M	Closed
T–T	Noon–5:00
F	Noon–7:00
S	Noon–6:00
S	Closed

SERVICES: Walk-in Store/Mail Order

SPECIALTIES: Rock, Rock & Roll, Popular, Vocal, Beatles, Comedy, Novelty, Big Band, Country & Western, Soul, Film Scores

VOLUME: 33⅓ – 25,000
              45 – 45,000
              78 – 200
           Other – 0

STOCK: Domestic & Import/New & Used

SEARCH: Available with service charge; Want lists maintained and requester notified when record comes in

COLLECTIONS: Not available for purchase; Will buy collections of rare records

PAYMENTS: Money Order, Personal Check

MAIL ORDER: Air Mail, 4th Class; Prepayment

DISCOUNTS: Not available

PUBLICATIONS: Free periodic catalog

HOLLYWOOD

SILBURY HILL RECORDS (I)
P.O. Box 2407
Hollywood 90028
   Telephone: I.N.A.

SERVICES: Mail Order Only

SPECIALTIES: Bluegrass, Blues, Ethnic, Folk, Traditional Jazz

VOLUME: 33⅓ – 100%
              45 – 0
              78 – 0
           Other – 0

STOCK: Domestic & Import/New & Used

SEARCH: Available with no service charge; Want lists maintained and requester notified when record comes in

COLLECTIONS: Will not buy collections of rare records

PAYMENTS: Master Charge, Money Order, Personal Check, VISA/BankAmericard

MAIL ORDER: Air Mail, 4th Class, U.P.S.; Prepayment

DISCOUNTS: Not available

PUBLICATIONS: I.N.A.

HOLLYWOOD

THE VINYL VAULT (I)
1456 North McCadden Place
Hollywood 90028
(213) 464-9099

M	Closed
T–F	Noon–7:30
S	Noon–6:00
S	Closed

SERVICES: Walk-in Store/Mail Order

SPECIALTIES: All Major Categories

VOLUME: 33⅓ – 15,000
          45 – 25,000
          78 – 1,500
   Other – 0

STOCK: Domestic & Import/New & Used

SEARCH: Available with no service charge; Want lists maintained and requester notified when record comes in

COLLECTIONS: Will buy collections of rare records

PAYMENTS: Master Charge, Money Order, Personal Check, VISA/Bank-Americard

MAIL ORDER: Air Mail, 4th Class; Prepayment or C.O.D.

DISCOUNTS: Not available

PUBLICATIONS: I.N.A.

ISLA VISTA

MORNINGLORY MUSIC (I)
910–C Embarcadero Del Norte
Isla Vista 93017
(805) 968-4665

M–S	10:00–10:00
S	Noon–8:00

SERVICES: Walk-in Store Only

SPECIALTIES: Classical, Contemporary Jazz, Rock & Roll

VOLUME: 33⅓ – 800
          45 – 0
          78 – 0
   Other – 0

STOCK: Domestic & Import/New & Used

SEARCH: Not available

COLLECTIONS: Will buy collections of rare records

PAYMENTS: Personal Check

MAIL ORDER: Not available

DISCOUNTS: Not available

PUBLICATIONS: I.N.A.

LEUCADIA

ROUNDSOUND WEST (I)
P.O. Box 2248
Leucadia 92024
 (714) 436-3131

SERVICES: Mail Order Only

SPECIALTIES: Most Major Categories

VOLUME: 33⅓ – 40,000
            45 – 1,000
            78 – 500
            Other – 0

STOCK: Domestic & Import/New & Used

SEARCH: Available with no service charge; Want lists maintained and requester notified when record comes in

COLLECTIONS: Not available

PAYMENTS: Master Charge, Money Order, Personal Check, VISA/Bank-Americard

MAIL ORDER: 4th Class, Whatever shipment method requested; Prepayment

DISCOUNTS: Not available

PUBLICATIONS: Several catalogs per year available for $2.50 per issue

LOMPOC

POC RECORDS (I)
203 North H Street
Lompoc 93436
 (805) 736-3035

M–F	10:00–9:00
S	10:00–7:00
S	Noon–5:00

SERVICES: Walk-in Store/Mail Order

SPECIALTIES: (Alphabetical) Contemporary Jazz, Disco, Folk-Rock, Reggae, Rock, Rock & Roll, Soul

VOLUME: 33⅓ – 1,000
            45 – 0
            78 – 0
            Other – 0

STOCK: Domestic & Import/New & Used

SEARCH: Available with no service charge; Want lists maintained and requester notified when record comes in

COLLECTIONS: Will buy collections of rare records

PAYMENTS: Personal Check

MAIL ORDER: Air Mail, 4th Class; Prepayment

DISCOUNTS: Available

PUBLICATIONS: Free periodic auction list

LONG BEACH

BAGATELLE RECORDS (I)
140 East 3rd Street
Long Beach 91744
  (213) 432-7534

M	11:00–6:00
T–T	11:00–11:00
F–S	11:00–6:00
S	Closed

SERVICES: Walk-in Store/Mail Order

SPECIALTIES: Rock & Roll, Vocal, Sound Tracks, Traditional Jazz, Easy Listening, Rhythm & Blues, Rockabilly, Surfing, Country & Western, Comedy

VOLUME: 33⅓ – 50,000
           45   – 20,000
           78   – 0
    Other   – 0

STOCK: Domestic/New & Used

SEARCH: Not available

COLLECTIONS: Will buy collections of rare records

PAYMENTS: Money Order, Personal Check (Local)

MAIL ORDER: 4th Class, U.P.S.; Prepayment or C.O.D.

DISCOUNTS: Not available

PUBLICATIONS: Not available

LOS ANGELES

A-1 RECORD FINDERS (I)
5639 Melrose Avenue (Rear Entrance)
Los Angeles 90038
  (213) REC-ORDS or 732-6737

M–F	11:00–6:00
S	11:00–5:00
S	Closed

SERVICES: Walk-in Store/Mail Order

SPECIALTIES: (Alphabetical) British Musical Shows, Broadway Shows, Comedy, Contemporary Jazz, Dance, Easy Listening, Film Scores, Nostalgia, Rock, Sinatra, Sound Tracks, Television Shows

VOLUME: 33⅓ – 175,000
           45   – 65,000
           78   – 10,000
    Other   – 0

STOCK: Domestic & Import/New & Used

SEARCH: Available with no service charge; Want lists maintained and requester notified when record comes in

COLLECTIONS: Will buy collections of rare records

PAYMENTS: Money Order, Personal Charge Account, Personal Check

MAIL ORDER: Air Mail, 4th Class, U.P.S.; Prepayment or C.O.D.

DISCOUNTS: Available to dealers

PUBLICATIONS: Free annual catalog; Monthly set-sale list available for $6.00 per year U.S.A. and $12.00 per year non-U.S.A.

34

LOS ANGELES

AARDVARK MUSIC (I)
P.O. Box 69441
Los Angeles 90069
(213) 553-1766

SERVICES: Mail Order Only

SPECIALTIES: (Alphabetical) Blues, Bossa Nova, Contemporary Jazz, Country & Western, Easy Listening, Folk, Folk-Rock, Rhythm & Blues, Rock, Rock & Roll, Soul, Traditional Jazz

VOLUME: 33⅓ – I.N.A.
45 – I.N.A.
78 – I.N.A.
Other – I.N.A.

STOCK: Domestic/New & Used

SEARCH: Available with no service charge; Want lists maintained and requester notified when record comes in

COLLECTIONS: Will buy collections of rare records

PAYMENTS: Money Order, Personal Check

MAIL ORDER: Air Mail, 4th Class; Prepayment

DISCOUNTS: Available

PUBLICATIONS: I.N.A.

LOS ANGELES

ARON'S RECORD SHOP (II)
7725 Melrose Avenue
Los Angeles 90046
(213) 653–8170

M–S   10:00–10:00
S   11:00–7:00

SERVICES: Walk-in Store Only

SPECIALTIES: Rock, Soul, Punk Rock /New Wave, Contemporary Jazz, Film Scores, Classical, Broadway Shows, Traditional Jazz, Folk, Nostalgia

VOLUME: 33⅓ – I.N.A.
45 – I.N.A.
78 – I.N.A.
Other – I.N.A.

STOCK: Domestic & Import/New & Used

SEARCH: Not available

COLLECTIONS: Available for purchase; Will buy collections of rare records

PAYMENTS: Master Charge, Money Order, Personal Check, VISA/Bank-Americard

MAIL ORDER: Not available

DISCOUNTS: Not available

PUBLICATIONS: Not available

LOS ANGELES

THE COLLECTOR SOUND (I)
P.O. Box 48154
Los Angeles 90048
  Telephone: I.N.A.

SERVICES: Mail Order Only

SPECIALTIES: (Alphabetical) Blue-
grass, Blues, Comedy, Country &
Western, Disco, Folk, Folk-Rock,
Hillbilly, Rhythm & Blues, Rock &
Roll, Rockabilly, Soul, Traditional
Jazz

VOLUME: 33⅓ – 10,000
                45   – 10,000
                78   – 1,000
             Other – 0

STOCK: Domestic & Import/New &
Used

SEARCH: Available with no service
charge; Want lists maintained and requester notified when record comes in

COLLECTIONS: Will buy collections of
rare records

PAYMENTS: Money Order, Personal
Charge Account, Personal Check

MAIL ORDER: Air Mail, 1st Class, 4th
Class; Prepayment or C.O.D.

DISCOUNTS: Available

PUBLICATIONS: I.N.A.

LOS ANGELES

DISC-CONNECTION RECORDS AND TAPES (I)   M 10:00 A.M.–mid.
1051 Gayley Avenue   T-W   10:00–7:00
Los Angeles 90024   T-S 10:00 A.M.–mid.
  (213) 477-0211   S   Noon–6:00

SERVICES: Walk-in Store/Mail Order

SPECIALTIES: Sound Tracks, Broad-
way Shows, British Musical Shows,
Film Scores, Television Shows, Tra-
ditional Jazz, Contemporary Jazz,
Beatles, Big Band, Easy Listening,
Promotional

VOLUME: 33⅓ – 10,000
                45   – 3,000
                78   – 0
             Other – 0

STOCK: Domestic & Import/New &
Used

SEARCH: Available with no service
charge; Want lists maintained and requester notified when record comes in

COLLECTIONS: Will buy collections of
rare records

PAYMENTS: Master Charge, Money
Order, Personal Check, VISA/Bank-
Americard

MAIL ORDER: Whatever shipment
method requested; Prepayment

DISCOUNTS: Available

PUBLICATIONS: Not available

LOS ANGELES

FRENCH & SPANISH BOOK	M–F	10:00–6:00
CORPORATION (II)	S	10:00–4:00
652 South Olive Street	S	Closed
Los Angeles 90014		
(213) 489-7963		

SERVICES: Walk-in Store/Mail Order

SPECIALTIES: (Alphabetical) Children's, Christmas, Educational, Folk, Foreign Language, Instrumental, Spoken Word

VOLUME: 33⅓ – 50%
             45 – 50%
             78 – 0
          Other – 0

STOCK: Import/New

SEARCH: Not available

COLLECTIONS: Will not buy collections of rare records

PAYMENTS: American Express, Diners Club, Master Charge, Money Order, VISA/BankAmericard

MAIL ORDER: 4th Class, U.P.S.; Prepayment

DISCOUNTS: Not available

PUBLICATIONS: Not available

LOS ANGELES

HOUSE OF RECORDS (I)	M	Closed
11511 West Pico Boulevard	T–S	11:00–6:00
Los Angeles 90064	S	Closed
(213) 477-8847		

SERVICES: Walk-in Store/Mail Order

SPECIALTIES: All Major Categories

VOLUME: 33⅓ – 3,000
             45 – 200,000
             78 – 300
          Other – 0

STOCK: Domestic/Used

SEARCH: Available with no service charge

COLLECTIONS: Available for purchase

PAYMENTS: American Express, Master Charge, Money Order, VISA/BankAmericard

MAIL ORDER: 4th Class, Whatever shipment method requested; Prepayment

DISCOUNTS: I.N.A.

PUBLICATIONS: Not available

LOS ANGELES

LANE AUDIO & RECORDS (I)
P.O. Box 29171
Los Angeles 90029
(213) 469-8007

SERVICES: Mail Order Only

SPECIALTIES: (Alphabetical) Brass Band, Chamber Music, Dance, Instrumental, Jazz, Opera, Swing, Symphonic, Vocal

VOLUME:
33⅓	– 1%
45	– 0
78	– 99%
Other	– Edison Discs/ Cylinders

STOCK: Domestic & Import/New & Used

SEARCH: Not available

COLLECTIONS: Will buy collections of rare records

PAYMENTS: Money Order, Personal Check

MAIL ORDER: 4th Class, U.P.S., Whatever shipment method requested; Prepayment

DISCOUNTS: Not available

PUBLICATIONS: Free quarterly auction list

LOS ANGELES

LEON LEAVITT'S RECORDS (I)
P.O. Box 38395
Los Angeles 90038
(213) 466-0079

SERVICES: Mail Order Only

SPECIALTIES: Bop Jazz, Jazz Vocal, Big Band, Swing, Traditional Jazz, Contemporary Jazz, Dixieland, Sinatra, Instrumental, Ragtime

VOLUME:
33⅓	– 10,000
45	– 0
78	– 0
Other	– 0

STOCK: Domestic/New & Used

SEARCH: Available with no service charge; Want lists maintained and requester notified when record comes in

COLLECTIONS: Available for purchase; Will buy collections of rare records

PAYMENTS: Money Order, Personal Check

MAIL ORDER: Whatever shipment method requested; Prepayment

DISCOUNTS: Not available

PUBLICATIONS: Free semiannual auction list

LOS ANGELES

MUSIC DEN (I)
226 West 9th Street
Los Angeles 90015
(213) 622-8466

M–S   10:00–5:00
S   Closed

SERVICES: Walk-in Store/Mail Order

SPECIALTIES: Nostalgia, Broadway Shows, Sound Tracks, Opera, Easy Listening, Traditional Jazz, Big Band, Vocal, Classical, Country & Western

VOLUME: 33⅓ – 4,000
      45 – 800
      78 – 75,000
     Other – 0

STOCK: Domestic & Import/New & Used

SEARCH: Available with no service charge; Want lists maintained and requester notified when record comes in

COLLECTIONS: Will buy collections of rare records

PAYMENTS: Master Charge, Money Order, Personal Check, VISA/Bank-Americard

MAIL ORDER: 4th Class, U.P.S.; Prepayment

DISCOUNTS: Available

PUBLICATIONS: Not available

LOS ANGELES

MUSIC MAN MURRAY (I)
5516 Santa Monica Boulevard
Los Angeles 90038
(213) 466-4000

M–S   11:00–5:00
S   Closed

SERVICES: Walk-in Store/Mail Order

SPECIALTIES: Film Scores, Broadway Shows, Opera, Traditional Jazz, Swing, Dance, Blues, Rock & Roll, Country & Western, Easy Listening

VOLUME: 33⅓ – 150,000
      45 – 150,000
      78 – 250,000
     Other – 0

STOCK: Domestic & Import/New & Used

SEARCH: Available with no service charge; Want lists maintained and requester notified when record comes in

COLLECTIONS: Will buy collections of rare records

PAYMENTS: Master Charge, Money Order, Personal Check, VISA/Bank-Americard

MAIL ORDER: 4th Class, Whatever shipment method requested; Prepayment

DISCOUNTS: Not available

PUBLICATIONS: Free occasional catalog; Free occasional auction list

LOS ANGELES

THE RECORD COLLECTOR (I)   M–S   10:00–5:00
1158 North Highland Avenue   S   Closed
Los Angeles 90038
  (213) 467-2875

SERVICES: Walk-in Store/Mail Order

SPECIALTIES: (Alphabetical)   Blues,
Classical, Contemporary Jazz, Ethnic,
Opera, Rhythm & Blues, Traditional
Jazz

VOLUME: 33⅓ – 20,000
             45   – 0
             78   – 100
          Other   – 0

STOCK: Domestic & Import/New &
Used

SEARCH: Not available; Want lists
maintained and requester notified
when record comes in

COLLECTIONS: Will buy collections of
rare records

PAYMENTS: Money Order, Personal
Check

MAIL ORDER: 4th Class; Prepayment

DISCOUNTS: Not available

PUBLICATIONS: I.N.A.

LOS ANGELES

RECORD CONNECTION–THE PLACE TO FIND   M–F   10:00–9:00
    THE HARD TO FIND RECORDS (I)   S   10:00–6:00
8505 Santa Monica Boulevard   S   11:00–6:00
Los Angeles 90046
  (213) 879-3518 or 820-8785

SERVICES: Walk-in Store/Mail Order

SPECIALTIES: Bop Jazz, Broadway
Shows, Big Band, Blues, Contempo-
rary Jazz, Traditional Jazz, Vocal,
Rock, Rhythm & Blues, Sound
Tracks, Classical, Promotional

VOLUME: 33⅓ – 200,000
             45   – 0
             78   – 0
          Other   – 0

STOCK: Domestic & Import/New &
Used

SEARCH: Available with no service
charge; Want lists maintained and requester notified when record comes in

COLLECTIONS: Available for purchase;
Will buy collections of rare records

PAYMENTS: Master Charge, Personal
Check, VISA/BankAmericard

MAIL ORDER: Air Mail, 1st Class,
Whatever shipment method requested;
Prepayment or C.O.D.

DISCOUNTS: Available

PUBLICATIONS: Not available; Annual
sit-down auction held

LOS ANGELES

RHINO RECORDS (II)   M–S   11:00–9:00
1720 Westwood Boulevard   S   Noon–5:00
Los Angeles 90025
  (213) 474-8685

SERVICES: Walk-in Store/Mail Order

SPECIALTIES: (Alphabetical) Bluegrass, Blues, Contemporary Jazz, Country & Western, Ethnic, Folk, Folk-Rock, Rhythm & Blues, Rock, Rock & Roll, Soul

VOLUME: 33⅓ – 100%
            45   – 0
            78   – 0
          Other – 0

STOCK: Domestic & Import/New & Used

SEARCH: Not available

COLLECTIONS: Will buy collections of rare records

PAYMENTS: Master Charge, Personal Check, VISA/BankAmericard

MAIL ORDER: 4th Class, U.P.S.; Prepayment or C.O.D.

DISCOUNTS: Not available

PUBLICATIONS: I.N.A.

LOS ANGELES

JOSEPH SACHS DISCOUNT RECORDS (II)   M–S   10:00–6:00
900 South Broadway   S   Closed
Los Angeles 90015
  (213) 622-3400

SERVICES: Walk-in Store/Mail Order

SPECIALTIES: All Major Categories

VOLUME: 33⅓ – I.N.A.
            45   – I.N.A.
            78   – I.N.A.
          Other – I.N.A.

STOCK: Domestic & Import/New

SEARCH: Not available

COLLECTIONS: Will not buy collections of rare records

PAYMENTS: Master Charge, Money Order, Personal Check, VISA/BankAmericard

MAIL ORDER: Whatever shipment method requested; Prepayment

DISCOUNTS: Available

PUBLICATIONS: I.N.A.

LOS ANGELES

SOUNDSENSATIONS (II)
8915 South Sepulveda Boulevard
Los Angeles 90045
  (213) 641-8877

M–T	10:00–7:00
F	10:00–8:00
S	10:00–7:00
S	Noon–5:00

SERVICES: Walk-in Store Only

SPECIALTIES: Rock & Roll, Beatles, Film Scores, Sound Tracks, Folk, Bop Jazz, British Musical Shows, Comedy, Disco, Television Shows, Swing

VOLUME: 33⅓ – 200
          45   – 0
          78   – 0
     Other   – 0

STOCK: Domestic & Import/New & Used

SEARCH: I.N.A.

COLLECTIONS: Will buy collections of rare records

PAYMENTS: Master Charge, VISA/ BankAmericard

MAIL ORDER: Not available

DISCOUNTS: Not available

PUBLICATIONS: Not available

LOS ANGELES

TOWER RECORDS (II)
8801 Sunset Boulevard
Los Angeles 90069
  (213) 657-7300 or 7330

M–S 9:00 A.M.–mid.

SERVICES: Walk-in Store/Mail Order (Limited)

SPECIALTIES: All Major Categories

VOLUME: 33⅓ – 100%
          45   – 0
          78   – 0
     Other   – 0

STOCK: Domestic & Import/New

SEARCH: Not available

COLLECTIONS: Will not buy collections of rare records

PAYMENTS: Master Charge, Money Order, Personal Charge Account, VISA/BankAmericard

MAIL ORDER: 4th Class, U.P.S.; Prepayment

DISCOUNTS: Available

PUBLICATIONS: Not available

LOS ANGELES

TOWER RECORDS (II)   M–S   9:00 A.M.–mid.
1028 Westwood Boulevard
Los Angeles 90024
  (213) 477-2021 or 478-2112

SERVICES: Walk-in Store/Mail Order (Limited)

SPECIALTIES: All Major Categories

VOLUME: 33⅓ – 100%
           45 – 0
           78 – 0
           Other – 0

STOCK: Domestic & Import/New

SEARCH: Not available

COLLECTIONS: Will not buy collections of rare records

PAYMENTS: Master Charge, Money Order, Personal Charge Account, VISA/BankAmericard

MAIL ORDER: 4th Class, U.P.S.; Prepayment

DISCOUNTS: Available

PUBLICATIONS: Not available

LOS GATOS

GALACTIC ZOO (I)   M–S   Noon–11:00
36 North Santa Cruz Avenue   S   Noon–6:00
Los Gatos 95030
  (408) 354-5690

SERVICES: Walk-in Store/Mail Order

SPECIALTIES: (Alphabetical) Contemporary Jazz, Folk, Folk-Rock, Punk Rock/New Wave, Rhythm & Blues, Rock, Rock & Roll

VOLUME: 33⅓ – 10,000
           45 – 1,000
           78 – 0
           Other – 0

STOCK: Domestic & Import/New & Used

SEARCH: Available with no service charge; Want lists maintained and requester notified when record comes in

COLLECTIONS: Will buy collections of rare records

PAYMENTS: Master Charge, Money Order, Personal Check, VISA/BankAmericard

MAIL ORDER: Whatever shipment method requested; Prepayment

DISCOUNTS: Available

PUBLICATIONS: I.N.A.

MONTEREY PARK

SOUND STAGE RECORDS AND TAPES (I)   M–S   10:00–6:00
121 East Garvey   S   Closed
Monterey Park 91754
  (213) 288-9600

SERVICES: Walk-in Store/Mail Order

SPECIALTIES: (Alphabetical) Beatles, Country & Western, Disco, Easy Listening, Elvis, Nostalgia, Rhythm & Blues, Rock, Rock & Roll, Rockabilly, Standards

VOLUME: 33⅓ – 1,000
             45 – 20,000
             78 – 0
           Other – 0

STOCK: Domestic Only/New Only

SEARCH: Available with no service charge

COLLECTIONS: I.N.A.

PAYMENTS: Master Charge, Money Order, Personal Check, VISA/BankAmericard

MAIL ORDER: 4th Class Mail, Whatever shipment method requested; Prepayment

DISCOUNTS: Not available

PUBLICATIONS: Not available

MOUNTAIN VIEW

TOWER RECORDS (II)   M–S   9:00 A.M.–mid.
630 San Antonio Road
Mountain View 94040
  (415) 941-7900

SERVICES: Walk-in Store/Mail Order (Limited)

SPECIALTIES: All Major Categories

VOLUME: 33⅓ – 100%
             45 – 0
             78 – 0
           Other – 0

STOCK: Domestic & Import/New

SEARCH: Not available

COLLECTIONS: Will not buy collections of rare records

PAYMENTS: Master Charge, Money Order, Personal Charge Account, VISA/BankAmericard

MAIL ORDER: 4th Class, U.P.S.; Prepayment

DISCOUNTS: Available

PUBLICATIONS: Not available

NORWALK

NORWALK RECORD SALES (I)
12143 Front Street
Norwalk 90650
  (213) 863-2403

M–W	10:00–6:00
T	Closed
F–S	10:00–6:00
S	Noon–6:00

SERVICES: Walk-in Store/Mail Order

SPECIALTIES: Soul, Rock

VOLUME: 33⅓ – 0
          45   – 3,500
          78   – 0
        Other – 0

STOCK: Domestic/New

SEARCH: Not available

COLLECTIONS: Not available for purchase

PAYMENTS: Master Charge, Personal Check, VISA/BankAmericard

MAIL ORDER: 1st Class; Prepayment

DISCOUNTS: Not available

PUBLICATIONS: Free biannual catalog

OAKLAND

RICHARD A. BASS RECORDS (I)
915 York Street
Oakland 94610
  (415) 451-2811

M–T	6:00 P.M.–10:00 P.M.
W–F	Closed
S–S	9:00 A.M.–10:00 P.M.

SERVICES: Walk-in Store (By Appointment)/Mail Order

SPECIALTIES: Blues, Rhythm & Blues, Soul, Rock & Roll, Rockabilly, Surfing, Country & Western, Folk, Gospel/Sacred, Political, Cajun, Rock

VOLUME: 33⅓ – 15,000
          45   – 60,000
          78   – 15,000
        Other – 0

STOCK: Domestic/New & Used

SEARCH: Not available

COLLECTIONS: Will buy collections of rare records

PAYMENTS: Money Order, Personal Check

MAIL ORDER: 4th Class, Whatever shipment method requested; Prepayment

DISCOUNTS: Not available

PUBLICATIONS: Free quarterly auction list

ORANGE

RECORD EXCHANGER (I)
P.O. Box 6144
Orange 92667
  (714) 639-3383

SERVICES: Mail Order Only

SPECIALTIES: (Alphabetical) Blues,
Country & Western, Easy Listening,
Folk, Folk-Rock, Religious, Rhythm
& Blues, Rock, Rock & Roll, Soul,
Traditional Jazz

VOLUME: 33⅓ – I.N.A.
           45 – I.N.A.
           78 – I.N.A.
           Other – I.N.A.

STOCK: Domestic & Import/New &
Used

SEARCH: Not available

COLLECTIONS: Will buy collections of
rare records

PAYMENTS: Money Order, Personal
Check

MAIL ORDER: Air Mail, 4th Class;
Prepayment

DISCOUNTS: Not available

PUBLICATIONS: I.N.A.

ORANGE

VINTAGE RECORDS (I)
P.O. Box 6144
Orange 92667
  (714) 639-3383

M–F   9:00–5:00
S–S   Closed

SERVICES: Mail Order Only (Above
Times for Telephone)

SPECIALTIES: (Alphabetical) Blues,
Country & Western, Folk, Folk-Rock,
Hillbilly, Religious, Rhythm & Blues,
Rock, Rock & Roll, Soul

VOLUME: 33⅓ – 0
           45 – 50,000
           78 – 0
           Other – 0

STOCK: Domestic & Import/New &
Used

SEARCH: Not available

COLLECTIONS: Will buy collections of
rare records

PAYMENTS: Money Order, Personal
Check

MAIL ORDER: 4th Class, Prepayment

DISCOUNTS: Not available

PUBLICATIONS: Quarterly auction list
available for $1.00 per issue

PANORAMA CITY

TOWER RECORDS (II)   M–S   9:00 A.M.–mid.
8717 Van Nuys Boulevard
Panorama City 91402
(213) 893-7808

SERVICES: Walk-in Store/Mail Order   COLLECTIONS: Will not buy collec-
(Limited)   tions of rare records

SPECIALTIES: All Major Categories   PAYMENTS: Master Charge, Money
                                            Order, Personal Charge Account,
VOLUME: 33⅓ – 100%   VISA/BankAmericard
             45   – 0
             78   – 0   MAIL ORDER: 4th Class, U.P.S.; Pre-
             Other – 0   payment

STOCK: Domestic & Import/New   DISCOUNTS: Available

SEARCH: Not available   PUBLICATIONS: Not available

PASADENA

POO-BAH RECORD SHOP (II)   M–S   Noon–9:00
1101 East Walnut   S   Noon–5:00
Pasadena 91106
(213) 449-3359

SERVICES: Walk-in Store Only   SEARCH: Not available

SPECIALTIES: All Major Categories   COLLECTIONS: Will not buy collec-
                                             tions of rare records
VOLUME: 33⅓ – I.N.A.
             45   – I.N.A.   PAYMENTS: Personal Check
             78   – I.N.A.
             Other – I.N.A.   MAIL ORDER: Not available

STOCK: Domestic & Import/New &   DISCOUNTS: Not available
Used   PUBLICATIONS: I.N.A.

PITTSBURG

BOB FERLINGERE RECORDS (I)
P.O. Box 1645
Pittsburg 94565
  (415) 754-7434

SERVICES: Mail Order Only

SPECIALTIES: Blues, Country & Western, Rhythm & Blues, Rock & Roll

VOLUME: 33⅓ – I.N.A.
                   45 – I.N.A.
                   78 – I.N.A.
                Other – I.N.A.

STOCK: Domestic/New & Used

SEARCH: Want lists maintained and requester notified when record comes in

COLLECTIONS: Will buy collections of rare records

PAYMENTS: Money Order, Personal Check

MAIL ORDER: Air Mail, 4th Class; Prepayment

DISCOUNTS: I.N.A.

PUBLICATIONS: I.N.A.

SACRAMENTO

AMERICAN MUSIC COMPANY (I)   M–S   9:00–10:00
5500 Sandburg Drive
Sacramento 95819
  (916) 454-4540

SERVICES: Walk-in Store/Mail Order

SPECIALTIES: Rock, Rock & Roll, Soul, Bop Jazz, Country & Western, Film Scores, Rhythm & Blues, Blues, Folk, Comedy

VOLUME: 33⅓ – 15,000
                   45 – 28,000
                   78 – 1,500
                Other – 0

STOCK: Domestic & Import/New & Used

SEARCH: Available with no service charge; Want lists maintained and requester notified when record comes in

COLLECTIONS: Available for purchase; Will buy collections of rare records

PAYMENTS: Master Charge, Money Order, Personal Check, VISA/Bank-Americard

MAIL ORDER: Air Mail, 4th Class, Whatever shipment method requested; Prepayment

DISCOUNTS: Not available

PUBLICATIONS: Quarterly catalog available for $2.00 per year; Quarterly auction list available for $2.00 per year

SACRAMENTO

DANCING BEAR RECORDS (1)
720 Alhambra Boulevard
Sacramento 95816
(916) 442-4858

M–S	11:00–7:00
S	Noon–5:00

SERVICES: Walk-in Store/Mail Order

SPECIALTIES: All Major Categories

VOLUME: 33⅓ – 90%
          45 – 5%
          78 – 5%
     Other – 0

STOCK: Domestic & Import/New & Used

SEARCH: Available with no service charge; Want lists maintained and requester notified when record comes in

COLLECTIONS: Will buy collections of rare records

PAYMENTS: Master Charge, Personal Check, VISA/BankAmericard

MAIL ORDER: 4th Class; Prepayment

DISCOUNTS: Available

PUBLICATIONS: I.N.A.

SACRAMENTO

NORTHERN LIGHTS RECORDS (II)
2425 J Street
Sacramento 95816
(916) 443-9292

M	Closed
T–S	11:00–6:00
S	Closed

SERVICES: Walk-in Store/Mail Order

SPECIALTIES: (Alphabetical) Classical, Elvis, Ethnic, Feminist, Film Scores, Folk, Meditative, Opera, Rock, Sound Tracks, Traditional Jazz

VOLUME: 33⅓ – I.N.A.
          45 – I.N.A.
          78 – I.N.A.
     Other – I.N.A.

STOCK: Domestic & Import/New & Used

SEARCH: Want lists maintained and requester notified when record comes in

COLLECTIONS: Will not buy collections of rare records

PAYMENTS: Master Charge, Money Order

MAIL ORDER: 1st Class; C.O.D.

DISCOUNTS: Available

PUBLICATIONS: Not available

SACRAMENTO

!RECORDS! (I)   M–S   10:00–5:30
806 K Street   S   11:00–4:00
Sacramento 95814
(916) 446-3973

SERVICES: Walk-in Store/Mail Order

SPECIALTIES: Rock, Rock & Roll, Sound Tracks, Beatles, Elvis, Country & Western, Traditional Jazz, Surfing, Nostalgia, Dixieland

VOLUME: 33⅓ – 25,000
           45   – 300,000
           78   – 10,000
           Other – Edison Discs/
                    Cylinders/
                    Berliners

STOCK: Domestic/New & Used

SEARCH: Available with no service charge; Want lists maintained and requester notified when record comes in

COLLECTIONS: Will buy collections of rare records

PAYMENTS: Master Charge, Money Order, Personal Check, VISA/Bank-Americard

MAIL ORDER: 4th Class, Whatever shipment method requested

DISCOUNTS: Available

PUBLICATIONS: Not available

SACRAMENTO

TOWER RECORDS (II)   M–S   9:00 A.M.–mid.
726 K Street
Sacramento 95816
(916) 446-3111

SERVICES: Walk-in Store/Mail Order (Limited)

SPECIALTIES: All Major Categories

VOLUME: 33⅓ – 100%
           45   – 0
           78   – 0
           Other – 0

STOCK: Domestic & Import/New

SEARCH: Not available

COLLECTIONS: Will not buy collections of rare records

PAYMENTS: Master Charge, Money Order, Personal Charge Account, VISA/BankAmericard

MAIL ORDER: 4th Class, U.P.S.; Prepayment

DISCOUNTS: Available

PUBLICATIONS: Not available

SACRAMENTO

TOWER RECORDS (II)   M–S   9:00 A.M.–mid.
2500 16th Street
Sacramento 95818
  (916) 444-3000

SERVICES: Walk-in Store/Mail Order   COLLECTIONS: Will not buy collec-
(Limited)   tions of rare records

SPECIALTIES: All Major Categories   PAYMENTS: Master Charge, Money
VOLUME: 33⅓ – 100%   Order, Personal Charge Account,
             45   – 0   VISA/BankAmericard
             78   – 0   MAIL ORDER: 4th Class, U.P.S.; Pre-
             Other – 0   payment

STOCK: Domestic & Import/New   DISCOUNTS: Available

SEARCH: Not available   PUBLICATIONS: Not available

SACRAMENTO

TOWER RECORDS (II)   M–S   9:00 A.M.–mid.
2520 Watt Avenue
Sacramento 95821
  (916) 482-6400 or 9191

SERVICES: Walk-in Store/Mail Order   COLLECTIONS: Will not buy collec-
(Limited)   tions of rare records

SPECIALTIES: All Major Categories   PAYMENTS: Master Charge, Money
VOLUME: 33⅓ – 100%   Order, Personal Charge Account,
             45   – 0   VISA/BankAmericard
             78   – 0   MAIL ORDER: 4th Class, U.P.S.; Pre-
             Other – 0   payment

STOCK: Domestic & Import/New   DISCOUNTS: Available

SEARCH: Not available   PUBLICATIONS: Not available

SAN BERNARDINO

S. A. LANGKAMMERER RECORD LISTS (I)   M–F   Closed
3238 Stoddard   S   9:00–4:00
San Bernardino 92405   S   Closed
  (714) 882-2175

SERVICES: Walk-in Store/Mail Order

SPECIALTIES: Popular, Big Band, Opera, Classical, Country & Western, Dance, Traditional Jazz, Dixieland, Contemporary Jazz, Sound Tracks

VOLUME: 33⅓ – 11,000
           45 – 7,000
           78 – 180,000
      Other – Edison Discs–
                2,000 16" Transcriptions–500

STOCK: Domestic & Import/New & Used

SEARCH: Want lists maintained and requester notified when record comes in

COLLECTIONS: Will buy collections of rare records

PAYMENTS: Money Order, Personal Check

MAIL ORDER: 4th Class, Prepayment

DISCOUNTS: Not available

PUBLICATIONS: Bimonthly auction list available for $1.00 per year

SAN DIEGO

FOLK ARTS RARE RECORDS (I)   M–S   10:00–7:00
3611 Adams Avenue   S   10:00–3:30
San Diego 92116
  (714) 282-7833

SERVICES: Walk-in Store/Mail Order/Library

SPECIALTIES: Traditional Field Recordings, Old-Time Radio, Hillbilly, Nostalgia, Old-Time Country, Bluegrass, Big Band, Traditional Jazz, Bop Jazz, Novelty

VOLUME: 33⅓ – 3,000
           45 – 0
           78 – 15,000
      Other – 0

STOCK: Domestic & Import/New & Used

SEARCH: Want lists maintained and requester notified when record comes in

COLLECTIONS: Will buy collections of rare records

PAYMENTS: Money Order, Personal Check

MAIL ORDER: Whatever shipment method requested; Prepayment

DISCOUNTS: Available

PUBLICATIONS: Auction list available five times per year for $5.00 per year

SAN DIEGO

TOWER RECORDS (II)   M–S   9:00 A.M.–mid.
6405 El Cajon Boulevard
San Diego 92115
(714) 287-1420

SERVICES: Walk-in Store/Mail Order
(Limited)

COLLECTIONS: Will not buy collections of rare records

SPECIALTIES: All Major Categories

PAYMENTS: Master Charge, Money Order, Personal Charge Account, VISA/BankAmericard

VOLUME: 33⅓ – 100%
           45   – 0
           78   – 0
           Other – 0

MAIL ORDER: 4th Class, U.P.S.; Prepayment

STOCK: Domestic & Import/New

DISCOUNTS: Available

SEARCH: Not available

PUBLICATIONS: Not available

SAN DIEGO

TOWER RECORDS (II)   M–S   9:00 A.M.–mid.
3601 Sports Arena Boulevard
San Diego 92110
(714) 224-3333 or 222-0882

SERVICES: Walk-in Store/Mail Order
(Limited)

COLLECTIONS: Will not buy collections of rare records

SPECIALTIES: All Major Categories

PAYMENTS: Master Charge, Money Order, Personal Charge Account, VISA/BankAmericard

VOLUME: 33⅓ – 100%
           45   – 0
           78   – 0
           Other – 0

MAIL ORDER: 4th Class, U.P.S.; Prepayment

STOCK: Domestic & Import/New

DISCOUNTS: Available

SEARCH: Not available

PUBLICATIONS: Not available

SAN FRANCISCO

THE MAGIC FLUTE (I)
510½ Frederick Street
San Francisco 94117
  (415) 661-4257

M	Closed
T–S	Noon–7:00
S	Noon–5:00

SERVICES: Walk-in Store/Mail Order

SPECIALTIES: All Major Categories

VOLUME: 33⅓ – 15,000
          45 – 350
          78 – 0
    Other – 0

STOCK: Domestic & Import/New & Used

SEARCH: Available with service charge; Want lists maintained and requester notified when record comes in

COLLECTIONS: Will buy collections of rare records

PAYMENTS: Money Order, Personal Check

MAIL ORDER: 4th Class; Prepayment

DISCOUNTS: Available

PUBLICATIONS: I.N.A.

SAN FRANCISCO

THE RECORD HOUSE (I)
389 Geary Street
San Francisco 94102
  (415) 434-3254

M–S	11:00–8:00
S	Closed

SERVICES: Walk-in Store/Mail Order

SPECIALTIES: Sound Tracks, Easy Listening, Classical, Instrumental, Nostalgia, Broadway Shows, Vocal, Opera, International, Standards

VOLUME: 33⅓ – 98%
          45 – 1%
          78 – 1%
    Other – 0

STOCK: Domestic & Import/New & Used

SEARCH: Available with no service charge; Want lists maintained and requester notified when record comes in

COLLECTIONS: Available for purchase; Will buy collections of rare records

PAYMENTS: Master Charge, Money Order, Personal Check, VISA/BankAmericard

MAIL ORDER: Air Mail, 1st Class, 4th Class; Prepayment

DISCOUNTS: Available

PUBLICATIONS: Not available

SAN FRANCISCO

RECYCLED RECORDS (II)   M–S   11:00–7:00
1415 Grant Avenue
San Francisco 94133
(415) 982-5442

SERVICES: Walk-in Store Only

SPECIALTIES: Rock, Rock & Roll,
Contemporary Jazz, Disco, Soul,
Classical, Comedy, Punk Rock/New
Wave, Reggae, Blues, Rhythm &
Blues, Rockabilly

VOLUME: 33⅓ – 100%
            45 – 0
            78 – 0
            Other – 0

STOCK: Domestic & Import/Used

SEARCH: Not available

COLLECTIONS: Will buy collections of
rare records

PAYMENTS: Personal Check

MAIL ORDER: Not available

DISCOUNTS: Not available

PUBLICATIONS: Not available

SAN FRANCISCO

RECYCLED RECORDS (II)   M–S   11:00–7:00
1377 Haight Street
San Francisco 94117
(415) 626-4075

SERVICES: Walk-in Store Only

SPECIALTIES: Rock, Rock & Roll,
Contemporary Jazz, Disco, Soul,
Classical, Comedy, Punk Rock/New
Wave, Reggae, Blues, Rhythm &
Blues, Rockabilly

VOLUME: 33⅓ – 100%
            45 – 0
            78 – 0
            Other – 0

STOCK: Domestic & Import/Used

SEARCH: Not available

COLLECTIONS: Will buy collections of
rare records

PAYMENTS: Personal Check

MAIL ORDER: Not available

DISCOUNTS: Not available

PUBLICATIONS: Not available

SAN FRANCISCO

STREETLIGHT RECORDS (II)
3979 24th Street
San Francisco 94114
  (415) 282-3550

M–S   11:00–10:00
S   11:00–7:00

SERVICES: Walk-in Store/Mail Order

SPECIALTIES: Rock, Bop Jazz, Folk, Vocal, Classical, Contemporary Jazz, Personality, Comedy, Blues, Soul

VOLUME: 33⅓ – 2,000
          45   – 0
          78   – 0
     Other – 0

STOCK: Domestic & Import/New & Used

SEARCH: Available with no service charge; Want lists maintained and requester notified when record comes in

COLLECTIONS: Will buy collections of rare records

PAYMENTS: Master Charge, Money Order, Personal Check, VISA/BankAmericard

MAIL ORDER: Whatever shipment method requested; Prepayment

DISCOUNTS: Available

PUBLICATIONS: Not available

SAN FRANCISCO

TOWER RECORDS (II)
2525 Jones Street
San Francisco 94133
  (415) 885-0500 or 0753

M–S 9:00 A.M.–mid.

SERVICES: Walk-in Store/Mail Order (Limited)

SPECIALTIES: All Major Categories

VOLUME: 33⅓ – 100%
          45 – 0
          78 – 0
     Other – 0

STOCK: Domestic & Import/New

SEARCH: Not available

COLLECTIONS: Will not buy collections of rare records

PAYMENTS: Master Charge, Money Order, Personal Charge Account, VISA/BankAmericard

MAIL ORDER: 4th Class, U.P.S.; Prepayment

DISCOUNTS: Available

PUBLICATIONS: Not available

SAN FRANCISCO

USED RECORD SHOPPE (I)   M–S   11:00–8:00
701 Irving Street   S   11:00–6:00
San Francisco 94122
(415) 665-2055

SERVICES: Walk-in Store Only

SPECIALTIES: Rock, Rock & Roll, Contemporary Jazz, Blues, Classical, Rhythm & Blues, Punk Rock/New Wave, Swing, Sound Tracks, Rockabilly

VOLUME: 33⅓ – 250
           45 – 10,000
           78 – 2,000
    Other – 0

STOCK: Domestic & Import/New & Used

SEARCH: Want lists maintained and requester notified when record comes in

COLLECTIONS: Available for purchase; Will buy collections of rare records

PAYMENTS: Money Order, Personal Check

MAIL ORDER: Not available

DISCOUNTS: Available

PUBLICATIONS: Not available

SAN JOSE

DEDICATED RECORD COLLECTOR (I)   M–T   Closed
56 North Bascom Avenue   W–S Noon–7:00
San Jose 95128   S   Closed
(408) 294–6868

SERVICES: Walk-in Store Only

SPECIALTIES: Rock & Roll, Contemporary Jazz, Blues, Country & Western, Folk, Classical, Sound Tracks, Soul, Reggae, Gospel/Sacred

VOLUME: 33⅓ – 100%
           45 – 0
           78 – 0
    Other – 0

STOCK: Domestic & Import/New & Used

SEARCH: Not available

COLLECTIONS: Will buy collections of rare records

PAYMENTS: Money Order, Personal Check

MAIL ORDER: Not available

DISCOUNTS: Not available

PUBLICATIONS: Not available

SAN JOSE

RECYCLE BOOKSTORE (I)
138 East Santa Clara
San Jose 95113
(408) 286-6275

M–S   10:00–9:00
S   10:00–6:00

SERVICES: Walk-in Store/Mail Order

SPECIALTIES: (Alphabetical) Bluegrass, Blues, Classical, Contemporary Jazz, Country & Western, Ethnic, Folk, Folk-Rock, Opera, Reggae, Rock & Roll, Traditional Jazz

VOLUME: 33⅓ – 3,500
            45 – 0
            78 – 0
            Other – 0

STOCK: Domestic & Import/Used

SEARCH: Not available; Want lists maintained and requester notified when record comes in

COLLECTIONS: Will buy collections of rare records

PAYMENTS: Master Charge, Personal Check, VISA/BankAmericard

MAIL ORDER: 1st Class; Prepayment

DISCOUNTS: Not available

PUBLICATIONS: I.N.A.

SAN JOSE

ROWE'S RARE RECORDS (I)
54 West Santa Clara Street
San Jose 95113
(408) 294-7200

M–F   10:00–6:00
S   Noon–5:00
S   Closed

SERVICES: Walk-in Store/Mail Order

SPECIALTIES: All Major Categories

VOLUME: 33⅓ – 20,000
            45 – 20,000
            78 – 25,000
            Other – 0

STOCK: Domestic/Used

SEARCH: Available with no service charge

COLLECTIONS: Will buy collections of rare records

PAYMENTS: Money Order, Personal Check

MAIL ORDER: 3rd Class, Whatever shipment method requested; Prepayment or C.O.D.

DISCOUNTS: Available

PUBLICATIONS: Not available

SAN LORENZO

WARPED RECORDS? (II)
65 East Lewelling Boulevard
San Lorenzo 94580
  (415) 278-9898

M	Closed
T–F	Noon–7:00
S–S	Noon–6:00

SERVICES: Walk-in Store/Mail Order

SPECIALTIES: Rock, Rock & Roll, Punk Rock/New Wave, Beatles, Reggae, Promotional, Comedy, Country & Western, Blues, Sound Tracks, Surfing, Film Scores

VOLUME:
  $33\frac{1}{3}$ – 2,000
  45 – 100
  78 – 0
  Other – 0

STOCK: Domestic & Import/New & Used

SEARCH: Available with no service charge; Want lists maintained and requester notified when record comes in

COLLECTIONS: Will not buy collections of rare records

PAYMENTS: Money Order, Personal Check

MAIL ORDER: Whatever shipment method requested; Prepayment

DISCOUNTS: Available

PUBLICATIONS: Not available

SAN LUIS OBISPO

SQUARE DEAL RECORD COMPANY (I)
169 Prado Road
P.O. Box 1002
San Luis Obispo 93401
  (805) 543-3636
Telex 910-321-2947

SERVICES: Walk-in Store (By Appointment Only)/Mail Order (Primarily)

SPECIALTIES: All Major Categories

VOLUME:
  $33\frac{1}{3}$ – 95%
  45 – 5%
  78 – 0
  Other – 0

STOCK: Domestic & Import/New & Used

SEARCH: Available with no service charge

COLLECTIONS: Will buy collections of rare records

PAYMENTS: Master Charge, Money Order, VISA/BankAmericard

MAIL ORDER: 4th Class, U.P.S., Whatever shipment method requested; Prepayment

DISCOUNTS: Available

PUBLICATIONS: Free catalog five times per year

SAN MATEO

BOOGIE MUSIC (I)
P.O. Box 2054
San Mateo 94401
(415) 348-5422

	M–F	9:00–4:00
	S	Closed
	S	Closed

SERVICES: Mail Order Only (Above Times for Telephone)

SPECIALTIES: Blues, Rock & Roll, Rockabilly, Soul, Vocal, Country & Western, Surfing, Elvis, Instrumental, Film Scores, Sound Tracks

VOLUME:
33⅓ – 8,000
45 – 30,000
78 – 2,000
Other – 0

STOCK: Domestic/New & Used

SEARCH: Available with no service charge; Want lists maintained and requester notified when record comes in

COLLECTIONS: Available for purchase; Will buy collections of rare records

PAYMENTS: Master Charge, Money Order, Personal Check, VISA/Bank-Americard

MAIL ORDER: Air Mail, 4th Class; Prepayment

DISCOUNTS: Not available

PUBLICATIONS: Free bimonthly catalog; Free occasional auction list

SAN MATEO

RARE RECORDS UNLIMITED (I)
1723 Lake Street
San Mateo 94403
(415) 349-5306

	M–F	10:00–6:00
	S	9:00–3:00
	S	Closed

SERVICES: Walk-in Store/Mail Order

SPECIALTIES: Rhythm & Blues, Rock & Roll, Blues, Rockabilly, Instrumental, Soul, Surfing, Country & Western, Elvis, Beatles

VOLUME:
33⅓ – 75,000
45 – 225,000
78 – 1,000
Other – 0

STOCK: Domestic & Import/New & Used

SEARCH: Not available

COLLECTIONS: Not available for purchase; Will buy collections of rare records

PAYMENTS: Master Charge, Money Order, Personal Check, VISA/Bank-Americard

MAIL ORDER: Whatever shipment method requested; Prepayment

DISCOUNTS: Available

PUBLICATIONS: Free bimonthly catalog available to anyone; Free wholesale catalog available to dealers

SAN PEDRO

JEFFY SALES (I)
P.O. Box 1962
San Pedro 90733
   Telephone: I.N.A.

SERVICES: Mail Order Only

SPECIALTIES: Bluegrass, Country & Western, Folk, Gospel/Sacred, Hillbilly

VOLUME: 33⅓ – 3,000
            45 – 3,000
            78 – 1,000
            Other – 0

STOCK: Domestic & Import/New & Used

SEARCH: Not available

COLLECTIONS: Will buy collections of rare records

PAYMENTS: Money Order, Personal Check

MAIL ORDER: Air Mail, 4th Class; Prepayment

DISCOUNTS: Not available

PUBLICATIONS: I.N.A.

SAN RAFAEL

SHANES RECORD FINDING SERVICE (I)   M–F   9:00–5:00
P.O. Box 6314   S–S   Closed
San Rafael 94903
   (415) 456-4631

SERVICES: Walk-in Store/Mail Order

SPECIALTIES: (Alphabetical) Folk, Promotional, Punk Rock/New Wave, Rock, Rock & Roll

VOLUME: 33⅓ – 15,000
            45 – 20,000
            78 – 0
            Other – 0

STOCK: Domestic & Import/New & Used

SEARCH: Available with service charge; Want lists maintained and requester notified when record comes in

COLLECTIONS: Will buy collections of rare records

PAYMENTS: Money Order, Personal Check

MAIL ORDER: 4th Class; Prepayment

DISCOUNTS: Available

PUBLICATIONS: Free periodic catalogs

SAN RAFAEL

USED RECORD SHOPPE (I)
555 Francisco Boulevard
San Rafael 94901
  (415) 665-2055

M–S	11:00–8:00
S	11:00–6:00

SERVICES: Walk-in Store Only

SPECIALTIES: Rock, Rock & Roll, Contemporary Jazz, Blues, Classical, Rhythm & Blues, Punk Rock/New Wave, Swing, Sound Tracks, Rockabilly

VOLUME:
  33⅓ – 250
  45 – 10,000
  78 – 2,000
  Other – 0

STOCK: Domestic & Import/New & Used

SEARCH: Want lists maintained and requester notified when record comes in

COLLECTIONS: Available for purchase; Will buy collections of rare records

PAYMENTS: Money Order, Personal Check

MAIL ORDER: Not available

DISCOUNTS: Available

PUBLICATIONS: Not available

SANTA MONICA

CHILDREN'S BOOK AND MUSIC CENTER (I)
2500 Santa Monica Boulevard
Santa Monica 90404
  (213) 829-0215

M–S	9:00–6:00
S	Closed

SERVICES: Walk-in Store/Mail Order

SPECIALTIES: Children's, Ethnic, Dance, Feminist, Foreign Language, Instructional, Folk

VOLUME:
  33⅓ – 50%
  45 – 50%
  78 – 0
  Other – 0

STOCK: Domestic & Import/New

SEARCH: Not available

COLLECTIONS: Not available for purchase

PAYMENTS: Master Charge, Money Order, Personal Check, VISA/BankAmericard

MAIL ORDER: Whatever shipment method requested; Prepayment

DISCOUNTS: Not available

PUBLICATIONS: Annual catalog available for $1.50 per issue

SANTA MONICA

JAZZ MAN RECORD SHOP (I)   M–F   10:00–5:00
3323 Pico Boulevard   S   10:00–8:00
Santa Monica 90405   S   Closed
 (213) 828-6939

SERVICES: Walk-in Store/Mail Order   SEARCH: Not available

SPECIALTIES: Traditional Jazz, Big   COLLECTIONS: Will buy collections of
Band, Swing, Vocal, Hillbilly, Dixie-   rare records
land, Blues, Rhythm & Blues, Rock &   PAYMENTS: Money Order, Personal
Roll, Sinatra   Check

VOLUME: 33⅓ – 1,000   MAIL ORDER: 4th Class; Prepayment
            45 – 5,000
            78 – 60,000   DISCOUNTS: Not available
            Other – 0   PUBLICATIONS: Not available

STOCK: Domestic & Import/New &
Used

SANTA MONICA

MUSIC ONE (II)   M–F   11:30–9:00
1902 Lincoln Boulevard   S   10:00–7:00
Santa Monica 90405   S   Noon–5:00
 (213) 399-2378

SERVICES: Walk-in Store Only   COLLECTIONS: Will buy collections of
                                          rare records
SPECIALTIES: All Major Categories
                                          PAYMENTS: Master Charge, Personal
VOLUME: 33⅓ – 200   Check, VISA/BankAmericard
            45 – 0
            78 – 0   MAIL ORDER: Not available
            Other – 0
                                          DISCOUNTS: Available
STOCK: Domestic/New & Used
                                          PUBLICATIONS: I.N.A.
SEARCH: Available with service
charge

SANTA MONICA

MUSKADINE MUSIC (I)
212 Pier Avenue
Santa Monica 90405
   (213) 392-1136

M	Closed
T-T	11:00-6:00
F	Closed
S	11:00-6:00
S	Noon-5:00

SERVICES: Walk-in Store/Mail Order

SPECIALTIES: Folk, Blues, Rhythm & Blues, Bluegrass, Traditional Jazz, Old-Time Country, Rockabilly, Hawaiian, Cajun, Hillbilly, Reggae

VOLUME: 33⅓ – 6,000
         45 – 0
         78 – 0
      Other – 0

STOCK: Domestic & Import/New & Used

SEARCH: Available with no service charge

COLLECTIONS: Not available for purchase

PAYMENTS: Master Charge, Money Order, Personal Check, VISA/Bank-Americard

MAIL ORDER: U.P.S.; Prepayment

DISCOUNTS: Not available

PUBLICATIONS: Free occasional catalog; Free occasional auction list; Free bimonthly newsletter

SEASIDE

HIGGINS RECORDS AND TAPES (I)
775 Broadway Avenue
Seaside 93955
   (408) 394-5924

M-S	11:00-6:00
S	Closed

SERVICES: Walk-in Store/Mail Order

SPECIALTIES: All Major Categories

VOLUME: 33⅓ – 2,500
         45 – 14,000
         78 – 200
      Other – 0

STOCK: Domestic/New & Used

SEARCH: Available with service charge; Available with no service charge; Want lists maintained and requester notified when record comes in

COLLECTIONS: Will buy collections of rare records

PAYMENTS: Master Charge, Money Order, Personal Check, VISA/Bank-Americard

MAIL ORDER: Air Mail, 1st Class, 4th Class, U.P.S.; Prepayment

DISCOUNTS: Not available

PUBLICATIONS: I.N.A.

SHERMAN OAKS

MOBY DISC (II)   M–S   11:00–9:00
14410 Ventura Boulevard   S   11:00–6:00
Sherman Oaks 91403
   (213) 990-2970 or 2975

SERVICES: Walk-in Store/Mail Order   COLLECTIONS: Will buy collections of
SPECIALTIES: All Major Categories   rare records

VOLUME: 33⅓ – 1,000   PAYMENTS: Money Order, Personal
             45 – 0   Check
             78 – 0   MAIL ORDER: Air Mail, 4th Class;
             Other – 0   Prepayment
STOCK: Domestic & Import/New &   DISCOUNTS: Available
Used   PUBLICATIONS: I.N.A.
SEARCH: Not available

STOCKTON

TOWER RECORDS (II)   M–S   9:00 A.M.–mid.
6475 Pacific Avenue
Stockton 95207
   (209) 951-3700

SERVICES: Walk-in Store/Mail Order   COLLECTIONS: Will not buy collec-
(Limited)   tions of rare records
SPECIALTIES: All Major Categories   PAYMENTS: Master Charge, Money
VOLUME: 33⅓ – 100%   Order, Personal Charge Account,
             45 – 0   VISA/BankAmericard
             78 – 0   MAIL ORDER: 4th Class, U.P.S.; Pre-
             Other – 0   payment
STOCK: Domestic & Import/New   DISCOUNTS: Available
SEARCH: Not available   PUBLICATIONS: Not available

TALMAGE

BLACK DAPHNE RECORDS (I)
P.O. Box 546
Talmage 95481
(707) 462-1252

SERVICES: Mail Order Only

SPECIALTIES: Rock & Roll, Contemporary Jazz, Rhythm & Blues, Sound Tracks, Folk, Country & Western, Blues, Broadway Shows, Comedy, Classical

VOLUME: 33⅓ – 8,000
          45 – 8,000
          78 – 2,000
          Other – 0

STOCK: Domestic & Import/New & Used

SEARCH: Not available

COLLECTIONS: Will buy collections of rare records

PAYMENTS: Money Order, Personal Check

MAIL ORDER: 4th Class, U.P.S., Whatever shipment method requested; Prepayment

DISCOUNTS: Not available

PUBLICATIONS: Semiannual catalog available for $1.00 per issue

TORRANCE

DISC-CONNECTION RECORDS AND TAPES (II)
2617 Pacific Coast Highway
Torrance 90505
(213) 530-7685

M 10:00 A.M.–mid.
T–W 10:00–7:00
T–S 10:00 A.M.–mid.
S Noon–6:00

SERVICES: Walk-in Store/Mail Order

SPECIALTIES: Sound Tracks, Broadway Shows, British Musical Shows, Film Scores, Television Shows, Traditional Jazz, Contemporary Jazz, Beatles, Big Band, Easy Listening, Promotional

VOLUME: 33⅓ – 10,000
          45 – 3,000
          78 – 0
          Other – 0

STOCK: Domestic & Import/New & Used

SEARCH: Available with no service charge; Want lists maintained and requester notified when record comes in

COLLECTIONS: Will buy collections of rare records

PAYMENTS: Master Charge, Money Order, Personal Check, VISA/BankAmericard

MAIL ORDER: Whatever shipment method requested; Prepayment

DISCOUNTS: Available

PUBLICATIONS: Not available

VAN NUYS

RAY MACKNIC OR THEO'S (I)
P.O. Box 7511
Department D
Van Nuys 91406
  (213) 892-6289

SERVICES: Mail Order Only

SPECIALTIES: Contemporary Jazz, Bop Jazz, Traditional Jazz, Swing, Film Scores, Easy Listening, Country & Western, Rock & Roll, Rhythm & Blues, Rock

VOLUME: 33⅓ – 60,000
            45 – 5,000
            78 – 0
            Other – 0

STOCK: Domestic & Import/Used

SEARCH: Not available

COLLECTIONS: Will buy collections of rare records

PAYMENTS: Money Order, Personal Check

MAIL ORDER: Air Mail, 4th Class; Prepayment

DISCOUNTS: Not available

PUBLICATIONS: Free auction list available 18 times per year

VAN NUYS

ROLLIN' ROCK RECORDS (I)
6918 Peach Avenue
Van Nuys 91406
  (213) 781-4805

SERVICES: Mail Order Only

SPECIALTIES: Rock & Roll, Rockabilly

VOLUME: 33⅓ – I.N.A.
            45 – I.N.A.
            78 – I.N.A.
            Other – I.N.A.

STOCK: Domestic & Import/New & Used

SEARCH: Available with no service charge; Want lists maintained and requester notified when record comes in

COLLECTIONS: Will buy collections of rare records

PAYMENTS: Money Order, Personal Check

MAIL ORDER: Air Mail, 4th Class, U.P.S.; Prepayment

DISCOUNTS: Available

PUBLICATIONS: I.N.A.

WEST COVINA

TOWER RECORDS (II)   M–S   9:00 A.M.–mid.
1205 West Covina Parkway
West Covina 91790
  (213) 962-8707

SERVICES: Walk-in Store/Mail Order   COLLECTIONS: Will not buy collec-
(Limited)   tions of rare records

SPECIALTIES: All Major Categories   PAYMENTS: Master Charge, Money
VOLUME: 33⅓ – 100%   Order, Personal Charge Account,
            45 – 0   VISA/BankAmericard
            78 – 0   MAIL ORDER: 4th Class, U.P.S.; Pre-
         Other – 0   payment

STOCK: Domestic & Import/New   DISCOUNTS: Available

SEARCH: Not available   PUBLICATIONS: Not available

WEST SACRAMENTO

CENTRAL VALLEY RECORD RACK (II)   M–S   9:00 A.M.–mid.
1600 Cebrian
West Sacramento 95691
  (916) 372-0341

SERVICES: Walk-in Store/Mail Order   COLLECTIONS: Will not buy collec-
(Limited)   tions of rare records

SPECIALTIES: All Major Categories   PAYMENTS: Master Charge, Money
VOLUME: 33⅓ – 100%   Order, Personal Charge Account,
            45 – 0   VISA/BankAmericard
            78 – 0   MAIL ORDER: 4th Class, U.P.S.; Pre-
         Other – 0   payment

STOCK: Domestic & Import/New   DISCOUNTS: Available

SEARCH: Not available   PUBLICATIONS: Not available

WESTMINSTER

SOUTHERN RECORD SALES (I)   M–S   11:00–6:00
5940 Westminster Avenue
Westminster 92683
   (714) 893-4959

SERVICES: Walk-in Store/Mail Order

SPECIALTIES: (Alphabetical) Bluegrass, Blues, Country & Western, Ethnic, Folk, Hillbilly, Reggae, Religious,
Rhythm & Blues, Rock, Rock & Roll,
Rockabilly, Soul

VOLUME: 33⅓ – 34%
             45   – 33%
             78   – 33%
          Other – 0

STOCK: Domestic & Import/New &
Used

SEARCH: Available with no service
charge; Want lists maintained and requester notified when record comes in

COLLECTIONS: Will buy collections of
rare records

PAYMENTS: Master Charge, Money
Order, Personal Charge Account, Personal Check, VISA/BankAmericard

MAIL ORDER: Air Mail, 3rd Class, 4th
Class; Prepayment or C.O.D.

DISCOUNTS: Available

PUBLICATIONS: Free periodic catalog

WHITTIER

FIRST EDITION RECORDS (I)
P.O. Box 1138
Whittier 90609
   (213) 947-4295

SERVICES: Mail Order Only

SPECIALTIES: Traditional Jazz, Con-
temporary Jazz, Bop Jazz, Big Band,
Dixieland, Swing, Vocal, Sound
Tracks, Sinatra

VOLUME: 33⅓ – 10,000
             45   – 0
             78   – 0
          Other – 0

STOCK: Domestic/New & Used

SEARCH: Available with no service
charge

COLLECTIONS: Will buy collections of
rare records

PAYMENTS: Money Order, Personal
Check

MAIL ORDER: 4th Class, Whatever
shipment method requested; Prepayment

DISCOUNTS: Not available

PUBLICATIONS: Free monthly catalog;
Free monthly auction list

WHITTIER

WHITTWOOD MUSIC (I)
15626 Whittwood Lane
Whittier 90603
(213) 943-0177

M–F	10:00–9:00
S	10:00–5:00
S	Noon–5:00

SERVICES: Walk-in Store/Mail Order

SPECIALTIES: Sinatra, Elvis, Nostalgia, Beatles, Big Band, Christmas, Classical, Comedy, Easy Listening, Foreign Language, Instructional, Hawaiian, Latin

VOLUME:
33⅓ – 250
45 – 5,000
78 – 300
Other – Edison Rolls– 125

STOCK: Domestic & Import/New

SEARCH: Not available

COLLECTIONS: Will not buy collections of rare records

PAYMENTS: Master Charge, Money Order, Personal Check, VISA/BankAmericard

MAIL ORDER: 4th Class, U.P.S.; Prepayment

DISCOUNTS: Not available

PUBLICATIONS: Not available

COLORADO

DENVER

DENVER FOLKLORE CENTER (I)
608 East Seventeenth Avenue
Denver 80203
(303) 831-7015

M–S	10:00–6:00
S	Closed

SERVICES: Walk-in Store/Mail Order

SPECIALTIES: Folk, Bluegrass, Banjo, Blues, Traditional Jazz, Hillbilly, Ethnic, Children's, Country & Western, Feminist

VOLUME:
33⅓ – 1,000
45 – 10
78 – 0
Other – 0

STOCK: Domestic & Import/New & Used

SEARCH: Available with no service charge; Want lists maintained and requester notified when record comes in

COLLECTIONS: Will buy collections of rare records

PAYMENTS: Master Charge, Money Order, Personal Check, VISA/BankAmericard

MAIL ORDER: U.P.S.; Prepayment or C.O.D.

DISCOUNTS: Not available

PUBLICATIONS: Not available

DENVER

NOSTALGIA SHOP (I)	M	Closed
2431 South University Boulevard	T–F	10:00–5:00
Denver 80210	S–S	Noon–5:00
(303) 778-6566		

SERVICES: Walk-in Store/Mail Order

SPECIALTIES: Blues, Broadway Shows, Classical, Personalities, Rock, Sound Tracks

VOLUME: 33⅓ – 5,000
             45 – 0
             78 – 65,000
             Other – Edison Cyl-
                     inders

STOCK: Domestic/Used

SEARCH: Available with no service charge; Want lists maintained and requester notified when record comes in

COLLECTIONS: Will buy collections of rare records

PAYMENTS: Master Charge, Money Order, Personal Check, VISA/Bank-Americard

MAIL ORDER: U.P.S.; Prepayment

DISCOUNTS: Not available

PUBLICATIONS: I.N.A.

DENVER

PEACHES RECORDS AND TAPES (II)	M–T	10:00 A.M.–mid.
1235 East Evans	F–S 10:00 A.M.–1:00 A.M.
Denver 80210	S	Noon–10:00
(303) 778-0320		

SERVICES: Walk-in Store Only

SPECIALTIES: All Major Categories

VOLUME: 33⅓ – I.N.A.
             45 – I.N.A.
             78 – I.N.A.
             Other – I.N.A.

STOCK: Domestic & Import/New

SEARCH: Not available

COLLECTIONS: Will not buy collections of rare records

PAYMENTS: American Express, Master Charge, Personal Check, VISA/BankAmericard

MAIL ORDER: Not available

DISCOUNTS: Not available

PUBLICATIONS: I.N.A.

ESTES PARK

ULTIMATE RECORD SERVICE (I)
P.O. Box 1130
Estes Park 80507
  (800) 525-8757

SERVICES: Mail Order Only

SPECIALTIES: All Major Categories

VOLUME:　33⅓ – I.N.A.
　　　　　45　– I.N.A.
　　　　　78　– I.N.A.
　　　Other　– I.N.A.

STOCK: Domestic & Import/New

SEARCH: Not available

COLLECTIONS: Will buy collections of rare records

PAYMENTS: Master Charge, Personal Check, VISA/BankAmericard

MAIL ORDER:　　3rd Class, U.P.S.; C.O.D.

DISCOUNTS: Not available

PUBLICATIONS: Not available

CONNECTICUT

AVON

RECYCLED RECORDS (I)
P.O. Box 139
Avon 06001
  (203) 693-2535

SERVICES: Mail Order Only

SPECIALTIES:　Bluegrass, Contemporary Jazz, Folk, Folk-Rock, Reggae, Rock, Rock & Roll

VOLUME:　33⅓ – 5,000
　　　　　45　– 0
　　　　　78　– 0
　　　Other　– 0

STOCK: Domestic & Import/New & Used

SEARCH: Available with no service charge; Want lists maintained and requester notified when record comes in

COLLECTIONS: Will buy collections of rare records

PAYMENTS: Money Order, Personal Check

MAIL ORDER: Air Mail, 4th Class, U.P.S.; Prepayment or C.O.D.

DISCOUNTS: Available

PUBLICATIONS: I.N.A.

EAST HARTFORD

RKNROL TRADER (II)
P.O. Box 18083
East Hartford 06118
  Telephone: I.N.A.

SERVICES: Mail Order Only

SPECIALTIES: Sinatra

VOLUME: 33⅓ – I.N.A.
           45 – I.N.A.
           78 – I.N.A.
        Other – I.N.A.

STOCK: Domestic/New

SEARCH: Available with service charge; Want lists maintained and requester notified when record comes in

COLLECTIONS: Not available for purchase

PAYMENTS: Money Order

MAIL ORDER: Whatever shipment method requested; Prepayment

DISCOUNTS: Not available

PUBLICATIONS: Free annual set-sale list

FAIRFIELD

TRIDENT RECORDS (II)
57 Unquowa Road
Fairfield 06430
  (203) 255-1838

SERVICES: Walk-in Store (By Appointment Only)/Mail Order (Occasional)

SPECIALTIES: (Alphabetical) Blues, Classical, Contemporary Jazz, Folk, Reggae, Rock, Rock & Roll, Traditional Jazz

VOLUME: 33⅓ – I.N.A.
           45 – I.N.A.
           78 – I.N.A.
        Other – I.N.A.

STOCK: Domestic & Import/New & Used

SEARCH: Available with no service charge; Want lists maintained and requester notified when record comes in

COLLECTIONS: Will not buy collections of rare records

PAYMENTS: Master Charge, Personal Check

MAIL ORDER: U.P.S.; C.O.D.

DISCOUNTS: Available

PUBLICATIONS: I.N.A.

GEORGETOWN

BROADWAY/HOLLYWOOD RECORDINGS (I) M–T 10:00–10:00
P.O. Box 496   F   10:00–4:00
Georgetown 06829   S–S   Closed
(203) 544-8288

SERVICES: Walk-in Store/Mail Order

SPECIALTIES: Broadway Shows, Film Scores, Sound Tracks, Nostalgia, Easy Listening, Instrumental, Comedy, British Musical Shows, Television Shows, Vocal

VOLUME: 33⅓ – 20,000
         45 – 5,000
         78 – 200
         Other – 0

STOCK: Domestic & Import/New & Used

SEARCH: Available with no service charge; Want lists maintained and requester notified when record comes in

COLLECTIONS: Available for purchase; Will buy collections of rare records

PAYMENTS: Money Order, Personal Check

MAIL ORDER: Whatever shipment method requested; Prepayment

DISCOUNTS: Not available

PUBLICATIONS: Triennial catalog available for $1.00 per issue; Free quarterly listing available

GLASTONBURY

ROBERT A. RYMARZICK RECORDS (I)
28 Courtney Circle
Glastonbury 06033
(203) 633-2385

SERVICES: Mail Order Only

SPECIALTIES: Rock & Roll, Soul, Rock, Instrumental, Rhythm & Blues, Promotional, Country & Western, Surfing, Sound Tracks, Comedy

VOLUME: 33⅓ – 5,000
         45 – 20,000
         78 – 500
         Other – 0

STOCK: Domestic/Used

SEARCH: Available with no service charge; Want lists maintained and requester notified when record comes in

COLLECTIONS: Will buy collections of rare records

PAYMENTS: Money Order, Personal Check

MAIL ORDER: Whatever shipment method requested; Prepayment or C.O.D.

DISCOUNTS: Not available

PUBLICATIONS: Free quarterly catalog; Free bimonthly auction list

HARTFORD

BELMONT RECORD SHOP (I)
163 Washington Street
Hartford 06106
(203) 522-2200

M–F   10:00–8:00
S   10:00–6:00
S   Noon–5:00

SERVICES: Walk-in Store/Mail Order

SPECIALTIES: All Major Categories

VOLUME: 33⅓ – 45%
            45 – 55%
            78 – 0
            Other – 0

STOCK: Domestic & Import/New

SEARCH: Not available

COLLECTIONS: Will buy collections of rare records

PAYMENTS: Master Charge, Money Order, VISA/BankAmericard

MAIL ORDER: 1st Class, U.P.S.; Prepayment

DISCOUNTS: Not available

PUBLICATIONS I.N.A.

MARION

RAMBLIN' RECORDS (I)
P.O. Box 4411
Marion 06444
  Telephone: I.N.A.

SERVICES: Mail Order Only

SPECIALTIES: All Major Categories

VOLUME: 33⅓ – 400
            45 – 20,000
            78 – 5,000
            Other – 0

STOCK: Domestic & Import/New & Used

SEARCH: Available with no service charge; Want lists maintained and requester notified when record comes in

COLLECTIONS: Will buy collections of rare records

PAYMENTS: Money Order

MAIL ORDER: Air Mail, 4th Class; Prepayment

DISCOUNTS: Available

PUBLICATIONS: I.N.A.

NEW BRITAIN

GARY KING RECORDS (I)
46 Bingham Street
New Britain 06050
(203) 229-7921

SERVICES: Mail Order Only

SPECIALTIES: Elvis, Nostalgia, Rock & Roll, Novelty, Surfing, Beatles, Country & Western, Punk Rock/New Wave, Rhythm & Blues, Rock, Rockabilly

VOLUME: 33⅓ – 1,000
           45   – 50,000
           78   – 0
           Other – 0

STOCK: Domestic & Import/New & Used

SEARCH: Not available; Want lists maintained and requester notified if record comes in

COLLECTIONS: Will buy collections of rare records

PAYMENTS: Money Order, Personal Check

MAIL ORDER: Whatever shipment method requested; Prepayment

DISCOUNTS: Not available

PUBLICATIONS: Free bimonthly auction list; Free bimonthly set-sale list

SOUTHINGTON

DAVE COOK RECORDS (I)
121 Oak Street
Southington 06489
(203) 628-4345

SERVICES: Mail Order Only

SPECIALTIES: Country & Western, Bluegrass, Hillbilly, Old-Time Country

VOLUME: 33⅓ – 4,000
           45   – 10,000
           78   – 5,000
           Other – 0

STOCK: Domestic/New & Used

SEARCH: Want lists maintained and requester notified when record comes in

COLLECTIONS: Will buy collections of rare records

PAYMENTS: Personal Check

MAIL ORDER: 4th Class; Prepayment

DISCOUNTS: Not available

PUBLICATIONS: Free monthly auction list

WETHERSFIELD

INTEGRITY 'N MUSIC (I)	M–W	11:00–7:00
506 Silas Deane Highway	T–F	11:00–9:00
Wethersfield 06109	S	10:00–6:00
(203) 563-4005	S	1:00–5:00

SERVICES: Walk-in Store/Mail Order

SPECIALTIES: (Alphabetical) Bluegrass, Blues, Bossa Nova, Classical, Contemporary Jazz, Disco, Folk, Folk-Rock, Reggae, Rhythm & Blues, Rock, Rock & Roll, Soul

VOLUME: 33⅓ – 2,500
            45 – 0
            78 – 0
            Other – 0

STOCK: Domestic & Import/New & Used

SEARCH: Not available

COLLECTIONS: Will buy collections of rare records

PAYMENTS: Master Charge, Money Order, Personal Check, VISA/BankAmericard

MAIL ORDER: Air Mail, 4th Class; Prepayment

DISCOUNTS: Available

PUBLICATIONS: I.N.A.

DELAWARE

CHESWOLD

DISC COLLECTOR PUBLICATIONS (I)
P.O. Box 169
Cheswold 19936
  Telephone: I.N.A.

SERVICES: Mail Order Only

SPECIALTIES: Bluegrass, Old- time Country, Hillbilly, Country & Western, Rockabilly

VOLUME: 33⅓ – 800
            45 – 1,800
            78 – 3,000
            Other – 0

STOCK: Domestic/New & Used

SEARCH: Available with no service charge; Want lists maintained and requester notified when record comes in

COLLECTIONS: Will not buy collections of rare records

PAYMENTS: Money Order

MAIL ORDER: Whatever shipment method requested; Prepayment

DISCOUNTS: Not available

PUBLICATIONS: Free quarterly auction list

WILMINGTON

BERT'S TAPE FACTORY (II) M–F   10:00–9:00
2501 Concord Pike S   10:00–6:00
Wilmington 19803 S   Noon–5:00
  (302) 478-3724

SERVICES: Walk-in Store Only

SPECIALTIES: (Alphabetical) Bluegrass, Blues, Classical, Disco, Folk, Folk-Rock, Reggae, Rhythm & Blues, Rock, Rock & Roll, Soul, Sound Tracks, Traditional Jazz

VOLUME: 33⅓ – I.N.A.
     45 – I.N.A.
     78 – I.N.A.
     Other – I.N.A.

STOCK: Domestic & Import/New & Used

SEARCH: Available with no service charge; Want lists maintained and requester notified when record comes in

COLLECTIONS: Will buy collections of rare records

PAYMENTS: Master Charge, Personal Check, VISA/BankAmericard

MAIL ORDER: Not available

DISCOUNTS: Available

PUBLICATIONS: I.N.A.

DISTRICT OF COLUMBIA

THE DISC SHOP (II) M–S   9:30–9:00
1815 Connecticut Avenue Northwest S   Noon–5:00
Washington 20009
  (202) 387-1353

SERVICES: Walk-in Store/Mail Order

SPECIALTIES: All Major Categories

VOLUME: 33⅓ – 100%
     45 – 0
     78 – 0
     Other – 0

STOCK: Domestic & Import/New

SEARCH: Available with service charge

COLLECTIONS: Will not buy collections of rare records

PAYMENTS: American Express, Central Charge, Master Charge, Money Order, Personal Check, VISA/BankAmericard

MAIL ORDER: Whatever shipment method requested; Prepayment or C.O.D.

DISCOUNTS: Available

PUBLICATIONS: I.N.A.

THE DISC SHOP (II)   M–S   9:30–9:00
5310 Wisconsin Avenue Northwest   S   Noon–5:00
Washington 20015
(202) 966-3466

SERVICES: Walk-in Store/Mail Order   PAYMENTS: American Express, Cen-
                                       tral Charge, Master Charge, Money
SPECIALTIES: All Major Categories   Order, Personal Check, VISA/Bank-
VOLUME: 33⅓ – 100%   Americard
             45   – 0
             78   – 0   MAIL ORDER: Whatever shipment
             Other – 0   method requested; Prepayment or
                                       C.O.D.
STOCK: Domestic & Import/New
                                       DISCOUNTS: Available
SEARCH: Available with service
charge   PUBLICATIONS: I.N.A.

COLLECTIONS: Will not buy collections of rare records

RECORD AND TAPE, LIMITED (II)   M–S   9:30–6:30
1900 L Street   S   Closed
Washington 20036
(202) 785-5037

SERVICES: Walk-in Store/Mail Order   COLLECTIONS: Will not buy collec-
                                       tions of rare records
SPECIALTIES: All Major Categories
                                       PAYMENTS: Master Charge, Money
VOLUME: 33⅓ – I.N.A.   Order, Personal Check, VISA/Bank-
             45   – I.N.A.   Americard
             78   – I.N.A.
             Other – I.N.A.   MAIL ORDER: 4th Class, U.P.S.; Pre-
                                       payment
STOCK: Domestic & Import/New
                                       DISCOUNTS: Not available
SEARCH: Available with no service
charge   PUBLICATIONS: I.N.A.

RECORD AND TAPE, LIMITED (II)
1239 Wisconsin Avenue
Washington 20016
(202) 338-6712

M–T   10:00–10:00
F–S 10:00 A.M.–mid.
S   Noon–5:00

SERVICES: Walk-in Store/Mail Order

SPECIALTIES: All Major Categories

VOLUME: 33⅓ – I.N.A.
            45   – I.N.A.
            78   – I.N.A.
            Other – I.N.A.

STOCK: Domestic & Import/New

SEARCH: Available with no service charge

COLLECTIONS: Will not buy collections of rare records

PAYMENTS: Master Charge, Money Order, Personal Check, VISA/Bank-Americard

MAIL ORDER: 4th Class, U.P.S.; Prepayment

DISCOUNTS: Not available

PUBLICATIONS: I.N.A.

FLORIDA

CLEARWATER

THE VINYL MUSEUM (I)
1665 Long Bow Lane
Clearwater 33516
Telephone: I.N.A.

SERVICES: Mail Order Only

SPECIALTIES: Rock, Soul, Rock & Roll, Folk, Blues, Easy Listening, Ethnic, Disco, Contemporary Jazz, Comedy, Rhythm & Blues, Punk Rock/New Wave

VOLUME: 33⅓ – 4,000
            45   – 0
            78   – 0
            Other – 0

STOCK: Domestic/New & Used

SEARCH: Available with no service charge; Want lists maintained and requester notified when record comes in

COLLECTIONS: Will buy collections of rare records

PAYMENTS: Money Order

MAIL ORDER: Whatever shipment method requested; Prepayment

DISCOUNTS: Available

PUBLICATIONS: Not available

CRYSTAL RIVER

ORANGE BLOSSOM RECORDS (I)　　　　　M–S　　5:00–11:00
c/o Marty W. Stonesifer/Joe Scott
Route 2
P.O. Box 159
Crystal River 32629
(904) 795-7512 or 3809

SERVICES: Mail Order Only (Above Times for Telephone)

SPECIALTIES: Rock, Rock & Roll, Rockabilly, Punk Rock/New Wave, Sound Tracks, Beatles, Rhythm & Blues, Broadway Shows, Elvis, Promotional

VOLUME:　　33⅓　–　3,500
　　　　　　45　–　4,500
　　　　　　78　–　100
　　　　　Other　–　0

STOCK: Domestic & Import/New & Used

SEARCH: Want lists maintained and requester notified when record comes in

COLLECTIONS: Will buy collections of rare records

PAYMENTS: Money Order, Personal Check

MAIL ORDER: 4th Class, Whatever shipment method requested; Prepayment or C.O.D.

DISCOUNTS: Available

PUBLICATIONS: Not available

CRYSTAL RIVER

JOSEPH SCOTT RECORDS (I)
Route 2
P.O. Box 194
Crystal River 32629
(904) 795-3809

SERVICES: Mail Order Only

SPECIALTIES: (Alphabetical) Blues, Bossa Nova, Contemporary Jazz, Country & Western, Easy Listening, Hillbilly, Reggae, Rhythm & Blues, Rock & Roll, Soul, Traditional Jazz

VOLUME:　　33⅓　–　2,000
　　　　　　45　–　35,000
　　　　　　78　–　1,000
　　　　　Other　–　0

STOCK: Domestic & Import/New & Used

SEARCH: Want lists maintained and requester notified when record comes in

COLLECTIONS: Will buy collections of rare records

PAYMENTS: Money Order, Personal Check

MAIL ORDER: Air Mail, 1st Class, 4th Class; Prepayment

DISCOUNTS: Available

PUBLICATIONS: I.N.A.

ELKTON

ROBERT BRENNAN RECORDS (I)
P.O. Box 118
Elkton 32033
  Telephone: I.N.A.

SERVICES: Mail Order Only

SPECIALTIES: (Alphabetical) Beatles, Blues, Contemporary Jazz, Country & Western, Elvis, Hillbilly, Instrumental, Rhythm & Blues, Rockabilly, Sinatra, Soul, Surfing

VOLUME: 33⅓ – 2,000
             45   – 15,000
             78   – 3,000
             Other – 0

STOCK: Domestic & Import/New & Used

SEARCH: Want lists maintained and requester notified when record comes in

COLLECTIONS: Available for purchase; Will buy collections of rare records

PAYMENTS: Money Order, Personal Check

MAIL ORDER: Whatever shipment method requested; Prepayment

DISCOUNTS: Not available

PUBLICATIONS: Free semiannual auction list available

FORT LAUDERDALE

DON CLEARY RECORD SALES (I)
P.O. Box 16265
Fort Lauderdale 33321
  Telephone: I.N.A.

SERVICES: Mail Order Only

SPECIALTIES: All Major Categories

VOLUME: 33⅓ – 30,000
             45   – 30,000
             78   – 40,000
             Other – 0

STOCK: Domestic & Import/New & Used

SEARCH: Available with no service charge; Want lists maintained and requester notified when record comes in

COLLECTIONS: Will buy collections of rare records

PAYMENTS: Money Order, Personal Check

MAIL ORDER: Air Mail, 4th Class; Prepayment

DISCOUNTS: Not available

PUBLICATIONS: Free periodic auction list; Free periodic set-sale list

FORT LAUDERDALE

HIT MAN RECORDS (I)
P.O. Box 9684
Fort Lauderdale 33310
(305) 733-2485

SERVICES: Mail Order Only

SPECIALTIES: Folk-Rock, Rhythm &
Blues, Rock, Rock & Roll

VOLUME: 33⅓ – 1,000
           45   – 30,000
           78   – 0
           Other – 0

STOCK: Domestic/New & Used

SEARCH: Available with no service
charge; Want lists maintained and requester notified when record comes in

COLLECTIONS: Will buy collections of
rare records

PAYMENTS: Money Order, Personal
Check

MAIL ORDER: 4th Class; Prepayment

DISCOUNTS: Available

PUBLICATIONS: I.N.A.

FORT LAUDERDALE

SID'S RECORDS AND TAPES
  INCORPORATED (I)
2896 East Sunrise Boulevard
Fort Lauderdale 33313
  (305) 563-9278 or 565-5855

M–S	10:00–9:00
S	Noon–6:00

SERVICES: Walk-in Store/Mail Order

SPECIALTIES: Beatles, Elvis, Rock,
Rock & Roll, Punk Rock/New Wave,
Promotional, Sound Tracks, Surfing,
Folk, Novelty

VOLUME: 33⅓ – 2,000
           45   – 1,000
           78   – 0
           Other – 0

STOCK: Domestic & Import/New &
Used

SEARCH: Available with no service
charge; Want lists maintained and requester notified when record comes in

COLLECTIONS: Will buy collections of
rare records

PAYMENTS: Master Charge, Money
Order, Personal Check, VISA/Bank-
Americard

MAIL ORDER: Whatever shipment
method requested; Prepayment

DISCOUNTS: Available

PUBLICATIONS: Free biannual auction
list

HOLLYWOOD

PHILIP SCHNEIDER RECORDS (I)
P.O. Box 1912
Hollywood 33022
   Telephone: I.N.A.

SERVICES: Mail Order Only

SPECIALTIES: Classical, Sound Tracks, Broadway Shows, Film Scores, Opera, Television Shows, Vocal

VOLUME: 33⅓ – 2,500
             45   – 0
             78   – 0
           Other – 0

STOCK: Domestic & Import/Used

SEARCH: Available with no service charge; Want lists maintained and requester notified when record comes in

COLLECTIONS: Will buy collections of rare records

PAYMENTS: Money Order, Personal Check

MAIL ORDER: 4th Class; Prepayment

DISCOUNTS: Not available

PUBLICATIONS: Not available

LAUDERDALE LAKES

SID'S RECORDS AND TAPES
   INCORPORATED (I)
3381 North State Road 7
Lauderdale Lakes 33319
   (305) 731-5559

M–S   10:00–9:00
S   Noon–6:00

SERVICES: Walk-in Store/Mail Order

SPECIALTIES: Beatles, Elvis, Rock, Rock & Roll, Punk Rock/New Wave, Promotional, Sound Tracks, Surfing, Folk, Novelty

VOLUME: 33⅓ – 2,000
             45   – 1,000
             78   – 0
           Other – 0

STOCK: Domestic & Import/New & Used

SEARCH: Available with no service charge; Want lists maintained and requester notified when record comes in

COLLECTIONS: Will buy collections of rare records

PAYMENTS: Master Charge, Money Order, Personal Check, VISA/Bank-Americard

MAIL ORDER: Whatever shipment method requested; Prepayment

DISCOUNTS: Available

PUBLICATIONS: Free biannual auction list

MIAMI

A.J.'S FILM AND STAGE RECORDINGS (I)
P.O. Box 557342
Miami 33155
  Telephone: I.N.A.

SERVICES: Mail Order Only

SPECIALTIES: Sound Tracks, Broadway Shows, Personalities, Television Shows, British Musical Shows, Elvis, Sinatra, Christmas

VOLUME: 33⅓ – 8,000
                 45 – 1,000
                 78 – 0
               Other – 0

STOCK: Domestic & Import/New & Used

SEARCH: Want lists maintained and requester notified when record comes in

COLLECTIONS: Will buy collections of rare records

PAYMENTS: Money Order

MAIL ORDER: 4th Class; Prepayment

DISCOUNTS: Not available

PUBLICATIONS: Free monthly auction list

MIAMI

HOME OF THE BLUES RECORD SHOP (I)   M–S   Noon–mid.
P.O. Box 557292
Miami 33155
  (305) 445-6797

SERVICES: Mail Order Only (Above Times for Telephone)

SPECIALTIES: (Alphabetical) Blues, Contemporary Jazz, Country & Western, Folk, Gospel/Sacred, Instrumental, Religious, Rhythm & Blues, Rock, Rock & Roll, Rockabilly, Soul

VOLUME: 33⅓ – 5,000
                 45 – 50,000
                 78 – 10,000
               Other – 0

STOCK: Domestic/New & Used

SEARCH: Want lists maintained and requester notified when record comes in

COLLECTIONS: Will buy collections of rare records

PAYMENTS: Money Order, Personal Check

MAIL ORDER: Air Mail, 4th Class; Prepayment

DISCOUNTS: Available

PUBLICATIONS: Free semiannual catalog

MIAMI

LEE'S MUSIC CENTER (I)   M–S   10:30–6:30
6265 Southwest 8th Street   S   Closed
Miami 33144
   (305) 264-0791

SERVICES: Walk-in Store/Mail Order

SPECIALTIES: (Alphabetical) Beatles, Broadway Shows, Country & Western, Dance, Disco, Dixieland, Elvis, Film Scores, Nostalgia, Rock & Roll, Soul, Sound Tracks

VOLUME: 33⅓ – 10,000
             45 – 500,000
             78 – 5,000
             Other – 0

STOCK: Domestic & Import/New & Used

SEARCH: Want lists maintained and requester notified when record comes in

COLLECTIONS: Available for purchase; Will buy collections of rare records

PAYMENTS: Money Order, Personal Check

MAIL ORDER: 4th Class, Whatever shipment method requested; Prepayment or C.O.D.

DISCOUNTS: Available

PUBLICATIONS: Biannual catalog available for $1.50 per issue; Free occasional auction list

MIAMI

JOHN MILLER MUSIC COMPANY (I)
P.O. Box 640116
Uleta Branch
Miami 33164
   (305) 652-0343

SERVICES: Mail Order Only

SPECIALTIES: Rock & Roll, Surfing, Rock, Elvis, Rockabilly, Instrumental, Novelty, Sound Tracks, Broadway Shows, Vocal

VOLUME: 33⅓ – 10,000
             45 – 30,000
             78 – 0
             Other – 0

STOCK: Domestic/New & Used

SEARCH: Want lists maintained and requester notified when record comes in

COLLECTIONS: Will buy collections of rare records

PAYMENTS: Money Order, Personal Check

MAIL ORDER: 4th Class; Prepayment

DISCOUNTS: Available

PUBLICATIONS: Monthly auction list available for $3.00 per year

MIAMI

RICHARD MINOR—MINORS THREE
  RECORDS (I)
9415 Southwest 42nd Street
Miami 33165
  (305) 552-7635

SERVICES: Mail Order Only

SPECIALTIES: (Alphabetical) Blue-
grass, Blues, Country & Western,
Disco, Easy Listening, Folk, Folk-
Rock, Hillbilly, Reggae, Rhythm &
Blues, Rock, Rock & Roll, Rockabilly

VOLUME: 33⅓ – 15,000
              45 – 200,000
              78 – 3,000
              Other – 0

STOCK: Domestic & Import/New &
Used

SEARCH: Available with no service
charge

COLLECTIONS: Will buy collections of
rare records

PAYMENTS: Money Order, Personal
Check

MAIL ORDER: Air Mail, 1st Class, 4th
Class; Prepayment or C.O.D.

DISCOUNTS: Available

PUBLICATIONS: I.N.A.

ORLANDO

MUSICAL MEMORIES (I)
P.O. Box 8382
Orlando 32806
  (305) 859-7980

SERVICES: Mail Order Only

SPECIALTIES: Big Band, Dance, Edi-
son Discs/Cylinders, Christmas,
Polka, Vocal, Children's, Country &
Western, Foreign Language, Nostalgia

VOLUME: 33⅓ – 4,000
              45 – 5,000
              78 – 117,000
              Other – Edison
                      Discs–4,500
                      Cylinders–4,500

STOCK: Domestic/New & Used

SEARCH: Not available

COLLECTIONS: Not available for purchase; Will buy collections of rare
records

PAYMENTS: Money Order, Personal
Check

MAIL ORDER: 4th Class, U.P.S.,
Whatever shipment method requested;
Prepayment

DISCOUNTS: Not available

PUBLICATIONS: Free quarterly auction
list

ORLANDO

ROCK & ROLL HEAVEN (I)
1819 North Orange Avenue
Orlando 32804
    (305) 896-1952

M	Closed
T–F	Noon–6:00
S	10:00–6:00
S	Closed

SERVICES: Walk-in Store Only

SPECIALTIES: (Alphabetical) Blues, Country & Western, Disco, Folk, Folk-Rock, Hillbilly, Rhythm & Blues, Rock, Rock & Roll, Soul

VOLUME: 33⅓ – I.N.A.
                45   – I.N.A.
                78   – I.N.A.
            Other – I.N.A.

STOCK: Domestic/Used

SEARCH: Want lists maintained and requester notified when record comes in

COLLECTIONS: Will buy collections of rare records

PAYMENTS: Personal Check

MAIL ORDER: Not available

DISCOUNTS: Not available

PUBLICATIONS: Not available

PLANTATION

SID-ARTHUR OLDIES (I)
Jacaranda Plaza Shops
8265 West Sunrise Boulevard
Plantation 33322
    (305) 472-3455

M–S	10:00–6:00
S	Closed

SERVICES: Walk-in Store/Mail Order

SPECIALTIES: (Alphabetical) Big Band, Easy Listening, Elvis, Film Scores, Nostalgia, Rhythm & Blues, Sinatra, Soul, Sound Tracks, Standards, Swing, Traditional Jazz

VOLUME: 33⅓ – 10,000
                45   – 150,000
                78   – 15,000
            Other – 0

STOCK: Domestic & Import/New & Used

SEARCH: Available with no service charge; Want lists maintained and requester notified when record comes in

COLLECTIONS: Will buy collections of rare records

PAYMENTS: Master Charge, Money Order, VISA/BankAmericard

MAIL ORDER: 4th Class, Whatever shipment method requested; Prepayment

DISCOUNTS: Available

PUBLICATIONS: Not available

ST. PETERSBURG

BOB BERNARD RECORDS (I)
P.O. Box 7885
St. Petersburg 33734
Telephone: I.N.A.

SERVICES: Mail Order Only

SPECIALTIES: (Alphabetical) Bossa Nova, Country & Western, Disco, Easy Listening, Folk-Rock, Hillbilly, Rhythm & Blues, Rock, Rock & Roll, Soul

VOLUME: 33⅓ – 1,000
            45 – 8,000
            78 – 100
     Other – 0

STOCK: Domestic/Used

SEARCH: Want lists maintained and requester notified when record comes in

COLLECTIONS: Will buy collections of rare records

PAYMENTS: Money Order, Personal Check

MAIL ORDER: Air Mail, 4th Class; Prepayment

DISCOUNTS: I.N.A.

PUBLICATIONS: I.N.A.

THONOTOSASSA

L & L ROCK BOTTOM RECORD COMPANY (I)
Route 2
P.O. Box 580
Thonotosassa 33592
  (813) 986-3698 (Call for Directions)

M–F	Noon–8:00
S–S	Closed

SERVICES: Walk-in Store/Mail Order

SPECIALTIES: All Major Categories

VOLUME: 33⅓ – 25,000
            45 – 20,000
            78 – 4,000
     Other – 0

STOCK: Domestic & Import/New & Used

SEARCH: Want lists maintained and requester notified when record comes in

COLLECTIONS: Will buy collections of rare records

PAYMENTS: Money Order, Personal Check

MAIL ORDER: 4th Class; Prepayment

DISCOUNTS: Available

PUBLICATIONS: I.N.A.

ROME

BO-JO'S RECORD COMPANY (I)
1507 Turner-McCall Boulevard
Rome 30161
(404) 232-2656

M–T	11:00–8:00
F	11:00–9:00
S	11:00–7:00
S	Closed

SERVICES: Walk-in Store/Mail Order

SPECIALTIES: Blues, Country & Western, Disco, Easy Listening, Rock, Rock & Roll, Soul

VOLUME:
33⅓ – 5,000
45 – 2,000
78 – 0
Other – 0

STOCK: Domestic & Import/New & Used

SEARCH: Want lists maintained and requester notified when record comes in

COLLECTIONS: Will not buy collections of rare records

PAYMENTS: Master Charge, Money Order, Personal Check, VISA/Bank-Americard

MAIL ORDER: U.P.S.; Prepayment

DISCOUNTS: Available

PUBLICATIONS: I.N.A.

UNION CITY

J. McCARTNEY RECORDS (I)
5148 Hilltop Drive
Union City 30291
(404) 964-2763

SERVICES: Mail Order Only

SPECIALTIES: Rock, Soul, Rock & Roll, Punk Rock/New Wave, Sound Tracks, Comedy, Rockabilly, Surfing, Folk, Country & Western

VOLUME:
33⅓ – 4,000
45 – 1,500
78 – 1,000
Other – 0

STOCK: Domestic & Import/New & Used

SEARCH: Available with no service charge; Want lists maintained and requester notified when record comes in

COLLECTIONS: Available for purchase; Will buy collections of rare records

PAYMENTS: Money Order, Personal Check

MAIL ORDER: 4th Class, Whatever shipment method requested; Prepayment

DISCOUNTS: Not available

PUBLICATIONS: Free auction list available eight times per year

HAWAII

HONOLULU

GOIN' BACK ENTERPRISES (I)
P.O. Box 7161
Honolulu 96821
  Telephone: I.N.A.

SERVICES: Mail Order Only

SPECIALTIES: Rock & Roll, Rock, Punk Rock/New Wave

VOLUME: 33⅓ – 50,000
         45 – 0
         78 – 0
     Other – 0

STOCK: Domestic & Import/New & Used

SEARCH: Available with no service charge

COLLECTIONS: Will buy collections of rare records

PAYMENTS: Money Order, Personal Check

MAIL ORDER: Air Mail, 1st Class, 4th Class, Whatever shipment method requested; Prepayment

DISCOUNTS: Available

PUBLICATIONS: Annual catalog available for $1.00 per issue

HONOLULU

MOM N' POP'S MUSIC (I)
2915 Kapiolani Boulevard
Honolulu 96814
  (808) 737-4348

M–W	9:00–6:00
T–F	9:00–8:00
S	9:00–6:00
S	Closed

SERVICES: Walk-in Store/Mail Order

SPECIALTIES: All Major Categories

VOLUME: 33⅓ – 10,000
         45 – 5,000
         78 – 1,000
     Other – 0

STOCK: Domestic/New & Used

SEARCH: Available with no service charge; Want lists maintained and requester notified when record comes in

COLLECTIONS: Will buy collections of rare records

PAYMENTS: Master Charge, Money Order, Personal Check, VISA/BankAmericard

MAIL ORDER: Air Mail, 4th Class; Prepayment or C.O.D.

DISCOUNTS: Not available

PUBLICATIONS: I.N.A.

IDAHO

BOISE

THE MUSICWORKS (I)	M–T	10:00–9:00
4212 Overland Road	F	10:00–10:00
Boise 83705	S	10:00–9:00
(208) 345-9730	S	Noon–8:00

SERVICES: Walk-in Store/Mail Order

SPECIALTIES: All Major Categories

VOLUME: 33⅓ – 2,000
          45 – 0
          78 – 0
          Other – 0

STOCK: Domestic & Import/New & Used

SEARCH: Available with no service charge; Want lists maintained and requester notified when record comes in

COLLECTIONS: Will buy collections of rare records

PAYMENTS: Master Charge, Money Order, Personal Check, VISA/BankAmericard

MAIL ORDER: Air Mail, 4th Class, U.P.S.; Prepayment

DISCOUNTS: Available

PUBLICATIONS: I.N.A.

ILLINOIS

BERWYN

JAZZ MUSIC MAGAZINES (I)   M–S 7:00 A.M.–10:00 P.M.
c/o Robert Fitzner
1942 South East Avenue
Berwyn 60402
  (312) 484-3587

SERVICES: Walk-in Store/Mail Order

SPECIALTIES: Big Band, Bop Jazz, Dixieland, Contemporary Jazz, Swing, Traditional Jazz, Classical, Documentary, Opera

VOLUME: 33⅓ – 2,000
          45 – 0
          78 – 400
          Other – 0

STOCK: Domestic & Import/New & Used

SEARCH: Available with no service charge; Want lists maintained and requester notified when record comes in

COLLECTIONS: I.N.A.

PAYMENTS: Money Order, Personal Check

MAIL ORDER: 4th Class; Prepayment

DISCOUNTS: Available

PUBLICATIONS: Free periodic catalog

CENTRALIA

YE OLDE RUMMAGE SHOPPE (II)   M–S   9:00–5:00
619 East 2nd
Centralia 62801
  (618) 532-3069

SERVICES: Walk-in Store/Mail Order

SPECIALTIES: All Major Categories

VOLUME: 33⅓ – 300
             45   – 5,000
             78   – 0
             Other – 0

STOCK: Domestic/New & Used

SEARCH: Not available; Want lists maintained and requester notified when record comes in

COLLECTIONS: Will not buy collections of rare records

PAYMENTS: Money Order, Personal Check

MAIL ORDER: 4th Class; Prepayment or C.O.D.

DISCOUNTS: Available

PUBLICATIONS: I.N.A.

CHICAGO

BEVERLY RECORD, COSTUME & NOVELTY   M–F   9:30–7:00
  SHOP (I)   S   9:30–6:00
11612 South Western Avenue   S   Closed
Chicago 60643
  (312) 779-0066 or 0067 or 0068

SERVICES: Walk-in Store/Mail Order

SPECIALTIES: All Major Categories

VOLUME: 33⅓ – 50,000
             45   – 100,000
             78   – 100,000
             Other – 0

STOCK: Domestic & Import/New & Used

SEARCH: Available with service charge; Want lists maintained and requester notified when record comes in

COLLECTIONS: Will buy collections of rare records

PAYMENTS: Master Charge, Money Order, VISA/BankAmericard

MAIL ORDER: U.P.S.; Prepayment or C.O.D.

DISCOUNTS: Available

PUBLICATIONS: Periodic catalog available for $2.00 per issue

CHICAGO

JAZZ RECORD MART (I)   M–F   10:30–8:00
4243 North Lincoln   S   10:30–6:00
Chicago 60618   S   1:30–6:30
  (312) 528-8834

SERVICES: Walk-in Store/Mail Order   SEARCH: Not available

SPECIALTIES: Contemporary Jazz,   COLLECTIONS: Will buy collections of
Bop Jazz, Blues, Traditional Jazz,   rare records
Swing, Rhythm & Blues, Soul, Rag-   PAYMENTS: Money Order, Personal
time, Gospel/Sacred, Sinatra   Check

VOLUME: 33⅓ – 50,000   MAIL ORDER: U.P.S.; Prepayment
             45 – 0
             78 – 0   DISCOUNTS: Available
          Other – 0   PUBLICATIONS: Free quarterly cata-
                                           log
STOCK: Domestic & Import/New &
Used

CHICAGO

JAZZ RECORD MART (I)   M–F   10:30–8:00
11 West Grand   S   10:30–6:00
Chicago 60610   S   1:30–6:30
  (312) 222-1467

SERVICES: Walk-in Store/Mail Order   COLLECTIONS: Will buy collections of
                                          rare records
SPECIALTIES: Contemporary Jazz,
Bop Jazz, Blues, Traditional Jazz,   PAYMENTS: Money Order, Personal
Swing, Rhythm & Blues, Soul, Rag-   Check
time, Gospel/Sacred, Sinatra   MAIL ORDER: U.P.S.; Prepayment

VOLUME: 33⅓ – 0   DISCOUNTS: Available
             45 – 5,000
             78 – 25,000   PUBLICATIONS: Free quarterly cata-
          Other – Transcriptions   log

STOCK: Domestic & Import/New &
Used

SEARCH: Not available

CHICAGO

JOE'S RECORDS AND TAPE CENTER (II)
550 East 43rd
Chicago 60653
 (312) 538-3232

M–T   9:30–9:00
F–S 9:30 A.M–10:00 P.M.
S   11:00–5:00

SERVICES: Walk-in Store Only

SPECIALTIES: Blues, Disco, Religious, Rhythm & Blues, Rock & Roll, Soul

VOLUME: 33⅓ – 0
            45 – 10,000
            78 – 0
          Other – 0

STOCK: Domestic/New

SEARCH: Not available

COLLECTIONS: Will not buy collections of rare records

PAYMENTS: Personal Check

MAIL ORDER: Not available

DISCOUNTS: Not available

PUBLICATIONS: Not available

CHICAGO

POLISH RECORD CENTER OF AMERICA (II)
3055 Milwaukee Avenue
Chicago 60618
 (312) 772-4044

M–T   11:00–8:00
W   Closed
T   11:00–8:00
F   11:00–6:00
S   10:00–5:00
S   Closed

SERVICES: Walk-in Store/Mail Order

SPECIALTIES: (Alphabetical) Polish Classical, Polish Ethnic, Polish Folk, Polish Foreign Language, Polish Instrumental, Polish Polka, Polish Religious, Polish Vocal

VOLUME: 33⅓ – 100%
            45 – 0
            78 – 0
          Other – 0

STOCK: Import/New

SEARCH: I.N.A.

COLLECTIONS: I.N.A.

PAYMENTS: Money Order

MAIL ORDER: 4th Class, U.P.S.; Prepayment or C.O.D.

DISCOUNTS: I.N.A.

PUBLICATIONS: Catalog available; further I.N.A.

CHICAGO

THE RECORD WAREHOUSE (II)   M–S   10:00–6:00
4025 North Ravenswood Avenue
Chicago 60613
  (312) 528-5600

SERVICES: Walk-in Store/Mail Order

SPECIALTIES: All Major Categories

VOLUME: 33⅓ – I.N.A.
          45 – I.N.A.
          78 – I.N.A.
     Other – I.N.A.

STOCK: Domestic & Import/New

SEARCH: Not available

COLLECTIONS: Will not buy collections of rare records

PAYMENTS: Money Order

MAIL ORDER: Whatever shipment method requested; Prepayment or C.O.D.

DISCOUNTS: Available

PUBLICATIONS: I.N.A.

CHICAGO

ROLLING STONE RECORDS (II)   M–S   10:00–6:30
175 West Washington   S   Closed
Chicago 60602
  (312) 346-3489

SERVICES: Walk-in Store Only

SPECIALTIES: (Alphabetical) Blues, Contemporary Jazz, Disco, Folk-Rock, Reggae, Rhythm & Blues, Rock, Rock & Roll, Soul, Traditional Jazz

VOLUME: 33⅓ – 2,000
          45 – 0
          78 – 0
     Other – 0

STOCK: Domestic & Import/New

SEARCH: Not available

COLLECTIONS: Will buy collections of rare records

PAYMENTS: Master Charge, Personal Check, VISA/BankAmericard

MAIL ORDER: Not available

DISCOUNTS: Available

PUBLICATIONS: I.N.A.

CHICAGO

ROSE DISCOUNT RECORDS (II)   M–S   9:00–5:45
165 West Madison   S   Closed
Chicago 60602
    (312) 332-2737

SERVICES: Walk-in Store/Mail Order

SPECIALTIES: All Major Categories

VOLUME: 33⅓ – 100%
                  45 – 0
                  78 – 0
                Other – 0

STOCK: Domestic & Import/New

SEARCH: I.N.A.

COLLECTIONS: Not available for purchase

PAYMENTS: American Express, Carte Blanche, Master Charge, Money Order, Personal Check, VISA/Bank-Americard

MAIL ORDER: U.P.S., Whatever shipment method requested; Prepayment

DISCOUNTS: Available

PUBLICATIONS: Not available

CHICAGO

ROSE RECORDS (II)   M   9:00–6:30
214 South Wabash   T–W   9:00–6:00
Chicago 60604   T   9:00–6:30
    (312) 663-0660   F–S   9:00–6:00
                                        S   Closed

SERVICES: Walk-in Store/Mail Order

SPECIALTIES: All Major Categories

VOLUME: 33⅓ – 70,000
                  45 – 0
                  78 – 0
                Other – 0

STOCK: Domestic & Import/New

SEARCH: Not available

COLLECTIONS: Not available for purchase

PAYMENTS: American Express, Carte Blanche, Master Charge, VISA/Bank-Americard

MAIL ORDER: 4th Class, U.P.S.; Prepayment

DISCOUNTS: Available

PUBLICATIONS: Free quarterly catalog

CHICAGO

SOUNDS GOOD (II)
3176 North Broadway
Chicago 60657
  (312) 281-5266

M–F	11:00–10:00
S	11:00–8:00
S	Noon–6:00

SERVICES: Walk-in Store Only

SPECIALTIES: All Major Categories

VOLUME: 33⅓ – 100%
         45 – 0
         78 – 0
      Other – 0

STOCK: Domestic & Import/New

SEARCH: Not available

COLLECTIONS: Will not buy collections of rare records

PAYMENTS: Master Charge, Personal Check, VISA/BankAmericard

MAIL ORDER: Not available

DISCOUNTS: Not available

PUBLICATIONS: Not available

CHICAGO

SOUNDS GOOD RECORDS AND TAPES (II)
3259 North Ashland Avenue
Chicago 60657
  (312) 528-8827

M	10:00–9:00
T–W	10:00–6:00
T–F	10:00–9:00
S	10:00–6:00
S	Noon–5:00

SERVICES: Walk-in Store Only

SPECIALTIES: (Alphabetical) Beatles, Christmas, Classical, Disco, Elvis, Rhythm & Blues, Rock, Rock & Roll, Sinatra, Soul, Standards, Traditional Jazz

VOLUME: 33⅓ – 50%
         45 – 50%
         78 – 0
      Other – 0

STOCK: Domestic & Import/New

SEARCH: Not available

COLLECTIONS: Not available for purchase

PAYMENTS: Carte Blanche, Master Charge, VISA/BankAmericard

MAIL ORDER: Not available

DISCOUNTS: Not available

PUBLICATIONS: Not available

DES PLAINES

ALGONQUIN RECORDS (I)   M–F   10:30–9:00
532 East Algonquin Road   S   10:30–7:00
Des Plaines 60016   S   Noon–5:00
(312) 827-0673

SERVICES: Walk-in Store/Mail Order   SEARCH: Available with no service
                                             charge
SPECIALTIES: (Alphabetical) Blue-
grass, Blues, Contemporary Jazz,   COLLECTIONS: Will not buy collec-
Country & Western, Disco, Easy Lis-   tions of rare records
tening, Ethnic, Folk, Folk-Rock, Hill-   PAYMENTS: Master Charge, Money
billy, Religious, Rhythm & Blues,   Order, Personal Check, VISA/Bank-
Rock & Roll, Soul, Traditional Jazz   Americard

VOLUME: 33⅓ – 2,000   MAIL ORDER: 4th Class, U.P.S.; Pre-
            45   – 2,000   payment
            78   – 50
            Other – 0   DISCOUNTS: Available

STOCK: Domestic & Import/New &   PUBLICATIONS: I.N.A.
Used

HIGHLAND PARK

A. LEVIN RARE RECORDS (I)   M–F   10:00–6:00
454 Central Avenue   S   10:00–5:00
Highland Park 60035   S   Closed
(312) 433-6090

SERVICES: Walk-in Store/Mail Order   SEARCH: Not available

SPECIALTIES: (Alphabetical) Blues,   COLLECTIONS: Will buy collections of
Country & Western, Easy Listening,   rare records
Hillbilly, Rhythm & Blues, Rock &   PAYMENTS: Money Order, Personal
Roll, Soul   Check

VOLUME: 33⅓ – 2,000   MAIL ORDER: Air Mail, 4th Class,
            45   – 35,000   U.P.S.; Prepayment
            78   – 0
            Other – 0   DISCOUNTS: Not available

STOCK: Domestic/New & Used   PUBLICATIONS: I.N.A.

MUNDELEIN

FRED W. BRANDT RECORDS (I)
P.O. Box 398
Mundelein 60060
  Telephone: I.N.A.

SERVICES: Mail Order Only

SPECIALTIES: Traditional Jazz, Dixieland, Swing, Dance

VOLUME: 33⅓ – 50%
             45   – 0
             78   – 50%
             Other – 0

STOCK: Domestic & Import/New &
Used

SEARCH: Want lists maintained and
requester notified when record comes
in

COLLECTIONS: Will buy collections of
rare records

PAYMENTS: Postal Money Order

MAIL ORDER: Whatever shipment
method requested; Prepayment

DISCOUNTS: Not available

PUBLICATIONS: Not available

ROCKFORD

BUFFALO RECORDS AND SUPPLIES (I)   M   Closed
1423 8th Street   T–S   1:00–8:00
Rockford 61104
  (815) 965-9926

SERVICES: Walk-in Store/Mail Order

SPECIALTIES: (Alphabetical) Blues,
Country & Western, Easy Listening,
Folk, Rhythm & Blues, Rock, Rock &
Roll, Rockabilly, Sound Tracks

VOLUME: 33⅓ – 10,000
             45   – 30,000
             78   – 1,000
             Other – 0

STOCK: Domestic/New & Used

SEARCH: Want lists maintained and
requester notified when record comes
in

COLLECTIONS: Will not buy collections of rare records

PAYMENTS: Money Order, Personal
Check

MAIL ORDER: 4th Class; Prepayment

DISCOUNTS: Not available

PUBLICATIONS: I.N.A.

INDIANA

CARMEL

SKID ROW RECORD SALES (I)   M–S   8:00–5:00
1764–A East 116th Street   S   Closed
Carmel 46032
  (317) 844-4384

SERVICES: Mail Order Only (Above Times for Telephone)

SPECIALTIES: (Alphabetical) Bluegrass, Blues, Contemporary Jazz, Country & Western, Folk, Folk-Rock, Hillbilly, Rhythm & Blues, Rock, Rock & Roll, Soul, Traditional Jazz

VOLUME: 33⅓ – 5,000
                   45 – 0
                   78 – 0
                   Other – 0

STOCK: Domestic & Import/New

SEARCH: Want lists maintained and requester notified when record comes in

COLLECTIONS: Will not buy collections of rare records

PAYMENTS: Money Order, Personal Check

MAIL ORDER: 4th Class; Prepayment

DISCOUNTS: Not available

PUBLICATIONS: I.N.A.

ELWOOD

NEW LIGHT DISTRIBUTORS (I)   M–F   9:00–5:00
521 North Anderson Street   S–S   Closed
Elwood 46036
  (317) 552-9846

SERVICES: Walk-in Store/Mail Order

SPECIALTIES: (Alphabetical) Bluegrass, Blues, Contemporary Jazz, Folk, Folk-Rock, Rhythm & Blues, Rock, Rock & Roll, Soul, Traditional Jazz

VOLUME: 33⅓ – 100,000
                   45 – 0
                   78 – 0
                   Other – 0

STOCK: Domestic & Import/New

SEARCH: Available with no service charge; Want lists maintained and requester notified when record comes in

COLLECTIONS: Will buy collections of rare records

PAYMENTS: Money Order, Personal Check

MAIL ORDER: U.P.S.; Prepayment or C.O.D.

DISCOUNTS: Available

PUBLICATION: Free periodic catalog

FORT WAYNE

SMOKY'S RECORD SHOP (I)   M–S   10:00–9:00
1632 Wells Street   S   Closed
Fort Wayne 46808
  (219) 743-7561

SERVICES: Walk-in Store/Mail Order

SPECIALTIES: All Major Categories

VOLUME: 33⅓ – 300
             45 – 300,000
             78 – 250
          Other – 0

STOCK: Domestic/New

SEARCH: Want lists maintained and requester notified when record comes in

COLLECTIONS: Will buy collections of rare records

PAYMENTS: Master Charge, Money Order, Personal Check, VISA/Bank-Americard

MAIL ORDER: Air Mail, 4th Class; Prepayment

DISCOUNTS: Not available

PUBLICATIONS: I.N. A.

MOORESVILLE

GOLDEN MEMORIES RECORDS (I)
P.O. Box 217
Mooresville 46158
  (317) 831-5207

SERVICES: Mail Order Only

SPECIALTIES: All Major Categories

VOLUME: 33⅓ – 600,000
             45 – 400,000
             78 – 50,000
          Other – 0

STOCK: Domestic & Import/New

SEARCH: Not available

COLLECTIONS: Will buy collections of rare records

PAYMENTS: American Express, Master Charge, Money Order, Personal Check, VISA/BankAmericard

MAIL ORDER: 4th Class; Prepayment or C.O.D.

DISCOUNTS: Available

PUBLICATION: Free periodic catalog

SHELBYVILLE

O. RODGER HARRIS RECORDS (I)
54 East Washington Street
Shelbyville 46176
  (317) 392-1447

SERVICES: Walk-in Store (By Appointment Only)/Mail Order

SPECIALTIES: Rock & Roll, Rhythm & Blues, Soul, Surfing, Easy Listening

VOLUME: 33⅓ – 7,000
           45   – 30,000
           78   – 0
           Other – 0

STOCK: Domestic/New & Used

SEARCH: Not available; Want lists maintained and requester notified when record comes in

COLLECTIONS: Will buy collections of rare records

PAYMENTS: Money Order, Personal Check

MAIL ORDER: Whatever shipment method requested; Prepayment

DISCOUNTS: Not available

PUBLICATIONS: Free semiannual auction list

KENTUCKY

MOREHEAD

ROCK 'N' READ SHOP (I)
151 East Main Street
P.O. Box 694
Morehead 40351
  (606) 784-8126

M–F   11:00–10:00
S   10:00–10:00
S By Appointment

SERVICES: Walk-in Store/Mail Order

SPECIALTIES: Rock, Rock & Roll, Sound Tracks, Country & Western, Disco, Easy Listening, Comedy, Elvis, Bluegrass, Religious

VOLUME: 33⅓ – 3,300
           45   – 12,500
           78   – 0
           Other – 0

STOCK Domestic & Import/New & Used

SEARCH: Want lists maintained and requester notified when record comes in

COLLECTIONS: Will buy collections of rare records

PAYMENTS: Money Order, Personal Check

MAIL ORDER: Whatever shipment method requested; Prepayment

DISCOUNTS: Available

PUBLICATIONS: Free monthly catalog

LOUISIANA

HARAHAN

THE GOLD MINE (I)
6469 Jefferson Highway
Harahan 70123
(504) 737-2233

M–S   10:00–6:00
S   Closed

SERVICES: Walk-in Store/Mail Order

SPECIALTIES: All Major Categories

VOLUME: 33⅓ – I.N.A.
           45 – I.N.A.
           78 – I.N.A.
           Other – I.N.A.

STOCK: Domestic & Import/New & Used

SEARCH: Available with no service charge; Want lists maintained and requester notified when record comes in

COLLECTIONS: Will buy collections of rare records

PAYMENTS: Money Order, Personal Check, VISA/BankAmericard

MAIL ORDER: Air Mail, 3rd Class, 4th Class, U.P.S.; Prepayment or C.O.D.

DISCOUNTS: Available

PUBLICATIONS: I.N.A.

METAIRIE

MEMORY LANE RECORDS (II)
6417 Airline Highway
Metairie 70003
(504) 733-2120

M–T   11:00–6:00
F–S   10:00–7:00
S   Closed

SERVICES: Walk-in Store/Mail Order

SPECIALTIES: (Alphabetical) Beatles, Blues, Country & Western, Disco, Elvis, Hillbilly, Nostalgia, Rhythm & Blues, Rock, Rock & Roll, Standards

VOLUME: 33⅓ – I.N.A.
           45 – I.N.A.
           78 – 0
           Other – 0

STOCK: Domestic & Import/New

SEARCH: Available with no service charge

COLLECTIONS: Will buy collections of rare records

PAYMENTS: Master Charge, Money Order, Personal Check, VISA/Bank-Americard

MAIL ORDER: Whatever shipment method requested; Prepayment

DISCOUNTS: Not available

PUBLICATIONS: Free periodic catalog

NEW ORLEANS

JIM RUSSELL RARE RECORDS (I)   M–S   10:00–6:00
1837 Magazine Street   S   Closed
New Orleans 70130
(504) 522-2602

SERVICES: Walk-in Store/Mail Order

SPECIALTIES: All Major Categories

VOLUME: 33⅓ – 30,000
           45   – 250,000
           78   – 10,000
           Other – 0

STOCK: Domestic & Import/New & Used

SEARCH: Available with no service charge; Want lists maintained and requester notified when record comes in

COLLECTIONS: Will buy collections of rare records

PAYMENTS: Money Order, Personal Check

MAIL ORDER: 4th Class; Prepayment or C.O.D.

DISCOUNTS: Available

PUBLICATIONS: I.N.A.

MAINE

PORTLAND

BONGO BREATH RECORDS! (I)   M–S   8:00 A.M.–mid.
P.O. Box 106–DTS
Portland 04112
(207) 772-9521

SERVICES: Mail Order Only (Above Times for Telephone)

SPECIALTIES: Punk Rock/New Wave, British Invasion, Surfing, Promotional, Christmas, Comedy, Novelty, Nostalgia, Sound Tracks, Rockabilly, Country & Western

VOLUME: 33⅓ – 20,000
           45   – 9,000
           78   – 350
           Other – Edison Discs—
                    100
                    Transcriptions,
                    Cardboard and
                    Flexi-Discs

STOCK: Domestic & Import/New & Used

SEARCH: Want lists maintained and requester notified when record comes in

COLLECTIONS: Will buy collections of rare records

PAYMENTS: Money Order, Personal Check (U.S.A.)

MAIL ORDER: 4th Class, Whatever shipment method requested; Prepayment or C.O.D.

DISCOUNTS: I.N.A.

PUBLICATIONS: Quarterly catalog available for $1.00 per year

MARYLAND

ANNAPOLIS

SEASONS FOUR (II)   M–S   10:00–9:00
Bay Ridge Plaza   S   10:00–5:00
Annapolis 21403
   (301) 269-0099

SERVICES: Walk-in Store Only

SPECIALTIES: (Alphabetical) Classical, Country & Western, Easy Listening, Rhythm & Blues, Rock, Rock & Roll

VOLUME: 33⅓ – I.N.A.
            45 – I.N.A.
            78 – I.N.A.
            Other – I.N.A.

STOCK: Domestic & Import/New

SEARCH: Available with no service charge

COLLECTIONS: Will not buy collections of rare records

PAYMENTS: Master Charge, VISA/-BankAmericard

MAIL ORDER: Not available

DISCOUNTS: Not available

PUBLICATIONS: I.N.A.

ANNAPOLIS

SEASONS FOUR (II)   M–S   10:00–9:00
Forest Plaza   S   10:00–5:00
Annapolis 21401
   (301) 841-6686

SERVICES: Walk-in Store Only

SPECIALTIES: (Alphabetical) Classical, Country & Western, Easy Listening, Rhythm & Blues, Rock, Rock & Roll

VOLUME: 33⅓ – I.N.A.
            45 – I.N.A.
            78 – I.N.A.
            Other – I.N.A.

STOCK: Domestic & Import/New

SEARCH: Available with no service charge

COLLECTIONS: Will not buy collections of rare records

PAYMENTS: Master Charge, VISA/BankAmericard

MAIL ORDER: Not available

DISCOUNTS: Not available

PUBLICATIONS: I.N.A.

BALTIMORE

AL'S RECORD HUT (I)
14 South Ellamont Street
Baltimore 21229
  (301) 233-4035

SERVICES: Mail Order Only

SPECIALTIES: Contemporary Jazz, Bop Jazz, Rhythm & Blues, Rock & Roll, Soul, Blues, Big Band, Vocal, Swing, Easy Listening

VOLUME: 33⅓ – 5,000
           45 – 1,500
           78 – 1,000
           Other – 0

STOCK: Domestic Only/New & Used

SEARCH: Not available; Want lists maintained and requester notified when record comes in

COLLECTIONS: Will buy collections of rare records

PAYMENTS: Money Order

MAIL ORDER: Whatever shipment method requested; Prepayment

DISCOUNTS: Not available

PUBLICATIONS: Monthly listings available for $15.00 per year

BALTIMORE

OUT-OF-PRINT RECORD LOCATOR (I)   M–S   2:00–10:00
6114 Gist Avenue
Baltimore 21215
  (301) 358-3033

SERVICES: Walk-in Store (By Appointment)/Mail Order (Limited to U.S.A.)/Library

SPECIALTIES: Vocal, Rock & Roll, Instrumental, Sound Tracks, Easy Listening, Big Band, Folk, Modern Jazz, Comedy, Novelty, Broadway Shows

VOLUME: 33⅓ – 50,000
           45 – 0
           78 – 0
           Other – 0

STOCK: Domestic/New & Used

SEARCH: Available with no service charge; Want lists maintained and requester notified when record comes in

COLLECTIONS: Will buy collections of rare records

PAYMENTS: Money Order, Personal Check

MAIL ORDER: 4th Class; Prepayment

DISCOUNTS: Not available

PUBLICATIONS: Free quarterly catalog

BALTIMORE

ROADHOUSE OLDIES OF BALTIMORE (I)
5200 Ritchie Highway
Baltimore 21225
   (301) 789-3142

M	Closed
T	5:00–8:00
W	Closed
T	5:00–8:00
F	Closed
S	Noon–6:00
S	Closed

SERVICES: Walk-in Store/Mail Order

SPECIALTIES: Rock & Roll, Rhythm & Blues, Soul, Elvis, Standards, Beatles, Rockabilly

VOLUME: 33⅓ – 2,000
          45 – 10,000
          78 – 0
    Other – 0

STOCK: Domestic/New & Used

SEARCH: Want lists maintained and requester notified when record comes in

COLLECTIONS: Will buy collections of rare records

PAYMENTS: Master Charge, Money Order, VISA/BankAmericard

MAIL ORDER: 4th Class; Prepayment

DISCOUNTS: Not available

PUBLICATIONS: Free semiannual catalog

BOWIE

SEASONS FOUR (II)
Free State Mall
Bowie 20715
   (301) 464-1191

M–S	10:00–9:30
S	10:00–5:00

SERVICES: Walk-in Store Only

SPECIALTIES: (Alphabetical) Classical, Contemporary Jazz, Country & Western, Rock, Rock & Roll

VOLUME: 33⅓ – I.N.A.
          45 – I.N.A.
          78 – I.N.A.
    Other – I.N.A.

STOCK: Domestic & Import/New

SEARCH: Available with no service charge

COLLECTIONS: Will not buy collections of rare records

PAYMENTS: Master Charge, VISA/-BankAmericard

MAIL ORDER: Not available

DISCOUNTS: Not available

PUBLICATIONS: I.N.A.

COCKEYSVILLE

RECORD SCAVENGERS (I)
P.O. Box 387
Cockeysville 21030
(301) 628-1090

SERVICES: Mail Order Only

SPECIALTIES: (Alphabetical) Blues,
Country & Western, Rhythm & Blues,
Rock, Rock & Roll, Soul

VOLUME: 33⅓ – 25,000
                  45 – 250,000
                  78 – 0
            Other – 0

STOCK: Domestic & Import/New &
Used

SEARCH: Want lists maintained and
requester notified when record comes
in

COLLECTIONS: Will buy collections of
rare records

PAYMENTS: Master Charge, Money
Order, Personal Check, VISA/Bank-
Americard

MAIL ORDER: U.P.S.; Prepayment or
C.O.D.

DISCOUNTS: Not available

PUBLICATIONS: I.N.A.

PHOENIX

RECORD SCAVENGERS (I)
Sunnybrook Shopping Center
13816 Jarrettsville Pike
Phoenix 21131
(301) 628-1090

M	Closed
T–S	Noon–7:00
S	Closed

SERVICES: Walk-in Store/Mail Order

SPECIALTIES: Beatles, Elvis, Rock,
Rock & Roll, Novelty, Rhythm &
Blues, Soul, Promotional, Rockabilly,
Surfing

VOLUME: 33⅓ – 50,000
                  45 – 250,000
                  78 – 0
            Other – 0

STOCK: Domestic & Import/New &
Used

SEARCH: Want lists maintained and
requester notified when record comes
in

COLLECTIONS: Will buy collections of
rare records

PAYMENTS: Master Charge, Money
Order, Personal Check, VISA/Bank-
Americard

MAIL ORDER: U.P.S.; Prepayment or
C.O.D.

DISCOUNTS: Not available

PUBLICATIONS: Free quarterly catalog; Free quarterly auction list

MASSACHUSETTS
BOSTON

BEACON HILL MUSIC (I)   M–S   11:00–5:30
17 Myrtle Street   S   Closed
Boston 02114
(617) 523-5807

SERVICES: Walk-in Store/Mail Order

SPECIALTIES: Rock & Roll, Rock, Sound Tracks, Beatles, Elvis, Folk, Rockabilly, Sinatra, Soul, Big Band, Traditional Jazz, Personalities

VOLUME: 33⅓ – 10,000
             45 – 6,000
             78 – 0
          Other – 0

STOCK: Domestic & Import/New & Used

SEARCH: Want lists maintained and requester notified when record comes in

COLLECTIONS: Will buy collections of rare records

PAYMENTS Master Charge, Money Order, Personal Charge Account, Personal Check, VISA/BankAmericard

MAIL ORDER: 1st Class, 4th Class; Prepayment

DISCOUNTS: Available

PUBLICATIONS: Not available

BOSTON

DEJA VU RECORDS (I)   M–S   10:00–7:00
151 Massachusetts Avenue   S   Noon–6:00
Boston 02115
(617) 267-8389

SERVICES: Walk-in Store/Mail Order

SPECIALTIES: (Alphabetical) Classical, Contemporary Jazz, Disco, Gospel/-Sacred, Punk Rock/New Wave, Reggae, Rock & Roll, Soul, Sound Tracks, Traditional Jazz

VOLUME: 33⅓ – 100%
             45 – 0
             78 – 0
          Other – 0

STOCK: Domestic & Import/New & Used

SEARCH: Available with no service charge

COLLECTIONS: Will buy collections of rare records

PAYMENTS: American Express, Master Charge, Money Order, Personal Check, VISA/BankAmericard

MAIL ORDER: Air Mail, 4th Class; Prepayment

DISCOUNTS: Not available

PUBLICATIONS: Not available

BOSTON

SKIPPY WHITE'S OLDIES BUT GOODIES   M–T   9:00–8:00
LAND (I)   F–S   9:00–9:00
1763 Washington Street   S   Closed
Boston 02118
  (617) 266-1002

SERVICES: Walk-in Store/Mail Order

SPECIALTIES: Rhythm & Blues, Soul, Rock & Roll, Blues, Gospel, Rockabilly, Elvis, Beatles, Disco, Comedy

VOLUME: 33⅓ – 30,000
            45 – 450,000
            78 – 0
            Other – 0

STOCK: Domestic & Import/New

SEARCH: Available with no service charge; Want lists maintained and requester notified when record comes in

COLLECTIONS: Will buy collections of rare records

PAYMENTS: Master Charge, Money Order, Personal Check, VISA/Bank-Americard

MAIL ORDER: U.P.S.; Prepayment

DISCOUNTS: Not available

PUBLICATIONS: Annual catalog available for $1.00; Free quarterly set-sale lists

BOSTON

ZOUNDZ (I)   M–T   10:00–10:00
P.O. Box 169   F–S   10:00–mid.
Boston 02199   S   Noon–6:00
  (617) 267-2555

SERVICES: Walk-in Store (By Appointment)/Mail Order

SPECIALTIES: All Major Categories

VOLUME: 33⅓ – 98%
            45 – 1%
            78 – 1%
            Other – 0

STOCK: Domestic & Import/New & Used

SEARCH: Available with no service charge

COLLECTIONS: Will buy collections of rare records

PAYMENTS: Master Charge, Money Order, Personal Check, VISA/Bank-Americard

MAIL ORDER: 4th Class; Prepayment

DISCOUNTS: Available

PUBLICATIONS: I.N.A.

CAMBRIDGE

BOJO RECORDS/JAZZ WORLD LIMITED (II)	M–F	10:00–10:00
P.O. Box 416	S	10:00–6:00
Cambridge 02138	S	Closed
(617) 899-6399		

SERVICES: Walk-in Store (By Appointment Only)/Mail Order

SPECIALTIES: Sound Tracks, Broadway Shows, Bop Jazz, Contemporary Jazz, Rock, Classical, Opera, Television Shows, Comedy, Documentary

VOLUME: 33⅓ – 22,000
       45 – 2,500
       78 – 0
    Other – 0

STOCK: Domestic & Import/New & Used

SEARCH: Available with no service charge; Want lists maintained and requester notified when record comes in

COLLECTIONS: Available for purchase; Will buy collections of rare records

PAYMENTS: Money Order

MAIL ORDER: 4th Class, Whatever shipment method requested; Prepayment

DISCOUNTS: Available

PUBLICATIONS: Semiannual catalog available for $1.00 per year; Free quarterly auction list

CAMBRIDGE

BRIGGS AND BRIGGS, INCORPORATED (II)	M–S	9:00–6:00
1270 Massachusetts Avenue	S	Closed
Cambridge 02138		
(617) 547-2007		

SERVICES: Walk-in Store/Mail Order

SPECIALTIES: All Major Categories

VOLUME: 33⅓ – 100%
       45 – 0
       78 – 0
    Other – 0

STOCK: Domestic & Import/New

SEARCH: Available with no service charge

COLLECTIONS: Will not buy collections of rare records

PAYMENTS: Master Charge, Money Order, Personal Charge Account, Personal Check, VISA/BankAmericard

MAIL ORDER: 4th Class; Prepayment or C.O.D.

DISCOUNTS: Available

PUBLICATIONS: I.N.A.

CAMBRIDGE

DEJA VU RECORDS (I)   M–S   10:00–7:00
1105 Massachusetts Avenue   S   Closed
Cambridge 02138
(617) 661-7869 or 7932

SERVICES: Walk-in Store/Mail Order

SPECIALTIES: (Alphabetical)   Folk,
Folk-Rock, Rock, Rock & Roll, Sound
Tracks

VOLUME: 33⅓ – 1,000
             45 – 0
             78 – 0
          Other – 0

STOCK: Domestic & Import/New &
Used

SEARCH: Not available

COLLECTIONS: Will buy collections of
rare records

PAYMENTS: Master Charge, Money
Order, VISA/BankAmericard

MAIL ORDER: Air Mail, 4th Class,
U.P.S.; Prepayment

DISCOUNTS: Not available

PUBLICATIONS: Annual catalog available for 50¢ U.S.A. and $1.00 non-
U.S.A.

CAMBRIDGE

FIGARO'S RECORD SHOP (I)   M   Closed
1287 Cambridge Street   T–W   11:00–6:00
Cambridge 02139   T   Noon–8:00
(617) 547–7228   F–S   11:00–6:00
                                                           S   Closed

SERVICES: Walk-in Store/Mail Order

SPECIALTIES: (Alphabetical) Classical,
Opera, Vocal

VOLUME: 33⅓ – 5,000
             45 – 500
             78 – 0
          Other – 0

STOCK: Domestic & Import/New &
Used

SEARCH: Available with no service
charge

COLLECTIONS: Will buy collections of
rare records

PAYMENTS: Money Order, Personal
Check

MAIL ORDER: 4th Class, Whatever
shipment method requested; Prepayment

DISCOUNTS: Not available

PUBLICATIONS: Free quarterly catalog; Free quarterly auction list

FRANKLIN

KING OF THE OLDIES–SEVY ALEXANDER
  RECORDS (I)
408 Pond Street
Franklin 02038
  (617) 528-6689

SERVICES: Mail Order Only

SPECIALTIES: (Alphabetical) Blues, Country & Western, Easy Listening, Hillbilly, Rhythm & Blues, Rock, Rock & Roll, Soul

VOLUME: 33⅓ – 3,000
              45 – 36,000
              78 – 2,000
       Other – 0

STOCK: Domestic/New & Used

SEARCH: Not available

COLLECTIONS: Will buy collections of rare records

PAYMENTS: Money Order, Personal Check

MAIL ORDER: Air Mail, 1st Class, 4th Class; Prepayment or C.O.D.

DISCOUNTS: Not available

PUBLICATIONS: I.N.A.

LOWELL

DYNAMITE SOUNDS/RICH GESNER (I)
8 Belmont Street
Lowell 01851
  Telephone: I.N.A.

SERVICES: Mail Order Only

SPECIALTIES: (Alphabetical) British Musical Shows, Broadway Shows, Contemporary Jazz, Edison Discs/-Cylinders, Film Scores, Novelty, Personality, Rhythm & Blues, Rock & Roll, Sound Tracks, Television Shows

VOLUME: 33⅓ – 500
              45 – 1,000
              78 – 1,500
       Other – Edison
                   Cylinders

STOCK: Domestic/New & Used

SEARCH: Not available

COLLECTIONS: Will buy collections of rare records

PAYMENTS: Master Charge, Money Order, VISA/BankAmericard

MAIL ORDER: 4th Class, Whatever shipment method requested; Prepayment

DISCOUNTS: Not available

PUBLICATIONS: Free occasional set-sale catalog

SOMERVILLE

ROUNDUP RECORDS (I)
P.O. Box 474
Somerville 02144
    Telephone: I.N.A.

SERVICES: Mail Order Only

SPECIALTIES: Folk, Bluegrass, Old-Time Country, Contemporary Jazz, Traditional Jazz, Rockabilly, Blues, British Isles Folk, Celtic Folk, Acoustic, Tex-Mex

VOLUME: 33⅓ – 4,000
           45 – 0
           78 – 0
           Other – 0

STOCK: Domestic & Import/New

SEARCH: Not available

COLLECTIONS: I.N.A.

PAYMENTS: Master Charge, Money Order, Personal Check, VISA/Bank-Americard

MAIL ORDER: Air Mail, 4th Class, U.P.S.; Prepayment

DISCOUNTS: Available

PUBLICATIONS: Free annual catalog; Free bimonthly record reviews for active customers

SPRINGFIELD

MUSIC IN THE ROUND (I)
311 Bridge Street
Springfield 01103
    (413) 788-0193

M–W	10:00–6:00
T–F	10:00–9:00
S	10:00–6:00
S	Closed

SERVICES: Walk-in Store/Mail Order

SPECIALTIES: (Alphabetical) Broadway Shows, Classical, Contemporary Jazz, Country & Western, Easy Listening, Opera, Sound Tracks, Traditional Jazz

VOLUME: 33⅓ – 4,500
           45 – 0
           78 – 12,000
           Other – 0

STOCK: Domestic & Import/New & Used

SEARCH: Want lists maintained and requester notified when record comes in

COLLECTIONS: Will not buy collections of rare records

PAYMENTS: Money Order, Personal Check

MAIL ORDER: 4th Class; Prepayment

DISCOUNTS: Available

PUBLICATIONS: I.N.A.

WORCESTER

VICTOR PEARLIN RECORDS (I)
P.O. Box 199–A
Greendale Station
Worcester 01606
  Telephone: I.N.A.

M–S   10:00–10:00

SERVICES: Mail Order Only (Above Times for Appointment)

SPECIALTIES: Rhythm & Blues, Blues, Rock & Roll, Rockabilly, Elvis, Novelty, Easy Listening, Soul, Surfing, Country & Western

VOLUME: 33⅓ – 2,500
           45 – 100,000
           78 – 5,500
           Other – 0

STOCK: Domestic/New & Used

SEARCH: Available with no service charge

COLLECTIONS: Will buy collections of rare records

PAYMENTS: Money Order, Personal Check

MAIL ORDER: 4th Class, Whatever shipment method requested; Prepayment

DISCOUNTS: Not available

PUBLICATIONS: Free quarterly catalog

MICHIGAN

ANN ARBOR

SCHOOLKIDS' RECORDS (I)
523 East Liberty
Ann Arbor 48104
  (313) 994-8031

M–S   10:00–9:00
S   Noon–8:00

SERVICES: Walk-in Store/Mail Order

SPECIALTIES: Rock, Rock & Roll, Bop Jazz, Contemporary Jazz, Soul, Swing, Folk, Bluegrass, Reggae, Punk Rock-/New Wave, Blues, Rhythm & Blues

VOLUME: 33⅓ – 1,000
           45 – 0
           78 – 0
           Other – 0

STOCK: Domestic & Import/New & Used

SEARCH: Not available

COLLECTIONS: Will buy collections of rare records

PAYMENTS: Master Charge, Money Order, Personal Check, VISA/Bank-Americard

MAIL ORDER: U.P.S.; Prepayment

DISCOUNTS: Not available

PUBLICATIONS: Free quarterly auction list

BAY CITY

THOMAS B. REINKE DISCOUNT TAPE OUT-   M–S   9:00–6:30
    LETS (I)
124 North Madison
Bay City 48706
    (517) 892-7407

SERVICES: Walk-in Store/Mail Order

SPECIALTIES: Rock, Rock & Roll, Country & Western, Easy Listening, Blues, Rockabilly, Hillbilly, Old-Time Country, Promotional, Contemporary Jazz

VOLUME: 33⅓ – 3,500
           45 – 25,000
           78 – 0
           Other – 0

STOCK: Domestic/New & Used

SEARCH: Want lists maintained and requester notified when record comes in

COLLECTIONS: Available for purchase; Will buy collections of rare records

PAYMENTS: Money Order, Personal Check

MAIL ORDER: Whatever shipment method requested; Prepayment or C.O.D.

DISCOUNTS: Available

PUBLICATIONS: Free bimonthly catalog; Free monthly auction list

DETROIT

MAYS RECORD & TALKING MACHINE CO. (I)   M–S   11:30–6:30
328 East 8 Mile Road   S   Closed
Detroit 48203
    (313) 368-0021

SERVICES: Walk-in Store/Mail Order

SPECIALTIES: (Alphabetical) Country & Western, Easy Listening, Motown, Rock, Rock & Roll, Rockabilly, Vocal

VOLUME: 33⅓ – 1,900
           45 – 250,000
           78 – 6,000
           Other – 0

STOCK: Domestic/Used

SEARCH: Not available

COLLECTIONS: Will buy collections of rare records

PAYMENTS: Money Order, Personal Check

MAIL ORDER: 4th Class; Prepayment

DISCOUNTS: Not available

PUBLICATIONS: Free quarterly auction list

FARMINGTON HILLS

TANT ENTERPRISES, INCORPORATED (II)   M–F   9:00–6:00
23745 Research Drive   S–S   Closed
Farmington Hills 48024
  (313) 478-5620

SERVICES: Walk-in Store/Mail Order

SPECIALTIES: (Alphabetical) Big
Band, Bluegrass, Blues, Classical,
Contemporary Jazz, Easy Listening,
Folk, Opera, Swing, Traditional Jazz

VOLUME: 33⅓ – I.N.A.
            45 – I.N.A.
            78 – I.N.A.
            Other – I.N.A.

STOCK: Domestic & Import/New

SEARCH: Not available

COLLECTIONS: Will not buy collections of rare records

PAYMENTS: Money Order

MAIL ORDER: U.P.S.; Prepayment or C.O.D.

DISCOUNTS: Not available

PUBLICATIONS: I.N.A.

FLINT

FLINT RECORD AND TAPE (I)   M–S   10:00–9:00
4945 Clio Road   S   Closed
Flint 48504
  (313) 785-4701

SERVICES: Walk-in Store Only

SPECIALTIES: All Major Categories

VOLUME: 33⅓ – 400
            45 – 200
            78 – 0
            Other – 0

STOCK: Domestic & Import/New

SEARCH: Available with no service charge; Want lists maintained and requester notified when record comes in

COLLECTIONS: Will not buy collections of rare records

PAYMENTS: American Express, Master Charge, Money Order, VISA/BankAmericard

MAIL ORDER: Not available

DISCOUNTS: Available

PUBLICATIONS: I.N.A.

FLINT

PROFFER SOUND CENTER (II)   M–S   10:00–5:30
463½ South Saginaw Street   S   Closed
Flint 48502
  (313) 235-2498

SERVICES: Walk-in Store Only

SPECIALTIES: (Alphabetical)   Blues,
Country & Western, Easy Listening,
Rhythm & Blues, Rock, Rock & Roll,
Soul

VOLUME: 33⅓ – 0
               45   – 5,000
               78   – 0
               Other – 0

STOCK: Domestic/New

SEARCH: Not available

COLLECTIONS: Will not buy collections of rare records

PAYMENTS: Master Charge, VISA/-
BankAmericard

MAIL ORDER: Not available

DISCOUNTS: Not available

PUBLICATIONS: I.N.A.

GRAND BLANC

L. M. BRUSH RECORDS—ESTATE OF RECORD
  SLEUTH (I)
P.O. Box 64
Grand Blanc 48439
  Telephone: I.N.A.

SERVICES: Mail Order Only

SPECIALTIES: All Major Categories

VOLUME: 33⅓ – 12,000
               45   – 25,000
               78   – 3,300
               Other – Edison Discs–12
                       Transcriptions

STOCK: Domestic & Import/New &
Used

SEARCH: Available with no service
charge; Want lists maintained and requester notified when record comes in

COLLECTIONS: Will not buy collections of rare records

PAYMENTS: Money Order, Personal
Check

MAIL ORDER: Air Mail, Whatever
shipment method requested; Prepayment

DISCOUNTS: Available

PUBLICATIONS: Not available

GRAND RAPIDS

BILL DODGE RECORDS (II)
124 Honeoye Street Southwest
D–62
Grand Rapids 49508
  Telephone: I.N.A.

SERVICES: Mail Order Only

SPECIALTIES: Traditional Jazz, Dixieland, Contemporary Jazz, Big Band,
Easy Listening, Sound Tracks, Country & Western, Ragtime, Banjo, Blues

VOLUME: 33⅓ – I.N.A.
            45 – I.N.A.
            78 – I.N.A.
          Other – I.N.A.

STOCK: Domestic & Import/New &
Used

SEARCH: Want lists maintained and
requester notified when record comes
in

COLLECTIONS: Will not buy collections of rare records

PAYMENTS: Money Order, Personal
Check

MAIL ORDER: 4th Class; Prepayment

DISCOUNTS: Not available

PUBLICATIONS: Free periodic listings
available by category of recording

GRAND RAPIDS

SPECIAL PRODUCTIONS (I)
1038 Lake Michigan Drive Northwest
Grand Rapids 49504
  (616) 774-8509

SERVICES: Walk-in Store (By Appointment Only)/Mail Order

SPECIALTIES: (Alphabetical) Classical,
Dance, Disco, Easy Listening, Ethnic,
Historical, Instrumental, Nostalgia,
Opera, Polka, Religious, Rock

VOLUME: 33⅓ – 1,000
            45 – 0
            78 – 0
          Other – 0

STOCK: Domestic & Import/New

SEARCH: Available with service
charge; Want lists maintained and requester notified when record comes in

COLLECTIONS: Will not buy collections of rare records

PAYMENTS: Money Order, Personal
Charge Account, Personal Check

MAIL ORDER: 4th Class; Prepayment

DISCOUNTS: Available

PUBLICATIONS: Not available

KALAMAZOO

THE RECORD MAN (I)
316 Stuart–#1
Kalamazoo 49001
(616) 382-3278

SERVICES: Mail Order Only

SPECIALTIES: (Alphabetical) Bluegrass, Blues, Classical, Contemporary Jazz, Country & Western, Easy Listening, Folk, Rhythm & Blues, Rock, Rock & Roll, Soul, Traditional Jazz

VOLUME: 33⅓ – 5,000
          45   – 500
          78   – 50
          Other – 0

STOCK: Domestic & Import/New & Used

SEARCH: Available with no service charge; Want lists maintained and requester notified when record comes in

COLLECTIONS: Will buy collections of rare records

PAYMENTS: Money Order

MAIL ORDER: 4th Class; Prepayment

DISCOUNTS: Available

PUBLICATIONS: Periodic auction list available for $1.00 per issue

SAGINAW

BLACK KETTLE RECORDS (I)
524 Gratiot Avenue
Saginaw 48602
(517) 793-1021

M–T	11:00–7:00
F	11:00–8:00
S	11:00–6:00
S	Closed

SERVICES: Walk-in Store/Mail Order

SPECIALTIES: Rock & Roll, Big Band, Blues, Rhythm & Blues, Reggae, Contemporary Jazz, Bop Jazz, Traditional Jazz, Promotional, Dixieland

VOLUME: 33⅓ – 7,000
          45   – 20,000
          78   – 4,000
          Other – 0

STOCK: Domestic & Import/New & Used

SEARCH: Want lists maintained and requester notified when record comes in

COLLECTIONS: Will buy collections of rare records

PAYMENTS: Master Charge, Money Order, Personal Check, VISA/BankAmericard

MAIL ORDER: Whatever shipment method requested; Prepayment

DISCOUNTS: Available

PUBLICATIONS: Free monthly auction list

MINNESOTA

MINNEAPOLIS

PYRAMID RECORDS (I)   M–S   1:00–5:00
506 First Avenue North   S   Closed
Minneapolis 55403
(612) 333-3825

SERVICES: Walk-in Store/Mail Order   STOCK: Domestic & Import/New

SPECIALTIES: Rock, Big Band, Tradi-   SEARCH: Not available
tional Jazz, Ragtime, Dixieland,   COLLECTIONS: I.N.A.
Rhythm & Blues, Bluegrass, Country
& Western, Old-Time Country, Classi-   PAYMENTS: Money Order, Personal
cal   Check

VOLUME: 33⅓ – 10,000   MAIL ORDER: 4th Class; Prepayment
           45 – 300   DISCOUNTS: Not available
           78 – 0   PUBLICATIONS: Not available
        Other – 0

MISSISSIPPI

BILOXI

RECORDS–SOUTH (I)
P.O. Box 56
Biloxi 39533
(601) 374-2595

SERVICES: Mail Order Only   SEARCH: Want lists maintained and
                                        requester notified when record comes
SPECIALTIES: (Alphabetical) Blues,   in
Country & Western, Easy Listening,
Rhythm & Blues, Rock, Rock & Roll,   COLLECTIONS: Will not buy collec-
Soul   tions of rare records

VOLUME: 33⅓ – 1,000   PAYMENTS: Money Order
           45 – 15,000
           78 – 0   MAIL ORDER: 1st Class, 2nd Class,
        Other – 0   3rd Class, U.P.S.; Prepayment
STOCK: Domestic/Used   DISCOUNTS: Available
                                        PUBLICATIONS: I.N.A.

MISSOURI

CREVE COEUR

JAYBEE JAZZ (I)
P.O. Box 24504
Creve Coeur 63141
Telephone: I.N.A.

SERVICES: Mail Order Only

SPECIALTIES: Contemporary Jazz, Big Band, Bop Jazz

VOLUME: 33⅓ – 30,000
                    45   – 0
                    78   – 0
                    Other – 0

STOCK: Domestic & Import/New

SEARCH: Not available

COLLECTIONS: Not available for purchase

PAYMENTS: Direct bank-to-bank transfer, Master Charge, Money Order, Personal Check, VISA/Bank-Americard

MAIL ORDER: 4th Class, Whatever shipment method requested; Prepayment

DISCOUNTS: Available

PUBLICATIONS: Free bimonthly catalog

KANSAS CITY

PENNY LANE RECORDS (II)
7408–A Wornal
Kansas City 64114
(816) 363-4288

M–F	10:00–7:00
S	10:00–6:00
S	Closed

SERVICES: Walk-in Store/Mail Order

SPECIALTIES: (Alphabetical) Bluegrass, Blues, Classical, Contemporary Jazz, Ethnic, Folk, Folk-Rock, Reggae, Rhythm & Blues, Rock & Roll, Soul, Traditional Jazz

VOLUME: 33⅓ – 100%
                    45   – 0
                    78   – 0
                    Other – 0

STOCK: Domestic & Import/New & Used

SEARCH: Not available

COLLECTIONS: Will not buy collections of rare records

PAYMENTS: Master Charge, Money Order, Personal Check, VISA/Bank-Americard

MAIL ORDER: 4th Class; Prepayment

DISCOUNTS: Available

PUBLICATIONS: I.N.A.

SPRINGFIELD

BOB'S RECORD RACK (I)
Route 9
P.O. Box 120
Springfield 65804
  (417) 485-7186

M–F		9:00–6:00
S		9:00–9:00
S		Closed

SERVICES: Walk-in Store/Mail Order

SPECIALTIES: Bluegrass, Banjo, Cajun, Comedy, Country & Western, Gospel/Sacred, Hillbilly, Historical, Instrumental, Old-Time Country, Religious, Sound Effects, Steel Band

VOLUME: 33⅓ – 50,000
           45 – 3,500
           78 – 3,000
     Other – 0

STOCK: Domestic & Import/New & Used

SEARCH: Not available; Want lists maintained and requester notified when record comes in

COLLECTIONS: Available for purchase; Will buy collections of rare records

PAYMENTS: Money Order, Personal Check

MAIL ORDER: Whatever shipment method requested; Prepayment or C.O.D.

DISCOUNTS: Not available

PUBLICATIONS: Semiannual catalog available for 60¢ per issue; Quarterly auction list available for 60¢ per issue

ST. LOUIS

ENCORE RECORDS (I)
P.O. Box 12585
St. Louis 63141
  (314) 434-4121

SERVICES: Mail Order Only

SPECIALTIES: (Alphabetical) Bluegrass, Blues, Bossa Nova, Contemporary Jazz, Country & Western, Disco, Easy Listening, Folk, Folk-Rock, Hillbilly, Religious, Rhythm & Blues, Rock & Roll, Soul

VOLUME: 33⅓ – 10%
           45 – 90%
           78 – 0
     Other – 0

STOCK: Domestic/New & Used

SEARCH: Not available; Want lists maintained and requester notified when record comes in

COLLECTIONS: Will buy collections of rare records

PAYMENTS: Money Order, Personal Check

MAIL ORDER: Air Mail, 1st Class, 4th Class; Prepayment

DISCOUNTS: I.N.A.

PUBLICATIONS: I.N.A.

ST. LOUIS

MARK'S ONE STOP (I)
P.O. Box 5862
St. Louis 63134
  (314) 423-6053

SERVICES: Mail Order Only

SPECIALTIES: Soul, Rock, Rock & Roll, Rhythm & Blues, Punk Rock/ New Wave, Instrumental, Country & Western, Novelty, Blues, Folk

VOLUME: 33⅓ – 10,000
             45 – 1,000,000
             78 – 1,000
          Other – 0

STOCK: Domestic & Import/New & Used

SEARCH: Available with no service charge

COLLECTIONS: Will buy collections of rare records

PAYMENTS: Money Order, Personal Check

MAIL ORDER: Whatever shipment method requested; Prepayment or C. O. D.

DISCOUNTS: Available

PUBLICATIONS: Free quarterly catalog; Free quarterly auction list

ST. LOUIS

ST. LOUIS RECORD RESEARCH (I)
707 Washington Avenue
St. Louis 63101
  (314) 421-4661

M–S 8:00 A. M.–mid.
S   11:00–7:00

SERVICES: Walk-in Store (By Appointment Only)/Mail Order

SPECIALTIES: (Alphabetical) Big Band, Blues, Bop Jazz, Classical, Hillbilly, Old-Time Country, Rhythm & Blues, Rock & Roll, Swing, Traditional Jazz

VOLUME: 33⅓ – 5,000
             45 – 15,000
             78 – 75,000
          Other – 0

STOCK: Domestic/New & Used

SEARCH: Available with service charge; Want lists maintained and requester notified when record comes in

COLLECTIONS: Will buy collections of rare records

PAYMENTS: Master Charge, Money Order, Personal Check, VISA/BankAmericard

MAIL ORDER: Whatever shipment method requested; Prepayment

DISCOUNTS: Not available

PUBLICATIONS: Free periodic auction list

ST. LOUIS

STREET SIDE RECORDS (II)   M–S   10:00–9:00
6314 Delmar   S   Closed
St. Louis 63130
(314) 726-6277

SERVICES: Walk-in Store/Mail Order
(To Prisons Only)

SPECIALTIES: All Major Categories

VOLUME: 33⅓ – 50,000
            45 – 0
            78 – 0
            Other – 0

STOCK: Domestic & Import/New

SEARCH: Available with no service
charge

COLLECTIONS: Will not buy collections of rare records

PAYMENTS: Master Charge, Personal Check, VISA/BankAmericard

MAIL ORDER: 4th Class, U.P.S.; Prepayment

DISCOUNTS: Available

PUBLICATIONS: I.N.A.

NEBRASKA

DODGE

M. J. RECORDING, INCORPORATED (I)   M–S   8:00–6:00
Dodge 68633   S   Closed
(402) 693-2379

SERVICES: Walk-in Store/Mail Order

SPECIALTIES: Foreign Language,
Polka

VOLUME: 33⅓ – 1,000
            45 – 0
            78 – 0
            Other – 0

STOCK: Domestic & Import/New

SEARCH: I.N.A.

COLLECTIONS: Will not buy collections of rare records

PAYMENTS: Money Order, Personal Check

MAIL ORDER: 4th Class; Prepayment

DISCOUNTS: Available

PUBLICATIONS: I.N.A.

NEVADA

LAS VEGAS

TOWER RECORDS (II)   M–S   9:00 A.M.–mid.
4700 Maryland Parkway
Las Vegas 89109
(702) 733-3000

SERVICES: Walk-in Store/Mail Order   COLLECTIONS: Will not buy collec-
(Limited)   tions of rare records

SPECIALTIES: All Major Categories   PAYMENTS: Master Charge, Money

VOLUME: 33⅓ – 100%   Order, Personal Charge Account,
           45 – 0   VISA/BankAmericard
           78 – 0   MAIL ORDER: 4th Class, U.P.S.; Pre-
           Other – 0   payment

STOCK: Domestic & Import/New   DISCOUNTS: Available

SEARCH: Not available   PUBLICATIONS: Not available

SPARKS

RECORD CORRAL (I)   M–S   9:30–6:00
544 Greenbrae Drive   S   Closed
Sparks 89431
(702) 358-1502

SERVICES: Walk-in Store/Mail Order   SEARCH: Available with no service
                                                charge; Want lists maintained and re-
SPECIALTIES: Country & Western,   quester notified when record comes in
Easy Listening, Big Band, Banjo, In-
strumental, Hillbilly, Bluegrass, Reli-   COLLECTIONS: Will buy collections of
gious, Old- time Country, Promo-   rare records
tional, Ragtime   PAYMENTS: American Express, Mas-
VOLUME: 33⅓ – 30,000   ter Charge, Money Order, VISA/Bank-
           45 – 2,500   Americard
           78 – 0   MAIL ORDER: 4th Class Mail, U.P.S.;
           Other – 0   Prepayment or C.O.D.

STOCK: Domestic & Import/New &   DISCOUNTS: Not available
Used
                                                PUBLICATIONS: Not available

NEW HAMPSHIRE

CONWAY

SCONE (I)
P.O. Box 813
Conway 03818
 (603) 447-2110

M–T	9;00–5:00
F	9:00–9:00
S–S	9:00–5:00

SERVICES: Walk-in Store/Mail Order

SPECIALTIES: Sound Tracks, Broadway Shows, Television Shows, Film Scores, Vocal, Rock, Rock & Roll, Country & Western, Classical, Contemporary Jazz

VOLUME:
 33⅓ – 5,000
 45 – 2,000
 78 – 0
 Other – 0

STOCK: Domestic & Import/New & Used

SEARCH: Available with no service charge; Want lists maintained and requester notified when record comes in

COLLECTIONS: Will buy collections of rare records

PAYMENTS: Money Order, Personal Check

MAIL ORDER: Whatever shipment method requested; Prepayment

DISCOUNTS: Available

PUBLICATIONS: Bimonthly catalog available for $3.00 free bimonthly auction list; Free bimonthly set-sale list

NEW JERSEY

ATLANTIC CITY

RUSS MILLER RECORD SHOP (I)
1507 Atlantic Avenue
Atlantic City 08401
 (609) 348-9674

M–T	10:00–6:00
F	10:00–9:00
S	10:00–6:00
S	11:00–6:00

SERVICES: Walk-in Store/Mail Order

SPECIALTIES: All Major Categories

VOLUME:
 33⅓ – 4,000
 45 – 3,000
 78 – 600
 Other – 0

STOCK: Domestic & Import/New

SEARCH: Not available

COLLECTIONS: Will not buy collections of rare records

PAYMENTS: Master Charge, Money Order, Personal Check, VISA/BankAmericard

MAIL ORDER: Air Mail, 1st Class, 4th Class, U.P.S.; Prepayment or C.O.D.

DISCOUNTS: Available

PUBLICATIONS: I.N.A.

BOONTON

THE OLDE TYME MUSIC SCENE (I)	M–T	Closed
915 Main Street	W–S	10:00–5:00
Boonton 07005	S	Noon–4:00
(201) 335-5040		

SERVICES: Walk-in Store/Mail Order

SPECIALTIES: (Alphabetical) Big Band, Contemporary Jazz, Dance, Dixieland, Instrumental, Nostalgia, Ragtime, Rock & Roll, Standards, Swing, Traditional Jazz

VOLUME: 33⅓ – I.N.A.
          45 – I.N.A.
          78 – I.N.A.
          Other – Edison Diamond Discs/Cylinders

STOCK: Domestic & Import/New & Used

SEARCH: Available with no service charge; Want lists maintained and requester notified when record comes in

COLLECTIONS: Will buy collections of rare records

PAYMENTS: Master Charge, Personal Check, VISA/BankAmericard

MAIL ORDER: 4th Class, U.P.S.; Prepayment

DISCOUNTS: Not available

PUBLICATIONS: Not available

CLIFTON

GEORGE'S GOLDEN OLDIES RECORD SHOP	M	11:30–8:00
(I)	T–S	11:30–6:00
311 Crooks Avenue	S	Closed
Clifton 07011		
(201) 546-5405		

SERVICES: Walk-in Store/Mail Order

SPECIALTIES: Blues, Rhythm & Blues, Rock & Roll

VOLUME: 33⅓ – 24%
          45 – 74%
          78 – 2%
          Other – 0

STOCK: Domestic & Import/New & Used

SEARCH: Available with no service charge; Want lists maintained and requester notified when record comes in

COLLECTIONS: Will buy collections of rare records

PAYMENTS: Money Order, Personal Check

MAIL ORDER: 4th Class, Prepayment

DISCOUNTS: Not available

PUBLICATIONS: I.N.A.

CLIFTON PARK

RALPH WILLIAM SIM RECORDS (I)
Rural Delivery 6
P.O. Box 101
Riverview Road
Clifton Park 12065
Telephone: I.N.A.

SERVICES: Mail Order Only

SPECIALTIES: Big Band, Swing, Classical, Opera, Vocal, Blues, Edison Discs/Cylinders, Rhythm & Blues, Broadway Shows, Country & Western, Hillbilly, Rock & Roll, Spoken Word

VOLUME: 33⅓ – 5,000
          45   – 5,000
          78   – 240,000
          Other – Edison Diamond
                  Discs–3,000,
                  V-Discs,
                  H.O.W.

STOCK: Domestic & Import/New & Used

SEARCH: Available with and without service charge; Want lists maintained and requester notified when record comes in

COLLECTIONS: Available for purchase; Will buy collections of rare records

PAYMENTS: Money Order, Personal Check

MAIL ORDER: 4th Class, U.P.S., Whatever shipment method requested; Prepayment

DISCOUNTS: Available

PUBLICATIONS: Free occasional catalog; Free occasional auction list; Free occasional set-sale list

CONVENT

HARMONY STREET MUSIC (I)
P.O. Box 2C
Convent 07961
Telephone: I.N.A.

SERVICES: Mail Order Only (Domestic Sales Only)

SPECIALTIES: Rhythm & Blues, Rock & Roll, Gospel/Sacred, Blues

VOLUME: 33⅓ – 10
          45   – 200
          78   – 6,000
          Other – 0

STOCK: Domestic/New & Used

SEARCH: Available with no service charge; Want lists maintained and requester notified when record comes in

COLLECTIONS: Will buy collections of rare records

PAYMENTS: Money Order, Personal Check

MAIL ORDER: 4th Class, U.P.S., Whatever shipment method requested

DISCOUNTS: Not available

PUBLICATIONS: Free periodic auction list

ESSEX FELLS

PAYOLA RECORDS (I)
c/o Don Mennie
P.O. Box 23
Essex Fells 07021
  Telephone: I.N.A.

SERVICES: Mail Order Only

SPECIALTIES: Rhythm & Blues, Rock & Roll, Elvis, Beatles, Rock, Blues, Rockabilly, Novelty, Surfing, Promotional

VOLUME: 33⅓ – 1,000
             45   – 10,000
             78   – 100
             Other – 0

STOCK: Domestic/New & Used

SEARCH: Not available

COLLECTIONS: Will buy collections of rare records

PAYMENTS: Money Order, Personal Check

MAIL ORDER: 4th Class; Prepayment

DISCOUNTS: Not available

PUBLICATIONS: Free semiannual auction list

HILLSIDE

MR. RECORDS (I)
P.O. Box 764
Hillside 07205
  (201) 688-2693

M–S 8:00 A.M.–9:00 P.M.
S   10:00–5:00

SERVICES: Walk-in Store/Mail Order

SPECIALTIES: Big Band, Sinatra, Nostalgia, Classical, Instrumental, Vocal, Dance, Country & Western, Contemporary Jazz, Sound Tracks

VOLUME: 33⅓ – 1,000
             45   – 0
             78   – 70,000
             Other – Edison
                      Discs/V-Discs

STOCK: Domestic/New & Used

SEARCH: Available with no service charge; Want lists maintained and requester notified when record comes in

COLLECTIONS: Not available for purchase

PAYMENTS: Money Order, Personal Check

MAIL ORDER: 4th Class; Prepayment or C.O.D.

DISCOUNTS: Not available

PUBLICATIONS: Free annual catalog

JERSEY CITY

JOURNAL SQUARE RECORDS INCORPO-
RATED (I)
737 Bergen Avenue
Jersey City 07306
(201) 653-5681

M	9:30–7:00
T–W	9:30–6:00
T	9:30–7:00
F	9:30–8:00
S	9:30–6:00
S	Closed

SERVICES: Walk-in Store/Mail Order

SPECIALTIES: Soul, Rock & Roll, Rhythm & Blues, Doo Wop, A Cappella, Vocal, Traditional Jazz, Rock, Disco, Blues

VOLUME: 33⅓ – 33%
45 – 67%
78 – 0
Other – 0

STOCK: Domestic & Import/New & Used

SEARCH: Want lists maintained and requester notified when record comes in

COLLECTIONS: Will buy collections of rare records

PAYMENTS: Money Order, Personal Check

MAIL ORDER: U.P.S., Whatever shipment method requested; Prepayment or C.O.D.

DISCOUNTS: Available

PUBLICATIONS: Annual catalog available for $1.00 per year

MARGATE

RUSS MILLER RECORD SHOP (I)
9414 Ventnor Avenue
Margate 08402
(609) 822-2646

M–T	10:00–6:00
F	10:00–9:00
S	10:00–6:00
S	11:00–6:00

SERVICES: Walk-in Store/Mail Order

SPECIALTIES: All Major Categories

VOLUME: 33⅓ – 4,000
45 – 3,000
78 – 600
Other – 0

STOCK: Domestic & Import/New

SEARCH: Not available

COLLECTIONS: Will not buy collections of rare records

PAYMENTS: Master Charge, Money Order, Personal Check, VISA/BankAmericard

MAIL ORDER: Air Mail, 1st Class, 4th Class, U.P.S.; Prepayment or C.O.D.

DISCOUNTS: Available

PUBLICATIONS: I.N.A.

NEWARK

PARK RECORDS (I)
100 Park Place
Newark 07102
 (201) 622-8453

M–T	9:00–5:30
F	9:00–6:30
S	9:00–5:30
S	Closed

SERVICES: Walk-in Store/Mail Order

SPECIALTIES: Rhythm & Blues, Disco, Contemporary Jazz, Soul, Rock & Roll, Religious, Vocal, Traditional Jazz, Dance, Blues

VOLUME: 33⅓ – 1,000
              45 – 55,000
              78 – 0
           Other – 0

STOCK: Domestic/New

SEARCH: Not available

COLLECTIONS: Will not buy collections of rare records

PAYMENTS: Master Charge, Money Order, Personal Check, VISA/Bank-Americard

MAIL ORDER: U.P.S., Whatever shipment method requested; Prepayment

DISCOUNTS: Not available

PUBLICATIONS: Free periodic catalog

ORADELL

THE RADIO STORE (I)
P.O. Box 203
Oradell 07649
 (201) 967-0373

SERVICES: Mail Order Only/Library

SPECIALTIES: Old Radio Shows

VOLUME: 33⅓ – I.N.A.
              45 – I.N.A.
              78 – I.N.A.
           Other – I.N.A.

STOCK: Domestic/New

SEARCH: Available with service charge

COLLECTIONS: Will not buy collections of rare records

PAYMENTS: Master Charge, Money Order, Personal Check, VISA/Bank-Americard

MAIL ORDER: Air Mail, 4th Class, U.P.S.; Prepayment

DISCOUNTS: Available

PUBLICATIONS: I.N.A.

NEW MEXICO

TAOS

INDIAN HOUSE (I)   M–S   9:00–5:00
P.O. Box 472   S   Closed
Taos 87571
(505) 776-2953

SERVICES: Walk-in Store/Mail Order

SPECIALTIES: American Indian

VOLUME: 33⅓ – 100
           45 – 0
           78 – 0
           Other – 0

STOCK: Domestic/New

SEARCH: Not available

COLLECTIONS: Not available for purchase

PAYMENTS: Money Order, Personal Check

MAIL ORDER: 4th Class; Prepayment

DISCOUNTS: Not available

PUBLICATIONS: Free semiannual catalog

NEW YORK

ALBANY

BLUE NOTE RECORD SHOP (I)   M   Closed
156 Central Avenue   T–W   10:00–6:00
Albany 12206   T   10:00–9:00
(518) 462-0221   F–S   10:00–6:00
                                           S   Closed

SERVICES: Walk-in Store/Mail Order (45 r.p.m., Only)

SPECIALTIES: All Major Categories

VOLUME: 33⅓ – 100
           45 – 20,000
           78 – 0
           Other – 0

STOCK: Domestic & Import/New

SEARCH: Available with no service charge

COLLECTIONS: Will not buy collections of rare records

PAYMENTS: Money Order

MAIL ORDER: Air Mail, 4th Class; Prepayment

DISCOUNTS: Not available

PUBLICATIONS: Periodic catalog available for $2.50 per issue U.S.A.; $5.00 per issue non-U.S.A.

BAYSIDE

ARCADE RECORDS (I)
P.O. Box 18
Bayside 11361
   Telephone: I.N.A.

SERVICES: Mail Order Only

SPECIALTIES: Rock & Roll, Rhythm & Blues, Soul, Disco, Rockabilly, Beatles, Elvis, Country & Western, Blues, Rock, Doo Wop

VOLUME: 33⅓ – 3,000
             45 – 30,000
             78 – 1,000
             Other – 0

STOCK: Domestic/New & Used

SEARCH: Available with no service charge; Want lists maintained and requester notified when record comes in

COLLECTIONS: Will buy collections of rare records

PAYMENTS: Money Order, Personal Check

MAIL ORDER: Air Mail, 4th Class, Whatever shipment method requested; Prepayment or C.O.D.

DISCOUNTS: Available

PUBLICATIONS: Annual catalog for $1.00 per year; Free quarterly auction list

BRONX

TIMES SQUARE RECORDS (II)
P.O. Box 985
Bronx 10463
   (212) 549-7497

M–S	1:00–4:00
S	Closed

SERVICES: Walk-in Store (By Appointment)/Mail Order

SPECIALTIES: Rhythm & Blues, Rock & Roll, Rockabilly

VOLUME: 33⅓ – I.N.A.
             45 – I.N.A.
             78 – I.N.A.
             Other – I.N.A.

STOCK: Domestic/New & Used

SEARCH: Want lists maintained and requester notified when record comes in

COLLECTIONS: Will buy collections of rare records

PAYMENTS: Money Order, Personal Check

MAIL ORDER: 1st Class, 4th Class; Prepayment

DISCOUNTS: Not available

PUBLICATIONS: Free periodic auction list

BROOKLYN

EUBIE BLAKE MUSIC (II)
284–A Stuyvesant Avenue
Brooklyn 11221
(212) 574-8511

SERVICES: Mail Order Only

SPECIALTIES: Eubie Blake, Ragtime, Nostalgia

VOLUME: 33⅓ – I.N.A.
          45 – I.N.A.
          78 – I.N.A.
    Other – I.N.A.

STOCK: Domestic/New

SEARCH: Not available

COLLECTIONS: I.N.A.

PAYMENTS: Money Order, Personal Check

MAIL ORDER: 4th Class; Prepayment

DISCOUNTS: Available

PUBLICATIONS: Free periodic catalog

BROOKLYN

K & J RECORDS (II)
1679 81st Street
Brooklyn 11214
   Telephone: I.N.A.

SERVICES: Mail Order Only

SPECIALTIES: Blues, Rhythm & Blues, Rock & Roll

VOLUME: 33⅓ – 20,000
          45 – 20,000
          78 – 0
    Other – 0

STOCK: Domestic/New

SEARCH: Not available

COLLECTIONS: Will not buy collections of rare records

PAYMENTS: Money Order

MAIL ORDER: 4th Class; Prepayment

DISCOUNTS: Available

PUBLICATIONS: I.N.A.

BROOKLYN

TITUS OAKS RECORD EXCHANGE (I)   M–S   10:30–8:00
893 Flatbush Avenue   S   Noon–6:00
Brooklyn 11226
 (212) 469-9384

SERVICES: Walk-in Store/Mail Order

SPECIALTIES: (Alphabetical) Bluegrass, Blues, Bossa Nova, Contemporary Jazz, Disco, Folk, Folk-Rock, Hillbilly, Reggae, Rhythm & Blues, Rock, Rock & Roll, Soul, Traditional Jazz

VOLUME: 33⅓ – 25,000
              45 – 0
              78 – 0
            Other – 0

STOCK: Domestic & Import/New & Used

SEARCH: Not available

COLLECTIONS: Will buy collections of rare records

PAYMENTS: Money Order, Personal Check

MAIL ORDER: Air Mail, 1st Class; Prepayment

DISCOUNTS: I.N.A.

PUBLICATIONS: I.N.A.

BROOKLYN

CHIN RANDY'S RECORDS, INCORPORATED   M–T   10:00–8:00
 (II)   F–S   10:00–9:00
1342 St. John's Place   S   Closed
Brooklyn 11213
 (212) 778-9470

SERVICES: Walk-in Store/Mail Order

SPECIALTIES: All Major Categories

VOLUME: 33⅓ – I.N.A.
              45 – I.N.A.
              78 – I.N.A.
            Other – I.N.A.

STOCK: Domestic & Import/New

SEARCH: Available with no service charge

COLLECTIONS: Will not buy collections of rare records

PAYMENTS: Master Charge, Money Order

MAIL ORDER: Whatever shipment method requested; Prepayment or C.O.D.

DISCOUNTS: I.N.A.

PUBLICATIONS: I.N.A.

BROOKLYN

THE RECORD FORUM, INCORPORATED (I)   M–T   11:00–8:00
892 Flatbush Avenue   F–S   11:00–8:30
Brooklyn 11226   S   Closed
 (212) 284-7268

SERVICES: Walk-in Store/Mail Order

SPECIALTIES: All Major Categories

VOLUME: 33⅓ – 400
           45   – 6,000
           78   – 400
           Other – 0

STOCK: Domestic/New

SEARCH: Not available; Want lists maintained and requester notified when record comes in

COLLECTIONS: Will not buy collections of rare records

PAYMENTS: Money Order, VISA/BankAmericard

MAIL ORDER: Air Mail, 4th Class, U.P.S.; Prepayment or C.O.D.

DISCOUNTS: Not available

PUBLICATIONS: I.N.A.

BUFFALO

PLAY IT AGAIN, SAM (I)   M–S   Noon–8:00
1115 Elmwood Avenue   S   Noon–6:00
Buffalo 14222
 (716) 883-0330

SERVICES: Walk-in Store Only

SPECIALTIES: (Alphabetical) Bluegrass, Blues, Broadway Shows, Classical, Comedy, Contemporary Jazz, Country & Western, Disco, Folk, Reggae, Rhythm & Blues, Rock & Roll, Soul

VOLUME: 33⅓ – 25,000
           45   – 1,000
           78   – 0
           Other – 0

STOCK: Domestic & Import/New & Used

SEARCH: Want lists maintained and requester notified when record comes in

COLLECTIONS: Will buy collections of rare records

PAYMENTS: Money Order, Personal Check

MAIL ORDER: Not available

DISCOUNTS: Not available

PUBLICATIONS: I.N.A.

BUFFALO

RUDA'S RECORD STORE (II)
915 Broadway
Buffalo 14212
  (716) 852-3121

M–W	10:00–5:30
T–F	10:00–8:00
S	10:00–5:30
S	Closed

SERVICES: Walk-in Store/Mail Order

SPECIALTIES: Country & Western, Folk-Rock, Rock

VOLUME: 33⅓ – I.N.A.
           45 – I.N.A.
           78 – I.N.A.
           Other – I.N.A.

STOCK: Domestic & Import/New

SEARCH: I.N.A.

COLLECTIONS: Will not buy collections of rare records

PAYMENTS: Master Charge, Money Order, VISA/BankAmericard

MAIL ORDER: 4th Class, U.P.S.; Prepayment

DISCOUNTS: Available

PUBLICATIONS: I.N.A.

CATSKILL

RECORD UNDERTAKER (I)
Rural Delivery 1
P.O. Box 152–C
Catskill 12414
  (914) 246-8748

SERVICES: Mail Order Only

SPECIALTIES: All Major Categories

VOLUME: 33⅓ – 40,000
           45 – 5,000
           78 – 15,000
           Other – 0

STOCK: Domestic & Import/New & Used

SEARCH: I.N.A.

COLLECTIONS: Will buy collections of rare records

PAYMENTS: Money Order, Personal Check

MAIL ORDER: U.P.S.; Prepayment

DISCOUNTS: Not available

PUBLICATIONS: Free periodic catalog

CHATHAM

BIOGRAPH RECORDS INCORPORATED (I)   M–T   9:00–4:00
16 River Street   F–S   Closed
Chatham 12037
(518) 392-3400

SERVICES: Walk-in Store/Mail Order

SPECIALTIES: (Alphabetical) Blue-grass, Blues, Contemporary Jazz, Country & Western, Dixieland, Folk, Historical, Nostalgia, Old-Time Country, Ragtime, Swing, Traditional Jazz

VOLUME: 33⅓ – 30,000
           45   – 0
           78   – 0
           Other – 0

STOCK: Domestic/New

SEARCH: I.N.A.

COLLECTIONS: Will buy collections of rare records

PAYMENTS: Money Order, Personal Check

MAIL ORDER: Whatever shipment method requested; Prepayment

DISCOUNTS: Available

PUBLICATIONS: Periodic catalog available for $1.25 per issue

FARMINGDALE

SAM BUCHMAN RECORDS (I)
1 Valpage Street
Farmingdale 11735
(516) 694-2691

SERVICES: Mail Order Only

SPECIALTIES: Rock & Roll, Sound Tracks, Broadway Shows, Standards, Comedy, Contemporary Jazz, Classical, Easy Listening, Traditional Jazz, Country & Western

VOLUME: 33⅓ – 10,000
           45   – 5,000
           78   – 1,000
           Other – Langworth L. P.
                   Records–1,000

STOCK: Domestic/Used

SEARCH: Available with no service charge

COLLECTIONS: Available for purchase

PAYMENTS: Money Order

MAIL ORDER: U.P.S.; Prepayment

DISCOUNTS: Available

PUBLICATIONS: Not available

FARMINGDALE

JOHN JACKSON RECORDS (I)
P.O. Box 724
Farmingdale 11735
   Telephone: I.N.A.

SERVICES: Mail Order Only

SPECIALTIES: Rock & Roll, Vocal, Rhythm & Blues, Surfing, Rockabilly, Country & Western, Reggae, Folk, Novelty, Punk Rock/New Wave

VOLUME: 33⅓ – 1,000
           45 – 2,000
           78 – 500
           Other – 0

STOCK: Domestic & Import/New & Used

SEARCH: Want lists maintained and requester notified when record comes in

COLLECTIONS: Will buy collections of rare records

PAYMENTS: Money Order, Personal Check

MAIL ORDER: 4th Class, Whatever shipment method requested; Prepayment

DISCOUNTS: Not available

PUBLICATIONS: Free semiannual auction list

FLUSHING

OLDIES UNLIMITED (I)
P.O. Box 389
Flushing 11352
   Telephone: I.N.A.

SERVICES: Mail Order Only

SPECIALTIES: Rockabilly, Rock & Roll, Rhythm & Blues, Elvis, Beatles, Surfing, Instrumental, Novelty, Country & Western, Soul

VOLUME: 33⅓ – 500
           45 – 15,000
           78 – 100
           Other – 0

STOCK: Domestic & Import/New & Used

SEARCH: Available with no service charge; Want lists maintained and requester notified when record comes in

COLLECTIONS: Will buy collections of rare records

PAYMENTS: Money Order, Personal Check

MAIL ORDER: Air Mail, 4th Class; Prepayment

DISCOUNTS: Available

PUBLICATIONS: Annual catalog available for $2.00 per year; Free periodic auction list

GETZVILLE

RARECORDS (I)
P.O. Box 254
Getzville 14068
  (716) 631-0855

M–T	10:00–9:30
W–T	Closed
F	10:00–9:30
S	10:00–1:00
S	11:00–1:00

SERVICES: Walk-in Store/Mail Order

SPECIALTIES: Sinatra

VOLUME: 33⅓ – 5,000
         45 – 5,000
         78 – 5,000
         Other – 0

STOCK: Domestic & Import/New & Used

SEARCH: Available with no service charge; Want lists maintained and requester notified when record comes in

COLLECTIONS: I.N.A.

PAYMENTS: Master Charge, Money Order, Personal Charge Account, Personal Check, VISA/BankAmericard

MAIL ORDER: Whatever shipment method requested; Prepayment or C.O.D.

DISCOUNTS: Available

PUBLICATIONS: Free quarterly catalog; Free quarterly auction list

GOVERNEUR

JACK WOLAK RECORDS (I)
171 Clinton Street
Governeur 13642
  (315) 287-4168

SERVICES: Mail Order Only

SPECIALTIES: Rock, Rock & Roll, Country & Western, Punk Rock/New Wave, Popular, Folk-Rock, Folk

VOLUME: 33⅓ – 25,000
         45 – 16,000
         78 – 0
         Other – 0

STOCK: Domestic & Import/New & Used

SEARCH: Want lists maintained and requester notified when record comes in

COLLECTIONS: Will buy collections of rare records

PAYMENTS: Money Order, Personal Check

MAIL ORDER: Whatever shipment method requested; Prepayment or C.O.D.

DISCOUNTS: Negotiable

PUBLICATIONS: Semiannual catalog available for $.25 each; Free monthly auction list available in Goldmine Magazine

GREENPORT

LIGHTFOOT COLLECTION (I)   M–S   9:00–9:00
P.O. Box A–F
Greenport 11944
(516) 477-2589

SERVICES: Mail Order (Above Times for Telephone)

SPECIALTIES: Classical, Traditional Jazz, Rhythm & Blues, Ethnic, Blues, Dixieland, Swing, Folk, Broadway Shows, Spoken Word

VOLUME: 33⅓ – 15,000
           45   – 1,000
           78   – 20,000
           Other – 0

STOCK: Domestic & Import/New & Used

SEARCH: Not available; Want lists maintained and requester notified when record comes in

COLLECTIONS: Will buy collections of rare records

PAYMENTS: Money Order, Personal Check

MAIL ORDER: 4th Class; Prepayment

DISCOUNTS: Not available

PUBLICATIONS: Not available

HICKSVILLE

JAZZ RECORD COMPANY (I)
P.O. Box 71
Hicksville 11801
(516) 997-3653

SERVICES: Mail Order Only

SPECIALTIES: All Major Categories

VOLUME: 33⅓ – 15,000
           45   – 100,000
           78   – 8,000
           Other – Edison
                   Discs–100
                   Transcrip-
                   tions–2,000

STOCK: Domestic & Import/New & Used

SEARCH: Available with no service charge; Want lists maintained and requester notified when record comes in

COLLECTIONS: Will buy collections of rare records

PAYMENTS: Money Order, Personal Check

MAIL ORDER: 4th Class, U.P.S., Whatever shipment method requested; Prepayment

DISCOUNTS: Available

PUBLICATIONS: Quarterly catalog available for $1.00 per year; Quarterly auction list available for $1.00 per year

JACKSON HEIGHTS

ARCADE RECORDS (I)
74–16 Roosevelt Avenue
Jackson Heights 11372
(212) 779-2728

M–F	11:00–8:00
S	Noon–6:00
S	Closed

SERVICES: Walk-in Store/Mail Order

SPECIALTIES: (Alphabetical) Disco, Rhythm & Blues, Rock, Rock & Roll, Soul

VOLUME: 33⅓ – 500
45 – 5,000
78 – 500
Other – 0

STOCK: Domestic/New & Used

SEARCH: Want lists maintained and requester notified when record comes in

COLLECTIONS: Will buy collections of rare records

PAYMENTS: Master Charge, Money Order, Personal Check

MAIL ORDER: 4th Class; Prepayment or C.O.D.

DISCOUNTS: Available

PUBLICATIONS: I.N.A.

JAMAICA

GREENLINE RECORDS (I)
92–36 New York Boulevard
Jamaica 11433
(212) 523-9782

| M–S | 9:00–7:00 |
| S | Closed |

SERVICES: Walk-in Store/Mail Order

SPECIALTIES: All Major Categories

VOLUME: 33⅓ – 30,000
45 – 45,000
78 – 2,000
Other – 0

STOCK: Domestic & Import/New & Used

SEARCH: Available with no service charge; Want lists maintained and requester notified when record comes in

COLLECTIONS: Available for purchase; Will buy collections of rare records

PAYMENTS: Master Charge, Money Order, VISA/BankAmericard

MAIL ORDER: Whatever shipment method requested; Prepayment

DISCOUNTS: Not available

PUBLICATIONS: Not available

LIVERPOOL

COLLECTOR-DEALER OUTLET (I)   M–S   Noon–6:00
113 Dollin Street
Liverpool 13088
  (315) 457-5789

SERVICES: Walk-in Store/Mail Order

SPECIALTIES: Rock & Roll, Rhythm & Blues, Rockabilly, Elvis, Beatles, Children's, Country & Western, Easy Listening, Surfing, Blues

VOLUME: 33⅓ – 300
            45 – 7,500
            78 – 0
            Other – 0

STOCK: Domestic/New & Used

SEARCH: Available with no service charge

COLLECTIONS: Will buy collections of rare records

PAYMENTS: Money Order, Personal Check

MAIL ORDER: 1st Class, 4th Class, Whatever shipment method requested; Prepayment

DISCOUNTS: Not available

PUBLICATIONS: Free semiannual auction list

LONG ISLAND CITY

RECORD SCENE (I)   M–W   10:00–7:00
30–73 Steinway Street   T–F   10:00–8:00
Long Island City 11103   S   10:00–6:00
  (212) 545-9211   S   Closed

SERVICES: Walk-in Store Only

SPECIALTIES: (Alphabetical)   Blues, Classical, Contemporary Jazz, Country & Western, Disco, Easy Listening, Rhythm & Blues, Rock, Rock & Roll, Soul, Traditional Jazz

VOLUME: 33⅓ – 1,000
            45 – 3,000
            78 – 0
            Other – 0

STOCK: Domestic/New

SEARCH: Available with no service charge; Want lists maintained and requester notified when record comes in

COLLECTIONS: Will not buy collections of rare records

PAYMENTS: Master Charge, VISA/-BankAmericard

MAIL ORDER: Not available

DISCOUNTS: Not available

PUBLICATIONS: I.N.A.

MASSAPEQUA

FRED STEINMETZ RECORDS (I)
One Seaview Avenue
Massapequa 11758
(516) 541-0597

SERVICES: Mail Order Only

SPECIALTIES: Classical, Opera, Nostalgia, Rock, Traditional Jazz, Country & Western, Film Scores, Broadway Shows, Comedy, Military

VOLUME: 33⅓ – 14,000
        45 – 1,000
        78 – 8,000
        Other – 0

STOCK: Domestic & Import/New & Used

SEARCH: Want lists maintained and requester notified when record comes in

COLLECTIONS: Will buy collections of rare records

PAYMENTS: Money Order, Personal Check

MAIL ORDER: U.P.S., Whatever shipment method requested; Prepayment

DISCOUNTS: Not available

PUBLICATIONS: Free catalog every four months

NEW YORK

AGM RARE RECORDS LIMITED (I)
1619 Broadway
New York 10019
(212) 581-0460

SERVICES: Walk-in Store (By Appointment Only)/Mail Order

SPECIALTIES: (Alphabetical) Bluegrass, Blues, Bossa Nova, Contemporary Jazz, Country & Western, Folk, Folk-Rock, Hillbilly, Rhythm & Blues, Rock & Roll, Soul, Traditional Jazz

VOLUME: 33⅓ – 100,000
        45 – 10,000
        78 – 0
        Other – 0

STOCK: Domestic/New

SEARCH: Available with no service charge; Want lists maintained and requester notified when record comes in

COLLECTIONS: Will buy collections of rare records

PAYMENTS: Money Order, Personal Check

MAIL ORDER: Air mail, 1st Class, 4th Class; Prepayment

DISCOUNTS: Not available

PUBLICATIONS: Free auction list

NEW YORK

ARF ARF (I)
P.O. Box 755
Cooper Station
New York 10003
    (212) 243-6484

SERVICES: Mail Order Only

SPECIALTIES: Fifties Vocal, Rock, Disco, Soul, Country & Western, Punk Rock/New Wave, Easy Listening, Rock & Roll, Promotional, Novelty

VOLUME: 33⅓ – 0
           45 – 50,000
           78 – 0
           Other – 0

STOCK: Domestic & Import/New & Used

SEARCH: Want lists maintained and in requester notified when record comes

COLLECTIONS: Will buy collections of rare records

PAYMENTS: Money Order, Personal Check

MAIL ORDER: 4th Class, Prepayment

DISCOUNTS: Available

PUBLICATIONS: Periodic catalog available for $3.00 per issue U.S.A. and for $4.00 per issue non-U.S.A.

NEW YORK

BIG HIT OLDIES SHOP (I)
170 Bleecker Street
Greenwich Village 10012
    (212) 475-9516

M–T Noon–2:00 A.M.
F–S Noon–4:00 A.M.
    S 1:00 P.M.–mid.

SERVICES: Walk-in Store/Mail Order

SPECIALTIES: (Alphabetical) Blues, Contemporary Jazz, Country & Western, Disco, Easy Listening, Folk, Folk-Rock, Punk Rock/New Wave, Rhythm & Blues, Rock & Roll, Soul, Traditional Jazz

VOLUME: 33⅓ – 20,000
           45 – 250,000
           78 – 1,000
           Other – 0

STOCK: Domestic & Import/New & Used

SEARCH: Available with no service charge; Want lists maintained and requester notified when record comes in

COLLECTIONS: Will buy collections of rare records

PAYMENTS: Money Order, Personal Check

MAIL ORDER: 4th Class; Prepayment

DISCOUNTS: Not available

PUBLICATIONS: Periodic catalog available for $1.25 per issue

NEW YORK

B.J.R. ENTERPRISES, INCORPORATED (I)   M–F   9:00–5:00
P.O. Box 330   S–S   Closed
Cathedral Station
New York 10025
  (212) 666-2834

SERVICES: Mail Order Only (Above Times for Telephone)

SPECIALTIES: Opera

VOLUME: 33⅓ – 100%
           45   – 0
           78   – 0
           Other – 0

STOCK: Domestic/New

SEARCH: Not available

COLLECTIONS: Will not buy collections of rare records

PAYMENTS: Money Order, Personal Check

MAIL ORDER: Air Mail, 4th Class, U.P.S.; Prepayment

DISCOUNTS: Available

PUBLICATIONS: I.N.A.

NEW YORK

BLEECKER BOB'S GOLDEN OLDIES   M–S Noon–1:00 A.M.
179 MacDougal Street
New York 10011
  (212) 475-9677

SERVICES: Walk-in Store/Mail Order

SPECIALTIES: Punk Rock/New Wave, Rock & Roll, Rockabilly

VOLUME: 33⅓ – 50%
           45   – 50%
           78   – 0
           Other – 0

STOCK: Domestic & Import/New & Used

SEARCH: Not available; Want lists checked but not maintained

COLLECTIONS: Will buy collections of rare records

PAYMENTS: Money Order

MAIL ORDER: 4th Class; Prepayment

DISCOUNTS: Not available

PUBLICATIONS: Annual catalog available for $2.00

NEW YORK

COLONY RECORD CENTER (II)
1619 Broadway
New York 10019
(212) 265-2050

M–F 9:30A.M.–2:30A.M.
S 10:00A.M.–3:00A.M.
S 10:00A.M.–2:00A.M.

SERVICES: Walk-in Store/Mail Order

SPECIALTIES: All Major Categories

VOLUME: 33⅓ – I.N.A.
           45   – I.N.A.
           78   – I.N.A.
           Other – I.N.A.

STOCK: Domestic & Import/New &
Used

SEARCH: Available with no service
charge

COLLECTIONS: Will buy collections of
rare records

PAYMENTS: American Express, Carte
Blanche, Diners Club, Master Charge,
Money Order, Personal Check,
VISA/BankAmericard

MAIL ORDER: Whatever shipment
method requested; Prepayment

DISCOUNTS: Not available

PUBLICATIONS: Not available

NEW YORK

DANNY'S RECORDS (I)
252 Bleecker Street
New York 10014
Telephone: I.N.A.

M   Closed
T   Noon–8:00
W   Closed
T   Noon–8:00
F–S   Noon–10:00
S   Noon–8:00

SERVICES: Walk-in Store/Mail Order

SPECIALTIES: Elvis, Rockabilly, Sound
Tracks, Sinatra, Beatles, Rock & Roll,
Rhythm & Blues

VOLUME: 33⅓ – 49%
           45   – 49%
           78   – 2%
           Other – 0

STOCK: Domestic & Import/New &
Used

SEARCH: Want lists maintained and
requester notified when record comes
in

COLLECTIONS: Will buy collections of
rare records

PAYMENTS: Personal Check, Money
Order

MAIL ORDER: 4th Class, Whatever
shipment method requested; Prepayment

DISCOUNTS: Available

PUBLICATIONS: Not available

NEW YORK

DARTON RECORDS (I)
160 West 56th Street
New York 10019
(212) 582-7350

| M–S | 9:00–6:00 |
| S | Closed |

SERVICES: Walk-in Store/Mail Order

SPECIALTIES: Opera, Classical, Instrumental, Broadway Shows, Sound Tracks

VOLUME: 33⅓ – 10,000
               45 – 0
               78 – 0
            Other – 0

STOCK: Domestic & Import/New

SEARCH: Not available

COLLECTIONS: Not available for purchase

PAYMENTS: Master Charge, Personal Charge Account, Personal Check, VISA/BankAmericard

MAIL ORDER: U.P.S.; Whatever shipment method requested; Prepayment

DISCOUNTS: Not available

PUBLICATIONS: Not available

NEW YORK

DAYTON'S (I)
824 Broadway
New York 10003
(212) 254-5084

M–F	10:00–6:00
S	10:00–5:00
S	Closed

SERVICES: Walk-in Store/Mail Order

SPECIALTIES: Classical, Vocal, Easy Listening, Contemporary Jazz, Sound Tracks, Broadway Shows, Rock & Roll, Opera, Traditional Jazz, Instrumental

VOLUME: 33⅓ – 100,000
               45 – 0
               78 – 0
            Other – 0

STOCK: Domestic & Import/New & Used

SEARCH: Not available

COLLECTIONS: Will buy collections of rare records

PAYMENTS: Money Order, Personal Check (New York City)

MAIL ORDER: Air Mail, 4th Class; Prepayment

DISCOUNTS: Not available

PUBLICATIONS: Not available

NEW YORK

DISCONNECTION (II)
P.O. Box 563
New York 10013
 Telephone: I.N.A.

SERVICES: Mail Order Only

SPECIALTIES: All Major Categories

VOLUME: 33⅓ – 100%
           45   – 0
           78   – 0
           Other – 0

STOCK: Domestic & Import/New & Used

SEARCH: Not available

COLLECTIONS: Will not buy collections of rare records

PAYMENTS: Money Order, Personal Check

MAIL ORDER: 4th Class; C.O.D.

DISCOUNTS: I.N.A.

PUBLICATIONS: I.N.A.

NEW YORK

DOWNSTAIRS RECORDS, INCORPORATED (I)   M–S   10:00–6:30
55 West 42nd Street   S   Closed
New York 10036
 (212) 221-8989 or 354-4684

SERVICES: Walk-in Store/Mail Order

SPECIALTIES: (Alphabetical) Bluegrass, Blues, Country & Western, Disco, Ethnic, Folk, Hillbilly, Reggae, Religious, Rhythm & Blues, Rock & Roll, Traditional Jazz

VOLUME: 33⅓ – 35%
           45   – 60%
           78   – 5%
           Other – 0

STOCK: Domestic & Import/New & Used

SEARCH: Want lists maintained and requester notified when record comes in

COLLECTIONS: Will buy collections of rare records

PAYMENTS: Master Charge, Money Order, VISA/BankAmericard

MAIL ORDER: Air Mail, 1st Class, U.P.S.; Prepayment or C.O.D.

DISCOUNTS: Available

PUBLICATIONS: I.N.A.

NEW YORK

FARFELS RECORDS (I)
179 West 4th Street
New York 10014
(212) 675-4126

M–F	12:30 P.M.–7:00
S	Noon–6:00
S	Closed

SERVICES: Walk-in Store/Mail Order

SPECIALTIES: Beatles, Rock, Rock & Roll, Punk Rock/New Wave, Rockabilly, Promotional, Surfing, Folk, Reggae

VOLUME: 33⅓ – 7,000
          45   – 2,000
          78   – 0
    Other – 0

STOCK: Domestic & Import/New & Used

SEARCH: I.N.A.

COLLECTIONS: Will buy collections of rare records

PAYMENTS: Money Order

MAIL ORDER: Whatever shipment method requested; Prepayment

DISCOUNTS: Not available

PUBLICATIONS: Free occasional auction list

NEW YORK

GOLDEN DISC RECORDS (I)
239 Bleecker Street
New York 10014
(212) 255-7899

M–S	11:00–9:00
S	12:30–7:00

SERVICES: Walk-in Store/Mail Order

SPECIALTIES: New Wave, Rock & Roll, Rhythm & Blues, Rockabilly, Elvis, Beatles, Blues

VOLUME: 33⅓ – 15,000
          45   – 100,000
          78   – 0
    Other – 0

STOCK: Domestic & Import/New & Used

SEARCH: Not available; Want lists checked but not maintained

COLLECTIONS: Will buy collections of rare records

PAYMENTS: Master Charge, Money Order, Personal Check, VISA/BankAmericard

MAIL ORDER: U.P.S. unless outside continental U.S.

DISCOUNTS: Not available

PUBLICATIONS: Catalog available; to be updated periodically

NEW YORK

HOUSE OF OLDIES (I)   M–S   11:00–7:00
267 Bleecker Street   S   Closed
New York 10014
(212) 243-0500

SERVICES: Walk-in Store/Mail Order

SPECIALTIES: Beatles, Elvis, Folk, Film Scores, Instrumental, Broadway Shows, Hillbilly, Blues, Dance, Country & Western, Big Band

VOLUME: 33⅓ – 25%
             45 – 74%
             78 – 1%
           Other – 0

STOCK: Domestic & Import/New & Used

SEARCH: Available with no service charge; Want lists maintained and requester notified when record comes in

COLLECTIONS: Available for purchase; Will buy collections of rare records

PAYMENTS: Money Order, Personal Check

MAIL ORDER: Air Mail, 1st Class, 4th Class, Whatever shipment method requested; Prepayment

DISCOUNTS: Available

PUBLICATIONS: Periodic catalog available for $1.50 per issue

NEW YORK

INFINITE RECORDS (I)   M–T   11:30–6:30
208 Mercer Street   F   11:30–9:30
New York 10012   S   Noon–7:00
(212) 473-7949   S   Noon–6:00

SERVICES: Walk-in Store/Mail Order

SPECIALTIES: Rock & Roll, Rock, Rhythm & Blues, Beatles

VOLUME: 33⅓ – 10,000
             45 – 20,000
             78 – 0
           Other – 0

STOCK: Domestic & Import/New & Used

SEARCH: Want lists maintained and requester notified when record comes in

COLLECTIONS: Will buy collections of rare records

PAYMENTS: Money Order, Personal Check

MAIL ORDER: Whatever shipment method requested; Prepayment

DISCOUNTS: Available

PUBLICATIONS: Free set-sale list

NEW YORK

DAVE KIESLER RECORDS (I)
188A East 93rd Street
New York 10028
(212) 534-5809

SERVICES: Mail Order Only

SPECIALTIES: Sound Tracks, Film Scores, Broadway Shows, Television Shows

VOLUME: 33⅓ – 350
           45   – 0
           78   – 0
           Other – 0

STOCK: Domestic & Import/New & Used

SEARCH: Want lists maintained and requester notified when record comes in

COLLECTIONS: Not available for purchase

PAYMENTS: Money Order, Personal Check

MAIL ORDER: 4th Class; Prepayment

DISCOUNTS: Not available

PUBLICATIONS: Semiannual catalog available for 50¢ per year

NEW YORK

LIBRAIRIE DE FRANCE (II)
115 Fifth Avenue
New York 10003
(212) 673-7400

M–F	9:00–6:00
S	10:00–6:00
S	Closed

SERVICES: Walk-in Store/Mail Order

SPECIALTIES: Foreign Language

VOLUME: 33⅓ – 50%
           45   – 50%
           78   – 0
           Other – 0

STOCK: Import/New

SEARCH: Not available

COLLECTIONS: Will not buy collections of rare records

PAYMENTS: American Express, Diners Club, Master Charge, Money Order, Personal Check, VISA/BankAmericard

MAIL ORDER: Air Mail, 4th Class, U.P.S.; Prepayment

DISCOUNTS: Not available

PUBLICATIONS: I.N.A.

NEW YORK

LIBRAIRIE DE FRANCE (II)
610 Fifth Avenue
New York 10020
(212) 581-8810

M–F   9:00–6:00
S   10:00–6:00
S   Closed

SERVICES: Walk-in Store/Mail Order

SPECIALTIES: Foreign Language

VOLUME: 33⅓ – 50%
           45 – 50%
           78 – 0
           Other – 0

STOCK: Import/New

SEARCH: Not available

COLLECTIONS: Will not buy collections of rare records

PAYMENTS: American Express, Diners Club, Master Charge, Money Order, Personal Check, VISA/BankAmericard

MAIL ORDER: Air Mail, 4th Class, U.P.S.; Prepayment

DISCOUNTS: Not available

PUBLICATIONS: I.N.A.

NEW YORK

LIST COMMUNICATIONS (I)
P.O. Box 916
New York 10023
(212) 362-3662

M–F   9:00–5:00
S–S   Closed

SERVICES: Walk-in Store/Mail Order

SPECIALTIES: (Alphabetical)   Blues, Bossa Nova, Broadway Shows, Classical, Contemporary Jazz, Ethnic, Folk, Personalities, Rhythm & Blues, Sound Tracks, Traditional Jazz

VOLUME: 33⅓ – 100%
           45 – 0
           78 – 0
           Other – 0

STOCK: Domestic/New

SEARCH: Available with no service charge

COLLECTIONS: Will not buy collections of rare records

PAYMENTS: Money Order, Personal Check

MAIL ORDER: Air Mail, 4th Class; Prepayment

DISCOUNTS: Available

PUBLICATIONS: I.N.A.

NEW YORK

ONCE IN A GREAT WHILE FINDS, LIMITED (I)
12 East 41st Street
Room 1006–Department 5088
New York 10017
   Telephone: I.N.A.

SERVICES: Mail Order Only

SPECIALTIES: Nostalgia, Easy Listening, Sound Tracks, Broadway Shows, Television Shows, Rhythm & Blues, Country & Western, Novelty, Christmas, Rock & Roll

VOLUME: 33⅓ – 98%
               45 – 1%
               78 – 1%
               Other – 0

STOCK: Domestic/New & Used

SEARCH: Want lists maintained and requester notified when record comes in

COLLECTIONS: Will buy collections of rare records

PAYMENTS: Money Order, Personal Check

MAIL ORDER: Whatever shipment method requested; Prepayment

DISCOUNTS: Not available

PUBLICATIONS: Free monthly auction list

NEW YORK

ROBERT PURCELL RECORDS (I)
P.O. Box 4669
New York 10017
   Telephone: I.N.A.

SERVICES: Mail Order Only

SPECIALTIES: (Alphabetical) Bluegrass, Country & Western, Hillbilly

VOLUME: 33⅓ – 28,000
               45 – 8,000
               78 – 12,000
               Other – 0

STOCK: Domestic & Import/New & Used

SEARCH: Available with no service charge; Want lists maintained and requester notified when record comes in

COLLECTIONS: Will buy collections of rare records

PAYMENTS Money Order

MAIL ORDER: 4th Class, U.P.S.; Prepayment

DISCOUNTS: Not available

PUBLICATIONS: I.N.A.

NEW YORK

THE RECORD HUNTER (II)   M–S   9:00–6:30
507 Fifth Avenue   S   Closed
New York 10017
(212) 697-8970

SERVICES: Walk-in Store/Mail Order   COLLECTIONS: Will buy collections of
                                          (new) rare records
SPECIALTIES: All Major Categories

VOLUME: 33⅓ – I.N.A.   PAYMENTS: American Express, Carte
               45 – I.N.A.   Blanche, Diners Club, Master Charge,
               78 – I.N.A.   Money   Order,   Personal   Check,
               Other – I.N.A.   VISA/BankAmericard

STOCK: Domestic & Import/New   MAIL ORDER: 1st Class, U.P.S.; Pre-
                                          payment
SEARCH: Available with no service
charge; Want lists maintained and re-   DISCOUNTS: Available
quester notified when record comes in   PUBLICATIONS: Free quarterly catalog

NEW YORK

RECORD LOFT INTERNATIONAL (I)   M–S   11:00–6:00
230 Seventh Avenue   S   Closed
New York 10011
(212) 691-2554 or 1934

SERVICES: Walk-in Store/Mail Order   COLLECTIONS: Will not buy collec-
                                          tions of rare records
SPECIALTIES: Classical, Opera
                                          PAYMENTS: Money Order, Personal
VOLUME: 33⅓ – 3,000   Check
               45 – 0
               78 – 0   MAIL ORDER: Air Mail, 4th Class,
               Other – 0   U.P.S.; Prepayment

STOCK: Import/New   DISCOUNTS: Not available

SEARCH: Want lists maintained and   PUBLICATIONS: I.N.A.
requester notified when record comes
in

NEW YORK

RECORD RUNNER (I)   M–S   Noon–7:00
5 Cornelia Street   S   Noon–6:00
New York 10014
(212) 255-4280

SERVICES: Walk-in Store/Mail Order

SPECIALTIES: (Alphabetical) Beatles, Elvis, Folk-Rock, Promotional, Punk Rock/New Wave, Rock, Rock & Roll, Surfing

VOLUME: 33⅓ – 75%
            45 – 25%
            78 – 0
            Other – 0

STOCK: Domestic & Import/New & Used

SEARCH: Want lists maintained and requester notified when record comes in

COLLECTIONS: Will buy collections of rare records

PAYMENTS: Personal Check, Money Order

MAIL ORDER: 4th Class, Whatever shipment method requested; Prepayment

DISCOUNTS: Not available

PUBLICATIONS: Free annual catalog available

NEW YORK

SECOND HAND ROSE'S 6th AVENUE SHOP,   M–S   10:30–7:00
   INC. (I)   S   Closed
525 Sixth Avenue
New York 10011
(212) 675-3735

SERVICES: Walk-in Store/Mail Order

SPECIALTIES: Vocal, Bop Jazz, Contemporary Jazz, Traditional Jazz, Rock, Classical, Sound Tracks, Broadway Shows, Nostalgia, Big Band, Rhythm & Blues

VOLUME: 33⅓ – 75,000
            45 – 5,000
            78 – 0
            Other – 0

STOCK: Domestic & Import/New & Used

SEARCH: Available with no service charge; Want lists maintained and requester notified when record comes in

COLLECTIONS: Will buy collections of rare records

PAYMENTS: Master Charge, Money Order, VISA/BankAmericard

MAIL ORDER: Whatever shipment method requested; Prepayment

DISCOUNTS: Not available

PUBLICATIONS: Not available

NEW YORK

C.S. SIERLE RECORDS (I)
155 West 95th Street
New York 10025
  (212) 222-0292

SERVICES: Mail Order Only

SPECIALTIES: Opera, Vocal, Classical, Spanish, Foreign Language

VOLUME: 33⅓ – 4,500
            45 – 0
            78 – 0
            Other – 0

STOCK: Domestic & Import/Used

SEARCH: Want lists maintained and requester notified when record comes in

COLLECTIONS: Available for purchase; Will buy collections of rare records

PAYMENTS: Money Order, Personal Check

MAIL ORDER: 4th Class; Prepayment

DISCOUNTS: Available

PUBLICATIONS: Periodic catalog available for $1.00

NEW YORK

STANTON RECORDS (I)
P.O. Box 468
Wall Street Station
New York 10005
  Telephone: I.N.A.

SERVICES: Mail Order Only

SPECIALTIES: (Alphabetical) Broadway Shows, Country & Western, Easy Listening, Folk, Rock & Roll, Sound Tracks, Vocal

VOLUME: 33⅓ – 4,000
            45 – 0
            78 – 0
            Other – 0

STOCK: Domestic & Import/New & Used

SEARCH: Available with no service charge; Want lists maintained and requester notified when record comes in

COLLECTIONS: Will buy collections of rare records

PAYMENTS: Money Order, Personal Check

MAIL ORDER: 4th Class; Prepayment

DISCOUNTS: Available

PUBLICATIONS: I.N.A.

NEW YORK

STRIDER RECORDS (I)
29 Cornelia Street
New York 10014
  (212) 675-3040

M–W	11:30–7:00
T	1:00–5:00
F–S	11:30–7:00
S	Closed

SERVICES: Walk-in Store/Mail Order

SPECIALTIES: Elvis, Rhythm & Blues, Sound Tracks, Rock, Rock & Roll, Personalities, Blues, Vocal

VOLUME: 33⅓ – 10,000
  45 – 100,000
  78 – 1,000
  Other – 0

STOCK: Domestic & Import/New & Used

SEARCH: Want lists maintained and requester notified when record comes in

COLLECTIONS: Will buy collections of rare records

PAYMENTS: Money Order

MAIL ORDER: 4th Class, Whatever shipment method requested; Prepayment

DISCOUNTS: Available

PUBLICATIONS: Free periodic catalog available

NEW YORK

STEPHEN J. TOKASH RECORDS (I)
G.P.O. Box 2302
New York 10001
  (212) 386-2560

SERVICES: Mail Order Only

SPECIALTIES: Elvis, Beatles, Rock, Rock & Roll, Rhythm & Blues, Rockabilly, Country & Western, Novelty, Sound Tracks, Easy Listening, Sinatra

VOLUME: 33⅓ – 5,000
  45 – 15,000
  78 – 500
  Other – 0

STOCK: Domestic & Import/New & Used

SEARCH: Want lists maintained and requester notified when record comes in

COLLECTIONS: Will buy collections of rare records

PAYMENTS: Money Order, Personal Check

MAIL ORDER: Whatever shipment method requested; Prepayment or C.O.D.

DISCOUNTS: Available

PUBLICATIONS: Free periodic catalog; Free periodic auction list

NEW YORK

LUDUS TONALIS (I)   M–S   10:30–6:30
24 Eighth Avenue   S   Closed
New York 10014
(212) 989-9758

SERVICES: Walk-in Store/Mail Order

SPECIALTIES: Opera, Classical, Vocal, Instrumental, Broadway Shows, British Musical Shows, Sound Tracks, Spoken Word, Nostalgia, Traditional Jazz

VOLUME: 33⅓ – 30,000
                  45   – 0
                  78   – 0
               Other – 0

STOCK: Domestic & Import/New & Used

SEARCH: Want lists maintained and requester notified when record comes in

COLLECTIONS: Will buy collections of rare records

PAYMENTS: Master Charge, Money Order, Personal Check, VISA/BankAmericard

MAIL ORDER: Air Mail, U.P.S., Whatever shipment method requested; Prepayment

DISCOUNTS: Available

PUBLICATIONS: Semiannual catalog available for $1.00 per year

NEW YORK

ANDREW VELEZ RECORDS (I)
101 West 12th Street
New York 10011
(212) 255-9562

SERVICES: Mail Order Only

SPECIALTIES: (Alphabetical)   Banjo, Bluegrass, Bossa Nova, Cajun, Calypso, Childrens, Christmas, Country & Western, Dance, Disco, Easy Listening, Educational

VOLUME: 33⅓ – 95%
                  45   – 5%
                  78   – 0
               Other – Edison
                          Discs/Cylinders

STOCK: Domestic & Import/New & Used

SEARCH: Available with no service charge; Want lists maintained and requester notified when record comes in

COLLECTIONS: Will buy collections of rare records

PAYMENTS: Money Order, Personal Check

MAIL ORDER: Whatever shipment method requested; Prepayment

DISCOUNTS: Not available

PUBLICATIONS: Not available

NEW YORK

WAVES (I)
32 East 13th Street
New York 10003
(212) 989-9284

M	Closed
T–S	Noon–6:00
S	Closed

SERVICES: Walk-in Store/Mail Order

SPECIALTIES: Edison Discs/Cylinders, Blues, Bop Jazz, Rock, Soul, Traditional Jazz

VOLUME: 33⅓ – 0
              45 – 500
              78 – 2,000
            Other – Edison
                    Cylinders–200

STOCK: Domestic & Import/Used

SEARCH: Not available; Want lists maintained and requester notified when record comes in

COLLECTIONS: Will buy collections of rare records

PAYMENTS: Master Charge, Money Order, Personal Check, VISA/Bank-Americard

MAIL ORDER: U.P.S., Whatever shipment method requested; Prepayment

DISCOUNTS: Dealer Only

PUBLICATIONS: Not available

OSSINING

ROCKABILIA (I)
P.O. Box 8
Ossining 10562
   Telephone: I.N.A.

SERVICES: Mail Order Only

SPECIALTIES: Rock & Roll, Folk, Blues, Beatles, Sound Tracks, Soul, Punk Rock/New Wave, Contemporary Jazz, Comedy, Country & Western

VOLUME: 33⅓ – 10,000
              45 – 10,000
              78 – 1,000
            Other – 0

STOCK: Domestic & Import/New & Used

SEARCH: Available with no service charge; Want lists maintained and requester notified when record comes in

COLLECTIONS: Will buy collections of rare records

PAYMENTS: Money Order

MAIL ORDER: 4th Class, Whatever shipment method requested; Prepayment

DISCOUNTS: Available

PUBLICATIONS: Free monthly catalog; Free quarterly auction list

PIERMONT

FAIR RECORDS (I)
c/o Mr. Robert Brennan
P.O. Box 412
Piermont 10968
  Telephone: I.N.A.

SERVICES: Mail Order Only

SPECIALTIES: (Alphabetical)   Bluegrass, Blues, Bossa Nova, Contemporary Jazz, Country & Western, Ethnic, Folk, Hillbilly, Religious, Rhythm & Blues, Rock & Roll, Soul, Traditional Jazz

VOLUME: 33⅓ – 1,500
             45   – 20,000
             78   – 2,000
             Other – 0

STOCK: Domestic & Import/New & Used

SEARCH: Available with no service charge; Want lists maintained and requester notified when record comes in

COLLECTIONS: Will buy collections of rare records

PAYMENTS: Money Order, Personal Check

MAIL ORDER: Air Mail, 4th Class; Prepayment

DISCOUNTS: Not available

PUBLICATIONS: Free periodic auction list

QUEENS

RESCUE RECORDS (II)
P.O. Box 1301
46–02 21st Street
Queens 11101
  Telephone: I.N.A.

SERVICES: Mail Order Only

SPECIALTIES: (Alphabetical)   Blues, Promotional, Rhythm & Blues, Rock, Rock & Roll, Rockabilly, Soul

VOLUME: 33⅓ – I.N.A.
             45   – I.N.A.
             78   – I.N.A.
             Other – I.N.A.

STOCK: Domestic & Import/New & Used

SEARCH: Not available

COLLECTIONS: I.N.A.

PAYMENTS: Money Order, Personal Check

MAIL ORDER: Whatever shipment method requested; Prepayment or C.O.D.

DISCOUNTS: Available

PUBLICATIONS: Free annual catalog; Free bimonthly auction/set-sale list

RENSSELAER

METRONOME RECORDS (II)
P.O. Box 313,
Rensselaer 12144
(518) 465-9969

SERVICES: Mail Order Only

SPECIALTIES: All Major Categories

VOLUME: 33⅓ – I.N.A.
          45 – I.N.A.
          78 – I.N.A.
          Other – I.N.A.

STOCK: Domestic & Import/New & Used

SEARCH: Available with no service charge; Want lists maintained and requester notified when record comes in

COLLECTIONS: Will buy collections of rare records

PAYMENTS: Money Order, Personal Check

MAIL ORDER: Whatever shipment method requested; Prepayment

DISCOUNTS: Available

PUBLICATIONS: I.N.A.

ROCHESTER

PLAY IT AGAIN SAM (I)
668 Monroe Avenue
Rochester 14607
(716) 442-1150

M–F	11:00–8:00
S	10:00–6:00
S	1:00–5:00

SERVICES: Walk-in Store Only

SPECIALTIES: All Major Categories

VOLUME: 33⅓ – 7,500
          45 – 10,000
          78 – 0
          Other – 0

STOCK: Domestic & Import/New & Used

SEARCH: Not available; Want lists maintained and requester notified when record comes in

COLLECTIONS: Will buy collections of rare records

PAYMENTS: Money Order, Personal Check

MAIL ORDER: Not available

DISCOUNTS: Available

PUBLICATIONS: I.N.A.

ROCHESTER

RECORD ARCHIVE (I)
1394 Mt. Hope Avenue
Rochester 14620
(716) 473-3820

M–F	11:00–8:00
S	11:00–6:00
S	Closed

SERVICES: Walk-in Store/Mail Order

SPECIALTIES: (Alphabetical) Bluegrass, Blues, Classical, Contemporary Jazz, Country & Western, Disco, Ethnic, Folk, Hillbilly, Opera, Rhythm & Blues, Rock & Roll, Soul, Traditional Jazz

VOLUME: 33⅓ – 30,000
           45 – 20,000
           78 – 10,000
           Other – 0

STOCK: Domestic & Import/New & Used

SEARCH: Available with service charge; Want lists maintained and requester notified when record comes in

COLLECTIONS: Will buy collections of rare records

PAYMENTS: Master Charge, Money Order

MAIL ORDER: U.P.S.; Prepayment or C.O.D.

DISCOUNTS: I.N.A.

PUBLICATIONS: I.N.A.

SAUGERTIES

PARNASSUS RECORDS (I)
2188 Stoll Road
Saugerties 12477
(914) 246-3332

SERVICES: Mail Order Only

SPECIALTIES: Opera

VOLUME: 33⅓ – 3,000
           45 – 300
           78 – 0
           Other – 0

STOCK: Domestic & Import/Used

SEARCH: Available with no service charge; Want lists maintained and requester notified when record comes in

COLLECTIONS: Not available for purchase; Will buy collections of rare records

PAYMENTS: Money Order, Personal Check

MAIL ORDER: U.P.S.; Prepayment

DISCOUNTS: Not available

PUBLICATIONS: Free monthly catalog

SEAFORD

DAVID A. REISS RECORDS (I)
3920 Eve Drive
Seaford 11783
(516) 785-8336

SERVICES: Mail Order Only

SPECIALTIES: All Major Categories

VOLUME: 33⅓ – 0
           45   – 0
           78   – 30,000
           Other – Disc
                   Recordings

STOCK: Domestic & Import/Used

SEARCH: Not available

COLLECTIONS: Will buy collections of rare records

PAYMENTS: Money Order, Personal Check

MAIL ORDER: 4th Class; Prepayment

DISCOUNTS: Not available

PUBLICATIONS: Free bimonthly auction list

SMITHTOWN

STEVE WEST RECORDS (I)
156 Oakside Drive
Smithtown 11787
Telephone: I.N.A.

SERVICES: Mail Order Only

SPECIALTIES: (Alphabetical) Blues, Classical, Comedy, Contemporary Jazz, Country & Western, Ethnic, Folk, Opera, Religious, Rhythm & Blues, Rock & Roll, Soul, Traditional Jazz

VOLUME: 33⅓ – 6,000
           45   – 20,000
           78   – 1,000
           Other – 0

STOCK: Domestic & Import/New & Used

SEARCH: Available with no service charge; Want lists maintained and requester notified when record comes in

COLLECTIONS: Will buy collections of rare records

PAYMENTS: Money Order, Personal Check

MAIL ORDER: 4th Class; Prepayment

DISCOUNTS: Not available

PUBLICATIONS: I.N.A.

STATEN ISLAND

R.T.O. RECORDS (I)
P.O. Box 176
Staten Island 10312
  (212) 356-2451

SERVICES: Mail Order Only

SPECIALTIES: (Alphabetical) Beatles, Elvis, Rhythm & Blues, Rock, Rock & Roll

VOLUME: 33⅓ – 20,000
              45 – 50,000
              78 – 0
           Other – 0

STOCK: Domestic & Import/New

SEARCH: Not available

COLLECTIONS: Will buy collections of rare records

PAYMENTS: Money Order

MAIL ORDER: 4th Class, U.P.S.; Prepayment or C.O.D.

DISCOUNTS: Available

PUBLICATIONS: Free quarterly catalog

SYRACUSE

DESERTSHORE RECORDS (I)
2810 James Street
Syracuse 13057
  (315) 437-3512

M–S		Noon–7:00
S		Closed

SERVICES: Walk-in Store/Mail Order

SPECIALTIES: (Alphabetical) Bluegrass, Blues, Classical, Contemporary Jazz, Country & Western, Disco, Folk, Reggae, Rock & Roll, Soul, Sound Tracks, Traditional Jazz

VOLUME: 33⅓ – 5,000
              45 – 5,000
              78 – 0
           Other – 0

STOCK: Domestic & Import/Used

SEARCH: Available with no service charge; Want lists maintained and requester notified when record comes in

COLLECTIONS: Will buy collections of rare records

PAYMENTS: Money Order, Personal Check

MAIL ORDER: 4th Class; Prepayment or C.O.D.

DISCOUNTS: Not available

PUBLICATIONS: I.N.A.

TAPPAN

ADLIBITUM RECORDS (I)
P.O. Box 103
Tappan 10983
  Telephone: I.N.A.

SERVICES: Mail Order Only
SPECIALTIES: Rock
VOLUME: 33⅓ – I.N.A.
     45 – I.N.A.
     78 – I.N.A.
   Other – I.N.A.
STOCK: Domestic & Import/New & Used

SEARCH: Available with no service charge; Want lists maintained and requester notified when record comes in

COLLECTIONS: Will buy collections of rare records

PAYMENTS: Money Order, Personal Check

MAIL ORDER: 4th Class, U.P.S., Whatever shipment method requested; Prepayment

DISCOUNTS: Not available

PUBLICATIONS: Free periodic catalog

VOORHEESVILLE

ANDY'S FRONT HALL (I)
Rural Delivery 1
Wormer Road
Voorheesville 12186
  (518) 765-4193

SERVICES: Walk-in Store (By Appointment)/Mail Order
SPECIALTIES: Bluegrass, Blues, Ethnic, Folk
VOLUME: 33⅓ – I.N.A.
     45 – I.N.A.
     78 – I.N.A.
   Other – I.N.A.
STOCK: Domestic & Import/New

SEARCH: Available with no service charge

COLLECTIONS: Will not buy collections of rare records

PAYMENTS: Money Order, Personal Check

MAIL ORDER: 4th Class; Prepayment

DISCOUNTS: Available

PUBLICATIONS: Free periodic catalog

WANTAGH

SANDRA BLANK RECORDS (I)
P.O. Box 91
Wantagh 11793
    Telephone: I.N.A.

M–T	5:00–10:00
W	Closed
T–F	5:00–10:00
S	4:00–8:00
S	Closed

SERVICES: Walk-in Store/Mail Order

SPECIALTIES: Sound Tracks, Vocal, Rock & Roll, Traditional Jazz, Comedy, Country & Western, Instrumental, Classical, Broadway Shows, Television Shows

VOLUME: 33⅓ – 11,000
                 45 – 6,000
                 78 – 0
                 Other – 0

STOCK: Domestic & Import/New & Used

SEARCH: Not available

COLLECTIONS: Will buy collections of rare records

PAYMENTS: Money Order, Personal Check

MAIL ORDER: 4th Class, Whatever shipment method requested; Prepayment

DISCOUNTS: Not available

PUBLICATIONS: Free quarterly auction list

WEST BABYLON

LOONEY TUNES (II)
25 Brookvale Avenue
West Babylon 11743
    (516) 587-4443

M–F	10:00–9:30
S	10:00–6:00
S	Noon–5:00

SERVICES: Walk-in Store Only

SPECIALTIES: (Alphabetical) Blues, Contemporary Jazz, Disco, Easy Listening, Folk, Folk-Rock, Reggae, Rhythm & Blues, Rock & Roll, Soul, Traditional Jazz

VOLUME: 33⅓ – 3,000
                 45 – 0
                 78 – 0
                 Other – 0

STOCK: Domestic & Import/New & Used

SEARCH: Available with no service charge

COLLECTIONS: Will buy collections of rare records

PAYMENTS: Master Charge

MAIL ORDER: Not available

DISCOUNTS: Available

PUBLICATIONS: I.N.A.

WHITE PLAINS

RECORD WORLD (I)   M–F   10:00–9:00
200 Hamilton Avenue   S   10:00–7:00
White Plains 10602   S   Noon–5:00
   (914) 948-7970

SERVICES: Walk-in Store Only

SPECIALTIES: All Major Categories

VOLUME: 33⅓ – 50%
            45 – 50%
            78 – 0
          Other – 0

STOCK: Domestic & Import/New

SEARCH: Available with no service charge; Want lists maintained and requester notified when record comes in

COLLECTIONS: Will not buy collections of rare records

PAYMENTS: American Express, Master Charge, Personal Check, VISA/-BankAmericard

MAIL ORDER: Not available

DISCOUNTS: Available

PUBLICATIONS: I.N.A.

WILLIAMSVILLE

MICHAEL S. SILVERMAN RECORDS (I)
3 Cindy Drive
Williamsville 14221
   (716) 632-0811

SERVICES: Mail Order Only

SPECIALTIES: (Alphabetical) Blues, Folk-Rock, Rhythm & Blues, Rock, Rock & Roll, Rockabilly

VOLUME: 33⅓ – 200
            45 – 5,000
            78 – 200
          Other – 0

STOCK: Domestic/New & Used

SEARCH: Not available; Want lists maintained and requester notified when record comes in

COLLECTIONS: Will buy collections of rare records

PAYMENTS: Money Order, Personal Check

MAIL ORDER: 4th Class; Prepayment

DISCOUNTS: Not available

PUBLICATIONS: I.N.A.

YONKERS

TIME BARRIER ENTERPRISES, INC. (I)
P.O. Box 206
Yonkers 10710
   (914) 337-8050

SERVICES: Mail Order Only

SPECIALTIES: (Alphabetical) A Cappella, Beatles, Elvis, Folk-Rock, Rhythm & Blues, Rock, Rock & Roll, Rockabilly, Soul, Surfing, Tex-Mex, Vocal

VOLUME: 33⅓ – 200
            45 – 10,000
            78 – 0
            Other – 0

STOCK: Domestic/New & Used

SEARCH: Available with no service charge; Want lists maintained and requester notified when record comes in

COLLECTIONS: Will buy collections of rare records

PAYMENTS: Money Order, Personal Check

MAIL ORDER: Whatever shipment method requested; Prepayment

DISCOUNTS: Available

PUBLICATIONS: Free annual catalog; Free bimonthly auction list

NORTH CAROLINA

BURLINGTON

GOLDEN DISCS UNLIMITED (I)
P.O. Box 2687
Burlington 27215
   (919) 584-0096

SERVICES: Mail Order Only

SPECIALTIES: Rock & Roll, Rhythm & Blues, Rockabilly, Country & Western, Blues, Novelty, Elvis, Instrumental, Bluegrass, Soul, Colored Wax

VOLUME: 33⅓ – 20,000
            45 – 90,000
            78 – 4,000
            Other – 0

STOCK: Domestic/New & Used

SEARCH: Not available

COLLECTIONS: Will buy collections of rare records

PAYMENTS: Bank Draft, Certified Cashier's Check, Money Order, Personal Check

MAIL ORDER: Air Mail, 1st Class, 4th Class, Parcel Post; Prepayment

DISCOUNTS: Available

PUBLICATIONS: Free annual catalog; Free bimonthly auction list

CHAPEL HILL

PIED PIPER RECORDS (I)
P.O. Box 2027
Chapel Hill 27514
  Telephone: I.N.A.
  Telex: 579337

SERVICES: Mail Order Only

SPECIALTIES: (Alphabetical)   Blues,
Contemporary Jazz, Folk, Folk-Rock,
Rock, Rock & Roll

VOLUME: 33⅓ – I.N.A.
             45 – I.N.A.
             78 – I.N.A.
             Other – I.N.A.

STOCK: Domestic & Import/New

SEARCH: Not available; Want lists
maintained and requester notified
when record comes in

COLLECTIONS: Will not buy collections of rare records

PAYMENTS: Money Order, Personal
Check

MAIL ORDER: Air Mail, 4th Class,
U.P.S.; Prepayment

DISCOUNTS: Not available

PUBLICATIONS: I.N.A.

CHAPEL HILL

STILL RARE RECORDS (I)
P.O. Box 994
Chapel Hill 27514
  (919) 942-8600 or 8627
  Telex: 579337 disctrade cpel

SERVICES: Mail Order Only (Wholesale)

SPECIALTIES: (Alphabetical) Hillbilly,
Punk Rock/New Wave, Rock, Rock
& Roll

VOLUME: 33⅓ – 80%
             45 – 20%
             78 – 0
             Other – 0

STOCK: Domestic & Import/New

SEARCH: Not available

COLLECTIONS: Will not buy collections of rare records

PAYMENTS: Money Order

MAIL ORDER: Air Mail, 4th Class,
U.P.S.; Prepayment or C.O.D.

DISCOUNTS: Not available

PUBLICATIONS: I.N.A.

CHARLOTTE

ERNIE'S RECORD SHOP (II)	M–F	10:00–9:00
Cotswold Center	S	10:00–6:00
Charlotte 28211	S	Closed
(704) 366-0135		

SERVICES: Walk-in Store/Mail Order

SPECIALTIES: (Alphabetical) Bluegrass, Classical, Country & Western, Easy Listening, Folk, Folk-Rock, Rock, Rock & Roll

VOLUME: 33⅓ – I.N.A.
45 – I.N.A.
78 – I.N.A.
Other – I.N.A.

STOCK: Domestic/New

SEARCH: Available with no service charge; Want lists maintained and requester notified when record comes in

COLLECTIONS: Will not buy collections of rare records

PAYMENTS: Master Charge, Money Order, Personal Check, VISA/BankAmericard

MAIL ORDER: 3rd Class, U.P.S.; Prepayment or C.O.D.

DISCOUNTS: Available

PUBLICATIONS: I.N.A.

CHARLOTTE

NEW WORLD RECORDS, INCORPORATED (I)	M–F	10:00–9:00
3629 East Independence Boulevard	S	10:00–6:00
Charlotte 28205	S	Closed
(704) 568-3010		

SERVICES: Walk-in Store Only

SPECIALTIES: (Alphabetical) Blues, Contemporary Jazz, Folk, Folk-Rock, Rhythm & Blues, Rock, Rock & Roll, Traditional Jazz

VOLUME: 33⅓ – 750
45 – 0
78 – 80
Other – 0

STOCK: Domestic & Import/New

SEARCH: Not available

COLLECTIONS: Will not buy collections of rare records

PAYMENTS: Master Charge, Money Order, VISA/BankAmericard

MAIL ORDER: Not available

DISCOUNTS: Not available

PUBLICATIONS: I.N.A.

CHARLOTTE

NEW WORLD RECORDS, INCORPORATED (I)	M–F	10:00–9:00
5611 South Boulevard	S	10:00–6:00
Charlotte 28210	S	Closed
(704) 525-6009		

SERVICES: Walk-in Store Only

SPECIALTIES: (Alphabetical) Blues, Contemporary Jazz, Folk, Folk-Rock, Rhythm & Blues, Rock, Rock & Roll, Soul, Traditional Jazz

VOLUME:
33⅓ – 750
45 – 0
78 – 0
Other – 0

STOCK: Domestic & Import/New

SEARCH: Not available

COLLECTIONS: Will not buy collections of rare records

PAYMENTS: Master Charge, Money Order, VISA/BankAmericard

MAIL ORDER: Not available

DISCOUNTS: Not available

PUBLICATIONS: I.N.A.

CHARLOTTE

THE WAX MUSEUM INCORPORATED (I)	M	Noon–6:00
1505 Elizabeth Avenue	T–F	Noon–9:00
Charlotte 28204	S	Noon–6:00
(704) 377-0700	S	Closed

SERVICES: Walk-in Store/Mail Order

SPECIALTIES: Rhythm & Blues, Rock & Roll, Blues, Rockabilly, Elvis, Country & Western

VOLUME:
33⅓ – 4,000
45 – 30,000
78 – 15,000
Other – 0

STOCK: Domestic/New & Used

SEARCH: Available with no service charge

COLLECTIONS: Will buy collections of rare records

PAYMENTS: Money Order, Personal Check

MAIL ORDER: 4th Class; Prepayment

DISCOUNTS: Available

PUBLICATIONS: Periodic catalog available for $1.00 per issue; Free quarterly auction list

CHARLOTTE

YESTERYEAR (I)	M	Noon–6:00
1505 Elizabeth Avenue	T–F	Noon–9:00
Charlotte 28204	S	Noon–6:00
(704) 377-0700	S	Closed

SERVICES: Walk-in Store/Mail Order

SPECIALTIES: Rhythm & Blues, Rock & Roll, Blues, Country & Western, Old-Time Country, Rockabilly, Soul, Swing, Big Band

VOLUME: 33⅓ – 0
             45 – 350,000
             78 – 10,000
             Other – 0

STOCK: Domestic/New & Used

SEARCH: Not available

COLLECTIONS: Will buy collections of rare records

PAYMENTS: Money Order, Personal Check

MAIL ORDER: 4th Class; Prepayment

DISCOUNTS: Not available

PUBLICATIONS: Free bimonthly auction list

PRINCETON

CARL R. GURLEY RECORDS (I)	M–W	8:00–5:00
128–130 South Pine Streeet	T	11:00–5:00
Princeton 27569	F	8:00–5:00
(919) 936-5121	S–S	Closed

SERVICES: Walk-in Store/Mail Order

SPECIALTIES: Sound Tracks, Blues, Broadway Shows, Big Band, Easy Listening, Film Scores, Rock & Roll, Rock, Dixieland, Dance, Country & Western

VOLUME: 33⅓ – 20,000
             45 – 10,000
             78 – 30,000
             Other – Edison
                     Discs–100
                     Cylinders–100

STOCK: Domestic & Import/New & Used

SEARCH: Available with no service charge; Want lists maintained and requester notified when record comes in

COLLECTIONS: Available for purchase

PAYMENTS: Master Charge, Money Order, Personal Check, VISA/Bank-Americard

MAIL ORDER: 1st Class, 4th Class, Whatever shipment method requested; Prepayment

DISCOUNTS: Available

PUBLICATIONS: Monthly catalog available for $2.00 per issue; Periodic auction list available for $1.00 per issue

CINCINNATI

PEGGY LIGON RECORDS (I)
2291 Wolff Street
Cincinnati 45211
  (513) 662-6723

SERVICES: Mail Order Only

SPECIALTIES: (Alphabetical) Bluegrass, Blues, Country & Western, Folk, Hillbilly, Religious, Rhythm & Blues, Rock & Roll, Soul, Traditional Jazz

VOLUME: 33⅓ – 2,000
45 – 6,000
78 – 3,000
Other – 0

STOCK: Domestic/New & Used

SEARCH: Available with no service charge

COLLECTIONS: Will buy collections of rare records

PAYMENTS: Money Order, Personal Check

MAIL ORDER: 4th Class; Prepayment or C.O.D.

DISCOUNTS: Available

PUBLICATIONS: I.N.A.

CINCINNATI

LISTEN (II)
117 Calhoun Street
Cincinnati 45219
  (513) 281-0606

M–S   Noon–7:00
S   Closed

SERVICES: Walk-in Store/Mail Order

SPECIALTIES: (Alphabetical) Bluegrass, Blues, Classical, Contemporary Jazz, Ethnic, Folk, Opera, Reggae, Rhythm & Blues, Rock & Roll, Soul, Traditional Jazz

VOLUME: 33⅓ – 70%
45 – 30%
78 – 0
Other – 0

STOCK: Domestic & Import/New

SEARCH: Not available

COLLECTIONS: Will not buy collections of rare records

PAYMENTS: Personal Check

MAIL ORDER: 4th Class, U.P.S.; Prepayment or C.O.D.

DISCOUNTS: Available

PUBLICATIONS: I.N.A.

CINCINNATI

MAKRIS FOREIGN RECORD SHOP (II)   M–S   9:00–5:00
1008 Walnut Street   S By appointment
Cincinnati 45202
(513) 621-0227

SERVICES: Walk-in Store/Mail Order   COLLECTIONS: Available for purchase

SPECIALTIES: All Major Categories   PAYMENTS: Master Charge

VOLUME: 33⅓ – I.N.A.   MAIL ORDER: Air Mail, 4th Class,
            45 – I.N.A.   U.P.S., Whatever shipment method re-
            78 – I.N.A.   quested; Prepayment
            Other – I.N.A.
                                        DISCOUNTS: Available
STOCK: Domestic & Import/New
                                        PUBLICATIONS: Free periodic catalog
SEARCH: Available with no service
charge

CINCINNATI

JOHN WADE RECORDS (I)
P.O. Box 991041
Cincinnati 45201
(513) 631-8374

SERVICES: Mail Order Only   COLLECTIONS: Will buy collections of
                                        rare records
SPECIALTIES: Rock & Roll, Rhythm
& Blues, Country & Western, Popular,   PAYMENTS: Money Order, Personal
Rockabilly, Elvis, Beatles, Surfing,   Check
Novelty, Blues
                                        MAIL ORDER: Air Mail, 4th Class,
VOLUME: 33⅓ – 200   Whatever shipment method requested;
            45 – 3,000   Prepayment
            78 – 100
            Other – 0   DISCOUNTS: Available

STOCK: Domestic/New & Used   PUBLICATIONS: Not available

SEARCH: Want lists maintained and
requester notified when record comes
in

CLEVELAND

TOMMY EDWARDS' RECORD HAVEN (I)   M–S   9:00–8:00
4237 Fulton Road   S   Noon–6:00
Cleveland 44144
(216) 351-9331

SERVICES: Walk-in Store/Mail Order

SPECIALTIES: (Alphabetical) Blue-grass, Country & Western, Easy Listening, Folk, Folk-Rock, Hillbilly, Rock, Rock & Roll

VOLUME: 33⅓ – 4,000
         45 – 25,000
         78 – 3,000
         Other – 0

STOCK: Domestic/New & Used

SEARCH: Want lists maintained and requester notified when record comes in

COLLECTIONS: Will not buy collections of rare records

PAYMENTS: Money Order, Personal Check

MAIL ORDER: Air Mail, 4th Class; Prepayment

DISCOUNTS: Not available

PUBLICATIONS: I.N.A.

CLEVELAND

TONY'S POLKA VILLAGE (I)   M–T   10:00–6:00
971 East 185th Street   F   10:00–8:00
Cleveland 44119   S   10:00–5:00
(216) 481-7512   S   Closed

SERVICES: Walk-in Store/Mail Order

SPECIALTIES: Ethnic, Polka

VOLUME: 33⅓ – I.N.A.
         45 – I.N.A.
         78 – I.N.A.
         Other – I.N.A.

STOCK: Domestic & Import/New

SEARCH: Want lists maintained and requester notified when record comes in

COLLECTIONS: Will buy collections of rare records

PAYMENTS: Money Order, Personal Check

MAIL ORDER: 4th Class; Prepayment

DISCOUNTS: Available

PUBLICATIONS: I.N.A.

COLUMBUS

TED DESPRES RECORDS (I)
5523 Parkville Street
Columbus 43229
 (614) 891-9353

SERVICES: Mail Order Only

SPECIALTIES: (Alphabetical) Easy Listening, Folk-Rock, Rock, Rock & Roll

VOLUME: 33⅓ – 500
            45 – 12,000
            78 – 0
            Other – 0

STOCK: Domestic/New & Used

SEARCH: Available with no service charge; Want lists maintained and requester notified when record comes in

COLLECTIONS: Will not buy collections of rare records

PAYMENTS: Money Order, Personal Check

MAIL ORDER: 1st Class, 4th Class; Prepayment

DISCOUNTS: Not available

PUBLICATIONS: I.N.A.

COLUMBUS

MOLE'S RECORD EXCHANGE (II)
1896 North High Street
Columbus 43201
 (614) 291-6133

M–S   11:00–7:00
 S   Closed

SERVICES: Walk-in Store Only

SPECIALTIES: All Major Categories

VOLUME: 33⅓ – 100%
            45 – 0
            78 – 0
            Other – 0

STOCK: Domestic & Import/Used

SEARCH: Not available

COLLECTIONS: Will buy collections of rare records

PAYMENTS: Money Order, Personal Check

MAIL ORDER: Not available

DISCOUNTS: Not available

PUBLICATIONS: I.N.A.

COLUMBUS

NORTHERN LIGHTS HARMONY HOUSE (II)   M–T   11:30–9:00
3507 Cleveland Avenue   F–S   10:00–9:00
Columbus 43224   S   Closed
  (614) 263-1434

SERVICES: Walk-in Store/Mail Order

SPECIALTIES: (Alphabetical) Bluegrass, Country & Western, Easy Listening, Religious, Rock, Rock & Roll, Soul

VOLUME: 33⅓ – 0
               45   – 100%
               78   – 0
               Other – 0

STOCK: Domestic/New

SEARCH: Not available

COLLECTIONS: Will not buy collections of rare records

PAYMENTS: Master Charge, Money Order, VISA/BankAmericard

MAIL ORDER: 4th Class; Prepayment

DISCOUNTS: Available

PUBLICATIONS: I.N.A.

COLUMBUS

ROBERT & COMPANY (I)   M–S   8:30–5:00
1910 Lockbourne Road   S   Closed
Columbus 43207
  (614) 444-9842

SERVICES: Walk-in Store/Mail Order

SPECIALTIES: All Major Categories

VOLUME: 33⅓ – 50%
               45   – 50%
               78   – 0
               Other – 0

STOCK: Domestic & Import/New & Used

SEARCH: Available with no service charge

COLLECTIONS: Will buy collections of rare records

PAYMENTS: Master Charge, Personal Check, VISA/BankAmericard

MAIL ORDER: Whatever shipment method requested; Prepayment

DISCOUNTS: Available

PUBLICATIONS: Free monthly auction list

DAYTON

BLUE NOTE RECORDS (I)	M–F	10:30–6:00
4897 North Dixie Drive	S	10:00–6:00
Dayton 45414	S	Closed
(513) 278-1192		

SERVICES: Walk-in Store/Mail Order

SPECIALTIES: Banjo, Beatles, Big Band, Rockabilly, Dixieland, Sound Tracks, Vocal, Bluegrass, Country & Western, Elvis

VOLUME: 33⅓ – 300
         45 – 9,000
         78 – 0
         Other – 0

STOCK: Domestic/New

SEARCH: Available with no service charge

COLLECTIONS: I.N.A.

PAYMENTS: Master Charge, Personal Check, VISA/BankAmericard

MAIL ORDER: 1st Class; Prepayment

DISCOUNTS: Not available

PUBLICATIONS: Not available

DAYTON

JAZZLAND (I)
P.O. Box 366
Dayton 45401
  (513) 222-4388

SERVICES: Mail Order Only/Inspection by Appointment

SPECIALTIES: Dixieland, Traditional Jazz, Big Band, Bluegrass, Bop Jazz, Blues, Contemporary Jazz, Swing, Ragtime, Nostalgia

VOLUME: 33⅓ – 2,000
         45 – 0
         78 – 2,000
         Other – 0

STOCK: Domestic & Import/New & Used

SEARCH: Available with no service charge; Want lists maintained and requester notified when record comes in

COLLECTIONS: Will buy collections of rare records

PAYMENTS: Money Order, Personal Check

MAIL ORDER: 4th Class; Prepayment or C.O.D.

DISCOUNTS: Available

PUBLICATIONS: Free quarterly catalog

OKLAHOMA

OKLAHOMA CITY

WILCOX RECORD SHOP (II)	M–F	9:00–7:00
1423 Northwest 23rd Street	S	9:00–6:00
Oklahoma City 73106	S	Closed
(405) 528-5517		

SERVICES: Walk-in Store/Mail Order

SPECIALTIES: All Major Categories

VOLUME: 33⅓ – 40%
            45 – 60%
            78 – 0
            Other – 0

STOCK: Domestic & Import/New & Used

SEARCH: Available with no service charge

COLLECTIONS: Will buy collections of rare records

PAYMENTS: Personal Check

MAIL ORDER: Air Mail, 4th Class; Prepayment

DISCOUNTS: Available

PUBLICATIONS: I.N.A.

OREGON

DRAIN

DAVID W. BELL RARE RECORDS (I)
P.O. Box 143
Drain 97435
  (503) 836-2306

SERVICES: Mail Order Only

SPECIALTIES: Film Scores, Sound Tracks, Rock, Rock & Roll, Rhythm & Blues, Vocal, Classical, Broadway Shows, Elvis, Beatles, Novelty, Spoken Word

VOLUME: 33⅓ – 10,000
            45 – 3,000
            78 – 1,500
            Other – 0

STOCK: Domestic & Import/New & Used

SEARCH: Available with no service charge; Want lists maintained and requester notified when record comes in

COLLECTIONS: Available for purchase

PAYMENTS: Money Order, Personal Check

MAIL ORDER: 4th Class, Whatever shipment method requested; Prepayment

DISCOUNTS: Available

PUBLICATIONS: Free periodic catalog

EUGENE

DJANGO RECORDS (I)	M–F	11:00–7:00
565 Willamette	S	10:00–6:00
Eugene 97401	S	Noon–6:00
(503) 343-1922		

SERVICES: Walk-in Store/Mail Order

SPECIALTIES: All Major Categories

VOLUME: 33⅓ – 13,000
           45   – 0
           78   – 1,000
           Other – 0

STOCK: Domestic/Used

SEARCH: Not available

COLLECTIONS: Will buy collections of rare records

PAYMENTS: Master Charge, Money Order, Personal Check, VISA/Bank-Americard

MAIL ORDER: 3rd Class, 4th Class; Prepayment

DISCOUNTS: I.N.A.

PUBLICATIONS: I.N.A.

EUGENE

HOUSE OF RECORDS (II)	M–S	11:30–9:00
258 East 13th	S	Noon–6:00
Eugene 97401		
(503) 342-7975		

SERVICES: Walk-in Store/Mail Order

SPECIALTIES: All Major Categories

VOLUME: 33⅓ – I.N.A.
           45   – I.N.A.
           78   – I.N.A.
           Other – I.N.A.

STOCK: Domestic & Import/New & Used

SEARCH: Want lists maintained and requester notified when record comes in

COLLECTIONS: Will not buy collections of rare records

PAYMENTS: Master Charge, Money Order, Personal Check, VISA/Bank-Americard

MAIL ORDER: 4th Class, U.P.S.; Prepayment

DISCOUNTS: Available

PUBLICATIONS: I.N.A.

EUGENE

LOONYLAND (I)   M–S   11:00–7:00
525 East Thirteenth Avenue
Eugene 97401
(503) 485-8554

SERVICES: Walk-in Store/Mail Order

SPECIALTIES: Rock, Rock & Roll, Punk Rock/New Wave, Rockabilly, Blues, Rhythm & Blues, Contemporary Jazz, Country & Western, Hebrew/Israeli, Reggae

VOLUME: 33⅓ – 1,000
           45   – 5,000
           78   – 0
           Other – 0

STOCK: Domestic & Import/New & Used

SEARCH: Not available

COLLECTIONS: Not available for purchase

PAYMENTS: Master Charge, Money Order, VISA/BankAmericard

MAIL ORDER: U.P.S.; Prepayment

DISCOUNTS: I.N.A.

PUBLICATIONS: Free occasional catalog

EUGENE

PREZ (I)   M–S   10:00–6:00
774 East Thirteenth Avenue   S   Closed
Eugene 97401
(503) 342-2088

SERVICES: Walk-in Store/Mail Order

SPECIALTIES: (Alphabetical) Blues, Classical, Comedy, Contemporary Jazz, Ethnic, Folk, Opera, Rhythm & Blues, Rock & Roll, Spoken Word, Traditional Jazz, Vocal

VOLUME: 33⅓ – I.N.A.
           45   – I.N.A.
           78   – I.N.A.
           Other – I.N.A.

STOCK: Domestic & Import/New & Used

SEARCH: Available with no service charge; Want lists maintained and requester notified when record comes in

COLLECTIONS: Will buy collections of rare records

PAYMENTS: Personal Check

MAIL ORDER: 4th Class; Prepayment

DISCOUNTS: Not available

PUBLICATIONS: I.N.A.

FLORENCE

LOONYLAND (I)   M–S   11:00–7:00
1348 Bay Street
Florence 97439
(503) 997-6060

SERVICES: Walk-in Store/Mail Order

SPECIALTIES: Rock, Rock & Roll, Punk Rock/New Wave, Rockabilly, Blues, Rhythm & Blues, Contemporary Jazz, Country & Western, Hebrew/Israeli, Reggae

VOLUME: 33⅓ – 1,000
                45   – 5,000
                78   – 0
               Other – 0

STOCK: Domestic & Import/New & Used

SEARCH: Not available

COLLECTIONS: Not available for purchase

PAYMENTS: Master Charge, Money Order, VISA/BankAmericard

MAIL ORDER: U.P.S.; Prepayment

DISCOUNTS: I.N.A.

PUBLICATIONS: Free occasional catalog

PORTLAND

BIRD'S SUITE (I)   M–T   10:00–8:00
720 Southwest Salmon   F   10:00–9:00
Portland 97205   S   10:00–6:00
(503) 222-3086   S   Noon–6:00

SERVICES: Walk-in Store/Mail Order

SPECIALTIES: All Major Categories

VOLUME: 33⅓ – 8,000
                45   – 200
                78   – 200
               Other – 0

STOCK: Domestic & Import/New & Used

SEARCH: Available with no service charge; Want lists maintained and requester notified when record comes in

COLLECTIONS: Will buy collections of rare records

PAYMENTS: Master Charge, Money Order, Personal Check, VISA/BankAmericard

MAIL ORDER: Whatever shipment method requested; Prepayment

DISCOUNTS: Available

PUBLICATIONS: I.N.A.

PORTLAND

BIRD'S SUITE (I)
3736 Southeast Hawthorne
Portland 97214
  (503) 235-6224

M–T	10:00–8:00
F	10:00–9:00
S	10:00–6:00
S	Noon–6:00

SERVICES: Walk-in Store/Mail Order

SPECIALTIES: All Major Categories

VOLUME: 33⅓ – 8,000
           45 – 200
           78 – 200
     Other – 0

STOCK: Domestic & Import/New & Used

SEARCH: Available with no service charge; Want lists maintained and requester notified when record comes in

COLLECTIONS: Will buy collections of rare records

PAYMENTS: Master Charge, Money Order, Personal Check, VISA/Bank-Americard

MAIL ORDER: Whatever shipment method requested; Prepayment

DISCOUNTS: Available

PUBLICATIONS: I.N.A.

PORTLAND

CHRYSTALSHIP (II)
921 Southwest Morrison
Portland 97221
  (503) 226-0416

M–S 9:30 A.M.–mid.

SERVICES: Walk-in Store/Mail Order

SPECIALTIES: All Major Categories

VOLUME: 33⅓ – 100%
           45 – 0
           78 – 0
     Other – 0

STOCK: Domestic & Import/New

SEARCH: Available with no service charge; Want lists maintained and requester notified when record comes in

COLLECTIONS: Will not buy collections of rare records

PAYMENTS: Master Charge, Money Order, Personal Check, VISA/Bank-Americard

MAIL ORDER: Air Mail, 4th Class; Prepayment or C.O.D.

DISCOUNTS: Not available

PUBLICATIONS: I.N.A.

PORTLAND

DJANGO (I)
1111 Southwest Stark Street
Portland 97205
(503) 227-4381

M–F	10:00–8:00
S	10:00–6:00
S	Noon–6:00

SERVICES: Walk-in Store/Mail Order

SPECIALTIES: Rock, Contemporary Jazz, Bop Jazz, Country & Western, Traditional Jazz, Classical, Film Scores, Soul, Broadway Shows, Big Band

VOLUME: 33⅓ – 1,000
                45 – 2,000
                78 – 1,000
            Other – 0

STOCK: Domestic & Import/New & Used

SEARCH: Want lists maintained and requester notified when record comes in

COLLECTIONS: Will buy collections of rare records

PAYMENTS: American Express, Master Charge, Money Order, Personal Check, VISA/BankAmericard

MAIL ORDER: 4th Class, Whatever shipment method requested; Prepayment

DISCOUNTS: Available

PUBLICATIONS: Not available

PORTLAND

BERNE GREENE RECORDS (I)
1833 Southeast Seventh Avenue
Portland 97214
(503) 232-5964

SERVICES: Mail Order Only

SPECIALTIES: Rock, Beatles, Promotional, Soul, Elvis, Comedy, Punk Rock/New Wave, Surfing, Folk, Political

VOLUME: 33⅓ – 20,000
                45 – 47,000
                78 – 0
            Other – 0

STOCK: Domestic & Import/New & Used

SEARCH: Available with no service charge; Want lists maintained and requester notified when record comes in

COLLECTIONS: Will buy collections of rare records

PAYMENTS: Money Order, Personal Check

MAIL ORDER: Air Mail, 1st Class, 2nd Class, 3rd Class, 4th Class; Prepayment

DISCOUNTS: Available

PUBLICATIONS: Free quarterly rock catalog available; free semiannual pop/soul catalog available

PORTLAND

MELODY TUNES (I)
2727 North Lombard
Portland 97217
  (503) 289-4610

SERVICES: Mail Order Only

SPECIALTIES: (Alphabetical) Country
& Western, Elvis, Folk Gospel/Sacred, Hawaiian, Hillbilly, Historical,
Instructional, Instrumental

VOLUME: 33⅓ – 500
          45 – 500
          78 – 3,000
       Other – 0

STOCK: Domestic & Import/New &
Used

SEARCH: Available with no service
charge; Want lists maintained and requester notified when record comes in

COLLECTIONS: Will not buy collections of rare records

PAYMENTS: American Express,
Money Order, Personal Check

MAIL ORDER: Air Mail, U.P.S. Whatever shipment method requested; Prepayment

DISCOUNTS: Not available

PUBLICATIONS: Not available

PORTLAND

CRAIG MOERER–RECORDS BY MAIL (I)   M–S 9:00 A.M.–10:00 P.M.
P.O. Box 13247   S   Closed
Portland 97213
  (503) 288-1777

SERVICES: Walk-in Store/Mail Order

SPECIALTIES: Rock & Roll, Rhythm &
Blues, Blues, Country & Western,
Rockabilly, Soul, Bluegrass, Instrumental, Surfing

VOLUME: 33⅓ – 3,000
           45 – 30,000
           78 – 0
        Other – 0

STOCK: Domestic/New & Used

SEARCH: Available with no service
charge

COLLECTIONS: Will buy collections of
rare records

PAYMENTS: Money Order, Personal
Check

MAIL ORDER: Whatever shipment
method requested; Prepayment or
C.O.D.

DISCOUNTS: Not available

PUBLICATIONS: Free quarterly catalog; Free quarterly auction list

PORTLAND

MUSIC ON RECORDS–ART GUENTHER (I)	M–S	10:00–5:30
1033 Southwest Morrison	S	Closed

Portland 97205
(503) 227-1311

SERVICES: Walk-in Store/Mail Order

SPECIALTIES: (Alphabetical) Classical, Nostalgia, Opera

VOLUME: 33⅓ – 100%
              45 – 0
              78 – 0
           Other – 0

STOCK: Domestic & Import/New

SEARCH: Not available; Want lists maintained and requester notified when record comes in

COLLECTIONS: Will not buy collections of rare records

PAYMENTS: Master Charge, Money Order, Personal Check, VISA/BankAmericard

MAIL ORDER: 4th Class; Prepayment

DISCOUNTS: I.N.A.

PUBLICATIONS: I.N.A.

PORTLAND

RENAISSANCE RECORDS (I)	M–F	Closed
220 Southwest Alder	S	11:00–4:00
Room 314	S	Closed

Portland 97205
(503) 223-9980

SERVICES: Walk-in Store/Mail Order

SPECIALTIES: Punk Rock/New Wave, Reggae, Rockabilly, Rock

VOLUME: 33⅓ – 50
              45 – 500
              78 – 0
           Other – 0

STOCK: Domestic & Import/New

SEARCH: Not available

COLLECTIONS: I.N.A.

PAYMENTS: Money Order, Personal Check

MAIL ORDER: U.P.S., Whatever shipment method requested; Prepayment or C.O.D.

DISCOUNTS: Not available

PUBLICATIONS: Free monthly catalog

PENNSYLVANIA

CARNEGIE

D & J RECORDS (I)
212 East Main Street
Carnegie 15106
(412) 279-8888

M–F	11:00–9:00
S	10:00–6:00
S	Closed

SERVICES: Walk-in Store/Mail Order

SPECIALTIES: Rhythm & Blues, Rock & Roll, Disco, Rock, Country & Western, Elvis, Beatles, Instrumental, Rockabilly, Polka

VOLUME: 33⅓ – 0
            45 – 200,000
            78 – 0
            Other – 0

STOCK: Domestic & Import/New & Used

SEARCH: Available with no service charge

COLLECTIONS: Will buy collections of rare records

PAYMENTS: Money Order

MAIL ORDER: Whatever shipment method requested; Prepayment or C.O.D.

DISCOUNTS: Available

PUBLICATIONS: Not available

CARNEGIE

FRANK B. POPE RECORDS UNLIMITED (I)   M–S   8:00 A.M.–4:00 P.M.
P.O. Box 510
Carnegie 15106
(412) 276-6076

SERVICES: Walk-in Store (By Appointment)/Mail Order

SPECIALTIES: All Major Categories

VOLUME: 33⅓ – 200,000
            45 – 400,000
            78 – 400,000
            Other – 0

STOCK: Domestic & Import/New

SEARCH: Not available

COLLECTIONS: Will buy collections of rare records

PAYMENTS: American Express, Master Charge, Money Order, Personal Charge Account, Personal Check, VISA/BankAmericard

MAIL ORDER: 4th Class; Prepayment

DISCOUNTS: Available

PUBLICATIONS: Free periodic catalog

ELKINS PARK

OWEN M. FELDMAN RECORDS (I)   M–F   11:00–7:00
7844 Montgomery Avenue   S–S   Closed
Elkins Park 19117
(215) 635-1487

SERVICES: Walk-in Store/Mail Order

SPECIALTIES: Classical, Rock

VOLUME: 33⅓ – 200
            45 – 0
            78 – 30
            Other – 0

STOCK: Domestic/New & Used

SEARCH: I.N.A.

COLLECTIONS: I.N.A.

PAYMENTS: Money Order, Personal Check

MAIL ORDER: 4th Class, Whatever shipment method requested; Prepayment

DISCOUNTS: I.N.A.

PUBLICATIONS: Free periodic auction list

ELKINS PARK

ROTMAN'S RECORDS (I)
8134 Cadwalader Avenue
Elkins Park 19117
(215) 635-1771

SERVICES: Mail Order Only

SPECIALTIES: Classical, Instrumental, Opera, Film Scores, Vocal, Broadway Shows

VOLUME: 33⅓ – 15,000
            45 – 0
            78 – 0
            Other – 0

STOCK: Domestic & Import/New & Used

SEARCH: Not available

COLLECTIONS: Will buy collections of rare records

PAYMENTS: Personal Check

MAIL ORDER: 4th Class; Prepayment

DISCOUNTS: Not available

PUBLICATIONS: Free monthly catalog

HARRISBURG

TREASURE HUNTERS RECORD FINDING
  SERVICE (I)
P.O. Box 2833
Harrisburg 17105
  (717) 761-2371

SERVICES: Mail Order Only

SPECIALTIES: (Alphabetical) Blues, Contemporary Jazz, Disco, Folk, Folk-Rock, Reggae, Rhythm & Blues, Rock, Rock & Roll, Soul

VOLUME: 33⅓ – 5,000
         45 – 3,000
         78 – 0
         Other – 0

STOCK: Domestic and Import/New & Used

SEARCH: Available with no service charge; Want lists maintained and requester notified when record comes in

COLLECTIONS: Will buy collections of rare records

PAYMENTS: Money Order, Personal Check

MAIL ORDER: Air Mail, 4th Class; Prepayment

DISCOUNTS: Available

PUBLICATIONS: I.N.A.

HORSHAM

MEMORY LANE RECORDS (I)
316 Easton Road
Horsham 19044
(Mail Address: P.O. Box 50, Horsham 19044)
  (215) 674-8864

M	Closed
T–W	1:30–7:30
T	1:30–8:00
F	1:30–9:00
S	11:30–5:30
S	By Appointment

SERVICES: Walk-in Store/Mail Order

SPECIALTIES: Rock & Roll, Rock, Rhythm & Blues, Easy Listening, Elvis, Beatles, Country & Western, Disco, Sinatra

VOLUME: 33⅓ – 8,000
         45 – 40,000
         78 – 0
         Other – 0

STOCK: Domestic/New & Used

SEARCH: Available with no service charge; Want lists maintained and requester notified when record comes in

COLLECTIONS: Available for purchase; Will buy collections of rare records

PAYMENTS: Money Order, Personal Charge Account, Personal Check

MAIL ORDER: 4th Class; Prepayment

DISCOUNTS: Available

PUBLICATIONS: Biannual catalog available for 50¢

HUNTINGDON VALLEY

RECORD KINGDOM (I)
P.O. Box 245
Huntingdon Valley 19006
 (215) 364-1230

M–F   10:00–5:00
S–S   Closed

SERVICES: Mail Order Only (Above Times for Telephone)

SPECIALTIES: Elvis, Rock & Roll, Rock, Beatles, Promotional, Punk Rock/New Wave, Surfing

VOLUME: 33⅓ – 10,000
            45 – 25,000
            78 – 0
            Other – 0

STOCK: Domestic & Import/New & Used

SEARCH: Want lists maintained and requester notified when record comes in

COLLECTIONS: Will buy collections of rare records

PAYMENTS: Money Order, Personal Check

MAIL ORDER: U.P.S., Whatever shipment method requested; Prepayment

DISCOUNTS: Available

PUBLICATIONS: Free periodic catalog

MILLVALE

C & L RECORDS (I)
1811 Babcock Boulevard
Millvale 15209
 (412) 821-4638

SERVICES: Walk-in Store (By Appointment)/Mail Order

SPECIALTIES: Soul, Rock & Roll, Rock, Rhythm & Blues, Popular, Country & Western, Big Band, Blues, Easy Listening, Instrumental

VOLUME: 33⅓ – 5,000
            45 – 60,000
            78 – 5,000
            Other – 0

STOCK: Domestic/New & Used

SEARCH: Want lists maintained and requester notified when record comes in

COLLECTIONS: Will buy collections of rare records

PAYMENTS: Money Order, Personal Check

MAIL ORDER: 4th Class, Whatever shipment method requested; Prepayment

DISCOUNTS: I.N.A.

PUBLICATIONS: Not available

OLYPHANT

FRANK ARMBRUSTER RECORDS (I)
306 Grant Street
Olyphant 18447
(717) 489-8991

SERVICES: Mail Order Only

SPECIALTIES: (Alphabetical) Bluegrass, Blues, Bossa Nova, Comedy, Contemporary Jazz, Country & Western, Disco, Folk, Hillbilly, Reggae, Rhythm & Blues, Rock & Roll, Soul, Traditional Jazz

VOLUME: 33⅓ – 2,500
           45   – 2,000
           78   – 500
           Other – 0

STOCK: Domestic & Import/New & Used

SEARCH: Available with no service charge; Want lists maintained and requester notified when record comes in

COLLECTIONS: Will not buy collections of rare records

PAYMENTS: Money Order, Personal Check

MAIL ORDER: Air Mail, 4th Class; Prepayment

DISCOUNTS: Available

PUBLICATIONS: I.N.A.

PHILADELPHIA

ALBUM ALLEY (I)   M–S   10:00–6:00
6325 Greene Street
Philadelphia 19144
(215) 438-1826

SERVICES: Walk-in Store/Mail Order

SPECIALTIES: Picture Discs, Underground/Bootleg, Rock, Rock & Roll, Promotional, Punk Rock/New Wave

VOLUME: 33⅓ – 5,000
           45   – 2,500
           78   – 0
           Other – 0

STOCK: Domestic & Import/New & Used

SEARCH: Want lists maintained and requester notified when record comes in

COLLECTIONS: Will buy collections of rare records

PAYMENTS: Diners Club, Master Charge, Money Order, Personal Check

MAIL ORDER: Whatever shipment method requested; Prepayment or C.O.D.

DISCOUNTS: Available

PUBLICATIONS: Not available

PHILADELPHIA

GARY JAFFE RECORDS (I)
2309 South Alder Street
Philadelphia 19148
(215) 462-3271

SERVICES: Mail Order Only

SPECIALTIES: Rhythm & Blues, Rock
& Roll

VOLUME: 33⅓ – 100
              45 – 600
              78 – 5
            Other – 0

STOCK: Domestic & Import/New &
Used

SEARCH: Not available; Want lists
maintained and requester notified
when record comes in

COLLECTIONS: Will buy collections of
rare records

PAYMENTS: Money Order, Personal
Check

MAIL ORDER: Air Mail, 4th Class;
Prepayment

DISCOUNTS: Available

PUBLICATIONS: I.N.A.

PHILADELPHIA

PARAMOUNT RECORD SHOP (I)
1801 Ridge Avenue
Philadelphia 19121
(215) 232-3814

M–T	10:00–7:00
F–S	10:00–9:00
S	11:00–5:00

SERVICES: Walk-in Store/Mail Order

SPECIALTIES: (Alphabetical) Blues,
Comedy, Contemporary Jazz, Disco,
Easy Listening, Reggae, Religious,
Rhythm & Blues, Rock & Roll, Soul,
Traditional Jazz

VOLUME: 33⅓ – 7,000
              45 – 15,000
              78 – 11,000
            Other – 0

STOCK: Domestic & Import/New

SEARCH: Available with no service
charge; Want lists maintained and requester notified when record comes in

COLLECTIONS: Will buy collections of
rare records

PAYMENTS: Master Charge, Money
Order, Personal Check, VISA/Bank-
Americard

MAIL ORDER: 4th Class, U.P.S.; Prepayment

DISCOUNTS: Available

PUBLICATIONS: Free periodic catalog

PHILADELPHIA

PARAMOUNT RECORD SHOP (I)
1519 South Street
Philadelphia 19146
(215) 735-6970

M–T	10:00–7:00
F–S	10:00–9:00
S	11:00–5:00

SERVICES: Walk-in Store/Mail Order

SPECIALTIES: (Alphabetical) Blues, Comedy, Contemporary Jazz, Disco, Easy Listening, Reggae, Religious, Rhythm & Blues, Rock, Rock & Roll, Soul, Traditional Jazz

VOLUME: 33⅓ – 7,000
45 – 15,000
78 – 11,000
Other – 0

STOCK: Domestic & Import/New

SEARCH: Available with no service charge; Want lists maintained and requester notified when record comes in

COLLECTIONS: Will buy collections of rare records

PAYMENTS: Master Charge, Money Order, Personal Check, VISA/Bank-Americard

MAIL ORDER: 4th Class, U.P.S.; Prepayment

DISCOUNTS: Available

PUBLICATIONS: Free periodic catalog

PHILADELPHIA

THIRD STREET JAZZ AND ROCK (II)
10 North 3rd Street
Philadelphia 19106
(215) 627-3366

M–T	11:00–6:00
F	11:00–7:00
S	10:00–6:00
S	Closed

SERVICES: Walk-in Store/Mail Order

SPECIALTIES: (Alphabetical) Contemporary Jazz, Disco, Folk-Rock, Reggae, Rhythm & Blues, Rock, Rock & Roll, Soul, Traditional Jazz

VOLUME: 33⅓ –100%
45 – 0
78 – 0
Other – 0

STOCK: Domestic & Import/New & Used

SEARCH: I.N.A.

COLLECTIONS: Will buy collections of rare records

PAYMENTS: Money Order, Personal Check

MAIL ORDER: U.P.S.; Prepayment

DISCOUNTS: I.N.A.

PUBLICATIONS: I.N.A.

PITTSBURGH

LARRY FIANDER RECORDS (I)
8 Allegheny Center
Pittsburgh 15212
(412) 322-8570

SERVICES: Mail Order Only

SPECIALTIES: Rock & Roll, Country &
Western, Easy Listening, Film Scores,
Rhythm & Blues, Religious, Comedy,
Classical, Broadway Shows, Tradi-
tional Jazz

VOLUME: 33⅓ – 15,000
            45   – 75,000
            78   – 10,000
            Other – 0

STOCK: Domestic/New

SEARCH: Available with no service
charge; Want lists maintained and requester notified when record comes in

COLLECTIONS: I.N.A.

PAYMENTS: Money Order, Personal
Check

MAIL ORDER: 4th Class; Prepayment

DISCOUNTS: Not available

PUBLICATIONS: Free monthly auction
list

PITTSBURGH

HEADS TOGETHER (II)
1914 Murray Avenue
Pittsburgh 15217
(412) 521-9632

M–T   11:00–11:00
F–S 11:00 A.M.–mid.
S   Noon–10:00

SERVICES: Walk-in Store/Mail Order

SPECIALTIES: All Major Categories

VOLUME: 33⅓ – 100%
            45   – 0
            78   – 0
            Other – 0

STOCK: Domestic & Import/New

SEARCH: Available with no service
charge; Want lists maintained and requester notified when record comes in

COLLECTIONS: Will buy collections of
rare records

PAYMENTS: Master Charge, Personal
Check, VISA/BankAmericard

MAIL ORDER: Air Mail, 4th Class,
U.P.S.; Prepayment

DISCOUNTS: Available

PUBLICATIONS: I.N.A.

PITTSBURGH

LOU'S MUSIC CONNECTION (I)
Noble Manor Shopping Center
2351 Noblestown Road
Pittsburgh 15205
   (412) 921-5535

M–F	11:00–9:00
S	Noon–6:00
S	Closed

SERVICES: Walk-in Store/Mail Order

SPECIALTIES: Gospel/Sacred, Contemporary Jazz, Disco, Rockabilly, Easy Listening, Soul, Dance, Rock & Roll, Rock, Rhythm & Blues

VOLUME: 33⅓ – 500
         45 – 50,000
         78 – 100
      Other – Picture Covers

STOCK: Domestic & Import/New & Used

SEARCH: Want lists maintained and requester notified when record comes in

COLLECTIONS: Will buy collections of rare records

PAYMENTS: Money Order, Personal Check

MAIL ORDER: Air Mail, 4th Class, Whatever shipment method requested; Prepayment

DISCOUNTS: Not available

PUBLICATIONS: Free monthly auction list

PITTSBURGH

MUSIC SCENE (II)
Crafton-Ingram Shopping Center
Pittsburgh 15205
   (412) 921-2828

M–S	10:00–9:00
S	Closed

SERVICES: Walk-in Store/Mail Order

SPECIALTIES: All Major Categories

VOLUME: 33⅓ – 70%
         45 – 30%
         78 – 0
      Other – 0

STOCK: Domestic & Import/New & Used

SEARCH: Not available

COLLECTIONS: Will buy collections of rare records

PAYMENTS: Money Order, Personal Check

MAIL ORDER: Air Mail, 4th Class, U.P.S.; Prepayment

DISCOUNTS: Not available

PUBLICATIONS: Free semiannual auction list

PITTSBURGH

OLD RECORD RACK (I)
P.O. Box 5888
Pittsburgh 15209
 Telephone: I.N.A.

SERVICES: Mail Order Only

SPECIALTIES: Rock & Roll, Popular, Rhythm & Blues, Sound Tracks, Country & Western, Contemporary Jazz, Folk, Instrumental, Blues, Classical, Crosby, Jolson

VOLUME: 33⅓ – 5,000
45 – 40,000
78 – 5,000
Other – 0

STOCK: Domestic & Import/New & Used

SEARCH: Want lists maintained and requester notified when record comes in

COLLECTIONS: Will buy collections of rare records

PAYMENTS: Money Order, Personal Check

MAIL ORDER: Air Mail, 4th Class; Prepayment

DISCOUNTS: Available

PUBLICATIONS: Annual set-sale list of 45 r.p.m. records available for $1.00 per year; Free monthly auction list

PITTSBURGH

RECORD HUT (I)
2019 Noble Street
Pittsburgh 15218
 (412) 271-9291

| M–S | 10:00–9:00 |
| S | Closed |

SERVICES: Walk-in Store/Mail Order

SPECIALTIES: (Alphabetical) Beatles, Broadway Shows, Children's, Country & Western, Easy Listening, Folk, Gospel/Sacred, Instrumental, Reggae, Rockabilly, Sinatra

VOLUME: 33⅓ – 20%
45 – 70%
78 – 10%
Other – 0

STOCK: Domestic/New & Used

SEARCH: Not available; Want lists maintained and requester notified when record comes in

COLLECTIONS: Available for purchase; Will buy collections of rare records

PAYMENTS: Master Charge, Money Order, Personal Check

MAIL ORDER: 4th Class; Prepayment

DISCOUNTS: Not available

PUBLICATIONS: Not available

PITTSBURGH

RECORD-RAMA (I)
635 Butler Street
Route 8 Etna
Pittsburgh 15223
(412) 781-2155

M–T	Closed
W–S	10:00–5:00
S	Closed

SERVICES: Walk-in Store/Mail Order

SPECIALTIES: Rock, Nostalgia, Easy Listening, Sound Tracks, Country & Western, Comedy, Polka, Rhythm & Blues, Sound Effects, Christmas

VOLUME:
33⅓ – 100,000
45 – 750,000
78 – 0
Other – 0

STOCK: Domestic & Import/New & Used

SEARCH: Available with service charge; Want lists maintained and requester notified when record comes in

COLLECTIONS: Will buy collections of rare records

PAYMENTS: Money Order, Personal Check

MAIL ORDER: 4th Class; Prepayment

DISCOUNTS: Available to dealers only

PUBLICATIONS: Monthly computerized want and trade lists available for $5.00 charge

PITTSBURGH

STEDEFORD'S RECORDS (I)
607 East Ohio Street
Pittsburgh 15212
(412) 321-8333

M–T	9:30–7:00
F	9:30–8:30
S	9:30–7:00
S	Closed

SERVICES: Walk-in Store/Mail Order

SPECIALTIES: (Alphabetical) Bluegrass, Blues, Contemporary Jazz, Country & Western, Disco, Easy Listening, Folk, Hillbilly, Reggae, Rhythm & Blues, Rock & Roll, Soul, Traditional Jazz

VOLUME:
33⅓ – 40%
45 – 60%
78 – 0
Other – 0

STOCK: Domestic & Import/New & Used

SEARCH: Available with no service charge; Want lists maintained and requester notified when record comes in

COLLECTIONS: Will buy collections of rare records

PAYMENTS: Master Charge, Personal Check, VISA/BankAmericard

MAIL ORDER: Whatever shipment method requested; Prepayment or C.O.D.

DISCOUNTS: Available

PUBLICATIONS: I.N.A.

QUARRYVILLE

SOUND TRACK ALBUM RETAILERS (I)   M–F   9:00–5:00
P.O. Box 7   S–S   Closed
Quarryville 17566
  (717) 284-2573

SERVICES: Walk-in Store/Mail Order

SPECIALTIES: Sound Tracks, Broadway Shows, British Musical Shows, Film Scores, Vocal, Television Shows

VOLUME: 33⅓ – 15,000
                   45   – 0
                   78   – 0
                Other – 0

STOCK: Domestic & Import/New & Used

SEARCH: Not available

COLLECTIONS: Not available for purchase; Will buy collections of rare records

PAYMENTS: Master Charge, Money Order, Personal Check, VISA/BankAmericard

MAIL ORDER: 4th Class; Prepayment

DISCOUNTS: Available

PUBLICATIONS: Free monthly catalog available

RADNOR

RECORDS RESURRECTED (I)
P.O. Box 143
Radnor 19087
  Telephone: I.N.A.

SERVICES: Mail Order Only

SPECIALTIES: Nostalgia, Personalities, Big Band, Easy Listening, British Musical Shows, Broadway Shows, Film Scores, Contemporary Jazz, Classical, Opera, Swing

VOLUME: 33⅓ – 10,000
                   45   – 0
                   78   – 0
                Other – 0

STOCK: Domestic & Import/New & Used

SEARCH: Not available

COLLECTIONS: Will buy collections of rare records

PAYMENTS: Master Charge, Money Order, Personal Check, VISA/BankAmericard

MAIL ORDER: 4th Class; Prepayment

DISCOUNTS: Not available

PUBLICATIONS: Free monthly auction list

ROSEMONT

BRYN MAWR RECORDS (I)
1121 Lancaster Avenue
Rosemont 19010
(215) 527-1175

M–T	10:00–6:00
F	10:00–9:00
S	10:00–6:00
S	Closed

SERVICES: Walk-in Store/Mail Order

SPECIALTIES: (Alphabetical) Blues, Bossa Nova, Classical, Contemporary Jazz, Country & Western, Disco, Ethnic, Folk, Opera, Religious, Rhythm & Blues, Rock & Roll, Soul, Traditional Jazz

VOLUME:
33⅓	–	100,000
45	–	100,000
78	–	200,000
Other	–	0

STOCK: Domestic & Import/New & Used

SEARCH: Available with no service charge; Want lists maintained and requester notified when record comes in

COLLECTIONS: Will buy collections of rare records

PAYMENTS: Master Charge, Money Order, Personal Check, VISA/Bank-Americard

MAIL ORDER: 4th Class; Prepayment or C.O.D.

DISCOUNTS: Available

PUBLICATIONS: I.N.A.

UPPER DARBY

VAL SHIVELY'S R & B RECORDS (I)
146 Garrett Road
Upper Darby 19082
(215) 352-2320

M–W	Noon–6:00
T	Noon–mid.
F	Closed
S	Noon–6:00
S	Closed

SERVICES: Walk-in Store/Mail Order

SPECIALTIES: (Alphabetical) Blues, Country & Western, Disco, Easy Listening, Folk, Religious, Rhythm & Blues, Rock, Rock & Roll, Soul, Traditional Jazz

VOLUME:
33⅓	–	3,000
45	–	200,000
78	–	2,000
Other	–	0

STOCK: Domestic/New & Used

SEARCH: Want lists maintained and requester notified when record comes in

COLLECTIONS: Will buy collections of rare records

PAYMENTS: Money Order, Personal Check

MAIL ORDER: 4th Class; Prepayment or C.O.D.

DISCOUNTS: Not available

PUBLICATIONS: I.N.A.

RHODE ISLAND

PROVIDENCE

ARTHUR E. KNIGHT RECORDS (I)
128 5th Street
Providence 02906
(401) 351-1546

SERVICES: Mail Order Only

SPECIALTIES: (Alphabetical) Classical,
Edison Discs, Historical, Instrumental, Opera, Vocal

VOLUME: 33⅓ – I.N.A.
           45 – I.N.A.
           78 – I.N.A.
           Other – Edison Discs

STOCK: Domestic & Import/New &
Used

SEARCH: Not available

COLLECTIONS: Not available for purchase; Will buy collections of rare
records

PAYMENTS: Personal Check

MAIL ORDER: Air Mail, 4th Class;
Prepayment

DISCOUNTS: Not available

PUBLICATIONS: Not available

PROVIDENCE

MUFFETT'S MUSIC SHOP INCORPORATED (I)	M–W	9:00–6:00
23 Empire Street	T	9:00–5:00
Providence 02903	F–S	9:00–6:00
(401) 621-9089	S	Closed

SERVICES: Walk-in Store/Mail Order

SPECIALTIES: All Major Categories

VOLUME: 33⅓ – 33%
           45 – 50%
           78 – 17%
           Other – 0

STOCK: Domestic & Import/New

SEARCH: Available with no service
charge; Want lists maintained and requester notified when record comes in

COLLECTIONS: Will not buy collections of rare records

PAYMENTS: Master Charge, Money
Order, VISA/BankAmericard

MAIL ORDER: Whatever shipment
method requested; Prepayment or
C.O.D.

DISCOUNTS: Available

PUBLICATIONS: I.N.A.

PROVIDENCE

WAX AGE RECORDS (II)
P.O. Box 9085
Providence 02940
  Telephone: I.N.A.

SERVICES: Mail Order Only

SPECIALTIES: (Alphabetical) Blues, Country & Western, Disco, Easy Listening, Folk, Folk-Rock, Hillbilly, Reggae, Rhythm & Blues, Rock, Rock & Roll

VOLUME: 33⅓ – I.N.A.
           45 – I.N.A.
           78 – I.N.A.
           Other – I.N.A.

STOCK: Domestic & Import/New & Used

SEARCH: Not available

COLLECTIONS: Will not buy collections of rare records

PAYMENTS: Money Order, Personal Check

MAIL ORDER: Air Mail, 4th Class; Prepayment

DISCOUNTS: Available

PUBLICATIONS: Free periodic catalog

SOUTH CAROLINA

BLUFFTON

GRAMMY'S ATTIC (I)
P.O. Box 181
Bluffton 29910
  (803) 757-2535

SERVICES: Mail Order Only

SPECIALTIES: Film Scores, Sound Tracks, Classical, Broadway Shows, Television Shows, Opera, British Musical Shows, Vocal,

VOLUME: 33⅓ – 98%
           45 – 2%
           78 – 0
           Other – 0

STOCK: Domestic & Import/New & Used

SEARCH: Available with no service charge; Want lists maintained and requester notified when record comes in

COLLECTIONS: Will buy collections of rare records

PAYMENTS: Money Order, Personal Check

MAIL ORDER: Whatever shipment method requested; Prepayment

DISCOUNTS: Not available

PUBLICATIONS: Quarterly catalog available for $1.00 per year

GOOSE CREEK

RECORD SHOWCASE (I)
P.O. Box 146
Old State Road
Goose Creek 29445
  (803) 553-1991

M–F	9:00–9:00
S	9:00–9:30
S	Closed

SERVICES: Walk-in Store/Mail Order

SPECIALTIES: (Alphabetical) Bluegrass, Blues, Contemporary Jazz, Country & Western, Disco, Folk-Rock, Hillbilly, Religious, Rhythm & Blues, Rock & Roll, Soul, Traditional Jazz

VOLUME: 33⅓ – 4,000
               45   – 70,000
               78   – 1,000
            Other – 0

STOCK: Domestic & Import/New & Used

SEARCH: Available with service charge; Want lists maintained and requester notified when record comes in

COLLECTIONS: Will buy collections of rare records

PAYMENTS: Money Order, Personal Check

MAIL ORDER: 1st Class; Prepayment

DISCOUNTS: Available

PUBLICATIONS: I.N.A.

TENNESSEE

CLARKSVILLE

DAVIS UNLIMITED RECORDS (I)
Route 7
P.O. Box 205–A
Clarksville 37040
  (615) 362-3845

SERVICES: Mail Order Only

SPECIALTIES: Bluegrass, Old-Time Country

VOLUME: 33⅓ – I.N.A.
               45   – I.N.A.
               78   – I.N.A.
            Other – I.N.A.

STOCK: Domestic/New

SEARCH: Not available

COLLECTIONS: Will not buy collections of rare records

PAYMENTS: Money Order, Personal Check

MAIL ORDER: Air Mail, 4th Class, U.P.S.; Prepayment or C.O.D.

DISCOUNTS: Available

PUBLICATIONS: I.N.A.

MEMPHIS

COLLECTOR'S RECORDLAND (I)
P.O. Box 16786
Memphis 38116
  (901) 396-6745

SERVICES: Mail Order Only

SPECIALTIES: (Alphabetical) Beatles, Blues, Cajun, Comedy, Country & Western, Easy Listening, Elvis, Hillbilly, Instrumental, Novelty, Rhythm & Blues, Rock, Rock & Roll, Rockabilly, Surfing

VOLUME: 33⅓ – 2,000
                45 – 500,000
                78 – 0
            Other – 0

STOCK: Domestic & Import/New & Used

SEARCH: Available with no service charge

COLLECTIONS: Will buy collections of rare records

PAYMENTS: Money Order, Personal Check

MAIL ORDER: Air Mail, 4th Class; Prepayment

DISCOUNTS: Available

PUBLICATIONS: Periodic annual catalog available for $1.00 per issue; Free bimonthly auction list

NASHVILLE

JEANNIE'S RECORDS (I)
P.O. Box 90700
Nashville 37209
  Telephone: I.N.A.

SERVICES: Mail Order Only

SPECIALTIES: (Alphabetical) Bluegrass, Blues, Bossa Nova, Contemporary Jazz, Country & Western, Folk, Hillbilly, Rhythm & Blues, Rock & Roll, Soul, Traditional Jazz

VOLUME: 33⅓ – 10,000
                45 – 5,000
                78 – 2,000
            Other – 0

STOCK: Domestic & Import/New & Used

SEARCH: Available with no service charge; Want lists maintained and requester notified when record comes in

COLLECTIONS: Will buy collections of rare records

PAYMENTS: Money Order, Personal Check

MAIL ORDER: Air Mail, 4th Class; Prepayment

DISCOUNTS: Not available

PUBLICATIONS: I.N.A.

NASHVILLE

MUSIC CITY ONE STOP (I)
127 Lafayette Street
Nashville 37210
(615) 256-4115

M–F	9:00–5:00
S	10:00–5:00
S	Closed

SERVICES: Walk-in Store Only

SPECIALTIES: (Alphabetical) Contemporary Jazz, Country & Western, Disco, Rhythm & Blues, Rock, Rock & Roll, Soul

VOLUME: 33⅓ – 0
45 – 100%
78 – 0
Other – 0

STOCK: Domestic/New

SEARCH: Available with no service charge

COLLECTIONS: Will not buy collections of rare records

PAYMENTS: Master Charge, Money Order, Personal Check, VISA/Bank-Americard

MAIL ORDER: Not available

DISCOUNTS: Available

PUBLICATIONS: I.N.A.

TEXAS

ARLINGTON

CONNOISSEURS GROOVY ORIGINALS (I)
P.O. Box 3672
Arlington 76010
(817) 461-0399

SERVICES: Walk-in Store (By Appointment)/Mail Order

SPECIALTIES: Rhythm & Blues, Rock & Roll, Rockabilly, Novelty, Elvis, Beatles, Broadway Shows, Film Scores, Sound Tracks, Blues, Big Band, Bop Jazz

VOLUME: 33⅓ – 3,000
45 – 18,000
78 – 0
Other – 0

STOCK: Domestic & Import/New & Used

SEARCH: Not available

COLLECTIONS: Not available for purchase

PAYMENTS: Money Order, Personal Check

MAIL ORDER: Whatever shipment method requested; Prepayment

DISCOUNTS: Available

PUBLICATIONS: Not available

ARLINGTON

FANTASIA (II)   M–S   10:00–10:00
c/o Mr. Robert Bobbitt   S   Closed
1313 South Cooper
Arlington 76010
  (814) 277-5011

SERVICES: Walk-in Store/Mail Order   COLLECTIONS: Will not buy collec-
(Limited)   tions of rare records

SPECIALTIES: All Major Categories   PAYMENTS: Master Charge, Money
                                            Order, Personal Check
VOLUME: 33⅓ – 100%
            45   – 0   MAIL ORDER: 3rd Class; Prepayment
            78   – 0   DISCOUNTS: Available
            Other – 0
                                            PUBLICATIONS: I.N.A.
STOCK: Domestic & Import/New

SEARCH: Not available; Want lists
maintained and requester notified
when record comes in

AUSTIN

HALF-PRICE BOOKS, RECORDS, & MAGA-   M–S   10:00–10:00
   ZINES (I)   S   Noon–6:00
1514 Lavaca
Austin 78701
  (512) 474-5209

SERVICES: Walk-in Store/Mail Order   SEARCH: Not available

SPECIALTIES: Rock, Big Band, Easy   COLLECTIONS: Will buy collections of
Listening, Film Scores, Classical, Con-   rare records
temporary Jazz, Promotional, Soul,
Sound Tracks   PAYMENTS: Master Charge, Money
                                            Order, Personal Check, VISA/Bank-
VOLUME: 33⅓ – 10,000   Americard
            45   – 1,000
            78   – 25,000   MAIL ORDER: Whatever shipment
            Other – 0   method requested; Prepayment

STOCK: Domestic & Import/New &   DISCOUNTS: Not available
Used
                                            PUBLICATIONS: Not available

AUSTIN

IMMORTAL PERFORMANCES (I)
P.O. Box 8316
Austin 78712
(512) 478-9954

SERVICES: Walk-in Store (By Appointment)/Mail Order

SPECIALTIES: (Alphabetical) Blues, Classical, Ethnic, Opera, Standards, Traditional Jazz, Vocal

VOLUME: 33⅓ – 1,000
           45 – 0
           78 – 5,000
           Other – 0

STOCK: Domestic & Import/New & Used

SEARCH: Not available

COLLECTIONS: Will buy collections of rare records

PAYMENTS: Money Order, Personal Check

MAIL ORDER: Air Mail, 4th Class; Prepayment or C.O.D.

DISCOUNTS: I.N.A.

PUBLICATIONS: Free periodic archives of historical recordings of classical music

AUSTIN

OK RECORDS (I)
200 East 6th Street
Austin 78701
(512) 477-7100

M–S	9:00–7:00
S	Closed

SERVICES: Walk-in Store/Mail Order

SPECIALTIES: Soul, Disco, Blues, Rhythm & Blues, Rock & Roll, Gospel/Sacred, Old-Time Country, Traditional Jazz, Rock, Cajun

VOLUME: 33⅓ – 1,000
           45 – 10,000
           78 – 25,000
           Other – 0

STOCK: Domestic & Import/New & Used

SEARCH: Want lists maintained and requester notified when record comes in

COLLECTIONS: Available for purchase; Will buy collections of rare records

PAYMENTS: Master Charge, Money Order, Personal Check, VISA/BankAmericard

MAIL ORDER: Whatever shipment method requested; Prepayment

DISCOUNTS: Available

PUBLICATIONS: Free semiannual auction list

AUSTIN

DAVID SHUTT RECORDS (I)
5510–A Ponciana Drive
Austin 78744
  (512) 447-6948

SERVICES: Mail Order Only

SPECIALTIES: (Alphabetical) Blues,
Country & Western, Easy Listening,
Religious, Rock, Rock & Roll, Soul

VOLUME: 33⅓ – 600
           45 – 3,000
           78 – 0
         Other – 0

STOCK: Domestic/New & Used

SEARCH: Want lists maintained and
requester notified when record comes
in

COLLECTIONS: Will not buy collections of rare records

PAYMENTS: Money Order, Personal
Check

MAIL ORDER: Air Mail, 4th Class;
Prepayment

DISCOUNTS: Available

PUBLICATIONS: I.N.A.

DALLAS

COLLECTORS RECORDS (I)
373 Casa Linda Plaza
Dallas 75218
  (214) 327-3313

M	10:00–6:00
T	Noon–6:00
W–T	10:00–6:00
F	10:00–9:00
S	10:00–6:00
S	Closed

SERVICES: Walk-in Store/Mail Order

SPECIALTIES: Rock & Roll, Rock,
Country & Western, Traditional Jazz,
Big Band, Sound Tracks, Ragtime,
Blues, Broadway Shows, Classical,
Easy Listening

VOLUME: 33⅓ – 3,500
           45 – 15,000
           78 – 2,000
         Other – 0

STOCK: Domestic & Import/New &
Used

SEARCH: Want lists maintained and
requester notified when record comes
in

COLLECTIONS: I.N.A.

PAYMENTS: Master Charge, Money
Order, Personal Check, VISA/Bank-
Americard

MAIL ORDER: 4th Class, Whatever
shipment method requested; Prepayment

DISCOUNTS: Not available

PUBLICATIONS: Not available

DALLAS

HALF-PRICE BOOKS, RECORDS, AND MAGA-	M–F	10:00–9:00
ZINES (I)	S	10:00–6:00
4528 McKinney Avenue	S	Noon–6:00
Dallas 75205		
(214) 526-8440		

SERVICES: Walk-in Store Only

SPECIALTIES: All Major Categories

VOLUME: 33⅓ – 10,000
              45 – 5,000
              78 – 10,000
              Other – 0

STOCK: Domestic & Import/New & Used

SEARCH: Not available

COLLECTIONS: Will buy collections of rare records

PAYMENTS: Master Charge, Personal Check, VISA/BankAmericard

MAIL ORDER: Not available

DISCOUNTS: Available

PUBLICATIONS: I.N.A.

DALLAS

HALF-PRICE BOOKS, RECORDS, AND MAGA-	M–F	10:00–9:00
ZINES (I)	S	10:00–6:00
4535 McKinney Avenue	S	Noon–6:00
Dallas 75205		
(214) 526-8440		

SERVICES: Walk-in Store Only

SPECIALTIES: All Major Categories

VOLUME: 33⅓ – 10,000
              45 – 2,500
              78 – 5,000
              Other – 0

STOCK: Domestic & Import/Used

SEARCH: Not available

COLLECTIONS: Will buy collections of rare records

PAYMENTS: Master Charge, Personal Check, VISA/BankAmericard

MAIL ORDER: Not available

DISCOUNTS: I.N.A.

PUBLICATIONS: I.N.A.

DALLAS

HALF-PRICE BOOKS AND RECORDS (I)   M–S   10:00–6:00
213 South Akard Street   S   Closed
Dallas 75202
   (214) 748-5920

SERVICES: Walk-in Store Only

SPECIALTIES: All Major Categories

VOLUME: 33⅓ – 500
            45 – 0
            78 – 0
          Other – 0

STOCK: Domestic & Import/Used

SEARCH: Not available

COLLECTIONS: Will buy collections of rare records

PAYMENTS: Master Charge, Money Order, VISA/BankAmericard

MAIL ORDER: Not available

DISCOUNTS: Not available

PUBLICATIONS: I.N.A.

DALLAS

METAMORPHOSIS RECORDS AND BOOKS (II)   M–W   10:00–5:30
2811 Allen Street   T–F   10:00–8:00
Dallas 75204   S   10:00–5:30
   (214) 742-3972   S   Noon–5:30

SERVICES: Walk-in Store/Mail Order

SPECIALTIES: Rock, Rock & Roll, Punk Rock/New Wave, Beatles, Contemporary Jazz, Disco, Big Band, Classical, Traditional Jazz, Sound Tracks

VOLUME: 33⅓ – I.N.A.
            45 – I.N.A.
            78 – I.N.A.
          Other – I.N.A.

STOCK: Domestic & Import/New & Used

SEARCH: Available with no service charge; Want lists maintained and requester notified when record comes in

COLLECTIONS: Will buy collections of rare records

PAYMENTS: Money Order, Personal Check

MAIL ORDER: Whatever shipment method requested; Prepayment or C.O.D.

DISCOUNTS: Not available

PUBLICATIONS: Not available

DALLAS

STACKS O'TRACKS (I)
2817 Greenville Avenue
Dallas 75206
 (214) 823-4261

M–S   10:00–8:00
S   Closed

SERVICES: Walk-in Store/Mail Order

SPECIALTIES: (Alphabetical) Beatles, Contemporary Jazz, Country & Western, Easy Listening, Elvis, Promotional, Punk Rock/New Wave, Rhythm & Blues, Rock & Roll, Soul

VOLUME: 33⅓ – 6,000
                45 – 1,000
                78 – 100
                Other – 0

STOCK: Domestic & Import/New & Used

SEARCH: Want lists maintained and requester notified when record comes in

COLLECTIONS: Will buy collections of rare records

PAYMENTS: Master Charge, Money Order, VISA/BankAmericard

MAIL ORDER: Whatever shipment method requested; Prepayment

DISCOUNTS: Available

PUBLICATIONS: Monthly auction list available for $1.00 per year

DEER PARK

ROCK-IT RECORDS (I)
P.O. Box 504
Deer Park 77536
 (713) 479-2061

SERVICES: Mail Order Only

SPECIALTIES: (Alphabetical) Bluegrass, Blues, Classical, Country & Western, Easy Listening, Hillbilly, Rhythm & Blues, Rock, Rock & Roll, Soul, Traditional Jazz

VOLUME: 33⅓ – 25,000
                45 – 125,000
                78 – 55,000
                Other – 0

STOCK: Domestic & Import/New & Used

SEARCH: Available with no service charge; Want lists maintained and requester notified when record comes in

COLLECTIONS: Will buy collections of rare records

PAYMENTS: Money Order, Personal Check

MAIL ORDER: Air Mail, 1st Class, 4th Class; Prepayment or C.O.D.

DISCOUNTS: Available

PUBLICATIONS I.N.A.

FARMERS BRANCH

HALF-PRICE BOOKS, RECORDS, AND MAGA-	M–S	10:00–6:00
ZINES (I)	S	Closed

Farmers Branch Shopping Center
Valley View Lane at Josey Lane
Farmers Branch 75234
  (214) 243-3347

SERVICES: Walk-in Store Only

SPECIALTIES: All Major Categories

VOLUME: 33⅓ – 3,000
           45   – 500
           78   – 0
         Other – 0

STOCK: Domestic & Import/Used

SEARCH: Not available

COLLECTIONS: Will buy collections of rare records

PAYMENTS: Master Charge, Personal Check, VISA/BankAmericard

MAIL ORDER: Not available

DISCOUNTS: Not available

PUBLICATIONS: I.N.A.

FORT WORTH

BROTHER SLIM'S RECORD REVIVAL (I)
103 Fondren
Fort Worth 76126
  (817) 249-2631

SERVICES: Mail Order Only

SPECIALTIES: (Alphabetical)   Blue-grass, Blues, Contemporary Jazz, Country & Western, Ethnic, Folk, Hillbilly, Religious, Rhythm & Blues, Rock & Roll, Rockabilly, Traditional Jazz

VOLUME: 33⅓ – 2,000
           45   – 1,000
           78   – 1,000
         Other – 0

STOCK: Domestic & Import/New & Used

SEARCH: Want lists maintained and requester notified when record comes in

COLLECTIONS: Will buy collections of rare records

PAYMENTS: Master Charge, Money Order, Personal Check, VISA/Bank-Americard

MAIL ORDER: 4th Class; Prepayment

DISCOUNTS: Available

PUBLICATIONS: I.N.A.

FORT WORTH

HALF-PRICE BOOKS, RECORDS, & MAGA-   M–S   9:00–7:00
   ZINES (I)   S   Noon–6:00
3306 Fairfield Drive
Fort Worth 76116
   (817) 732-4111

SERVICES: Walk-in Store/Mail Order

SPECIALTIES: (Alphabetical) Classical, Contemporary Jazz, Dance, Disco, Easy Listening, Gospel/Sacred, Religious, Rock, Rock & Roll, Traditional Jazz

VOLUME: 33⅓ – 7,000
           45   – 3,000
           78   – 1,000
           Other – 0

STOCK: Domestic & Import/New & Used

SEARCH: Not available

COLLECTIONS: Will buy collections of rare records

PAYMENTS: American Express, Carte Blanche, Master Charge, Money Order, Personal Check, VISA/Bank-Americard

MAIL ORDER: Whatever shipment method requested; Prepayment

DISCOUNTS: Not available

PUBLICATIONS: Not available

FORT WORTH

SELL 'DEM RECORDS (I)   M–F   10:00–6:00
7121 West Vickery–#118   S–S   Closed
Fort Worth 76116
   (817) 731-7375

SERVICES: Walk-in Store/Mail Order

SPECIALTIES: (Alphabetical) Bluegrass, Blues, Contemporary Jazz, Country & Western, Ethnic, Folk, Hillbilly, Religious, Rhythm & Blues, Rock & Roll, Rockabilly, Soul, Traditional Jazz

VOLUME: 33⅓ – 10,000
           45   – 2,000
           78   – 500
           Other – 0

STOCK: Domestic/New & Used

SEARCH: Want lists maintained and requester notified when record comes in

COLLECTIONS: Will buy collections of rare records

PAYMENTS: Money Order, Personal Check

MAIL ORDER: 4th Class; Prepayment

DISCOUNTS: Available

PUBLICATIONS: I.N.A.

FORT WORTH

SYBLE'S GOLDEN OLDIE RECORDS (I)   M–S   9:00–7:00
5411 East Lancaster
Fort Worth 76112
  (817) 457-1911 or 429-1702

SERVICES: Walk-in Store/Mail Order

SPECIALTIES: All Major Categories

VOLUME: 33⅓ – 50,000
            45   – 1,000,000
            78   – 15,000
            Other – Edison Discs

STOCK: Domestic & Import/New & Used

SEARCH: Available with no service charge; Want lists maintained and requester notified when record comes in

COLLECTIONS: Available for purchase; Will buy collections of rare records

PAYMENTS: Master Charge, Money Order, Personal Check, VISA/Bank-Americard

MAIL ORDER: 4th Class, Whatever shipment method requested; Prepayment

DISCOUNTS: Available

PUBLICATIONS: Free quarterly auction list

HOUSTON

ROY'S MEMORY SHOP (I)   M–S   10:00–6:00
2312 Bissonnet   S   Closed
Houston 77005
  (713) 529-1387

SERVICES: Walk-in Store/Mail Order

SPECIALTIES: Rock & Roll, Rhythm & Blues, Easy Listening, Rockabilly, Hillbilly, Country & Western, Blues, Beatles, Sinatra, Rock

VOLUME: 33⅓ – 500
            45   – 5,000
            78   – 0
            Other – 0

STOCK: Domestic/New & Used

SEARCH: Want lists maintained and requester notified when record comes in

COLLECTIONS: Will buy collections of rare records

PAYMENTS: Master Charge, Money Order, Personal Check, VISA/Bank-Americard

MAIL ORDER: 4th Class; Prepayment

DISCOUNTS: Not available

PUBLICATIONS: Not available

LUBBOCK

DEWITT ENTERPRISES (I)
4423 38th Street
Lubbock 79414
  (806) 792-0837

SERVICES: Mail Order Only

SPECIALTIES: (Alphabetical) Blues,
Country & Western, Easy Listening,
Rhythm & Blues, Rock & Roll

VOLUME: 33⅓ – 2,500
           45 – 2,500
           78 – 200
           Other – 0

STOCK: Domestic & Import/New &
Used

SEARCH: Available with no service
charge; Want lists maintained and requester notified when record comes in

COLLECTIONS: Will buy collections of
rare records

PAYMENTS: Money Order, Personal
Check

MAIL ORDER: Air Mail, 4th Class;
Prepayment

DISCOUNTS: Not available

PUBLICATIONS: I.N.A.

LUBBOCK

RALPH'S RARE RECORDS (I)
P.O. Box 3545
Lubbock 79452
  (806) 745-6868

SERVICES: Mail Order Only

SPECIALTIES: Rock, Rock & Roll,
Promotional, Surfing, Elvis, Punk
Rock/New Wave, Beatles, Sound
Tracks, Rhythm & Blues, Blues

VOLUME: 33⅓ – 7,500
           45 – 10,000
           78 – 500
           Other – 0

STOCK: Domestic & Import/New &
Used

SEARCH: Available with no service
charge; Want lists maintained and requester notified when record comes in

COLLECTIONS: Available for purchase;
Will buy collections of rare records

PAYMENTS: Money Order, Personal
Check

MAIL ORDER: Whatever shipment
method requested; Prepayment

DISCOUNTS: Available

PUBLICATIONS: Free monthly auction
list

RICHARDSON

HALF-PRICE BOOKS, RECORDS, AND MAGA-   M–S   10:00–6:00
   ZINES (I)   S   Closed
508 Lochwood Street
Richardson 75080
   (214) 234-4286

SERVICES: Walk-in Store Only

SPECIALTIES: All Major Categories

VOLUME: 33⅓ – 3,000
          45 – 500
          78 – 0
     Other – 0

STOCK: Domestic & Import/Used

SEARCH: Want lists maintained and requester notified when record comes in

COLLECTIONS: Will buy collections of rare records

PAYMENTS: Master Charge, Personal Check, VISA/BankAmericard

MAIL ORDER: Not available

DISCOUNTS: Not available

PUBLICATIONS: I.N.A.

SAN ANTONIO

LEIGH BROWN RECORDS (I)
434 Avant Avenue
San Antonio 78210
   (512) 534-3740

SERVICES: Mail Order Only

SPECIALTIES: (Alphabetical) Big Band, Blues, Broadway Shows, Classical, Contemporary Jazz, Country & Western, Opera, Personalities, Rhythm & Blues, Rock & Roll, Sound Tracks, Traditional Jazz

VOLUME: 33⅓ – I.N.A.
          45 – I.N.A.
          78 – I.N.A.
     Other – 0

STOCK: Domestic & Import/New & Used

SEARCH: Want lists maintained and requester notified when record comes in

COLLECTIONS: Will buy collections of rare records

PAYMENTS: Bank Check, Money Order, Personal Check

MAIL ORDER: Air Mail, 1st Class, 4th Class; Prepayment

DISCOUNTS: I.N.A.

PUBLICATIONS: Free periodic auction list; Free periodic set-sale list

SAN ANTONIO

L.R. DOCKS RECORDS (I)
P.O. Box 13685
San Antonio 78213
(512) 341-0978

SERVICES: Mail Order Only

SPECIALTIES: Blues, Rhythm & Blues, Rockabilly, Traditional Jazz, Hillbilly, Bluegrass, Big Band, Old-Time Country, Rock & Roll, Dixieland

VOLUME: 33⅓ – 10,000
          45 – 30,000
          78 – 30,000
    Other – Edison Discs

STOCK: Domestic & Import/New & Used

SEARCH: Want lists maintained and requester notified when record comes in

COLLECTIONS: Will buy collections of rare records

PAYMENTS: Money Order, Personal Check

MAIL ORDER: 4th Class, Whatever shipment method requested; Prepayment

DISCOUNTS: Not available

PUBLICATIONS: Free occasional auction list

SAN ANTONIO

FRANK HAECKER–THE TEXAS SOUND DISTRIBUTOR (I)
423 Woodcrest Drive
San Antonio 78209
(512) 826-0770

M–F	10:00–7:00
A	10:00–9:00
S	Closed

SERVICES: Walk-in Store/Mail Order

SPECIALTIES: Rock, Punk Rock/New Wave, Rock & Roll, Psychedelic, Country Rock, Country & Western, Tex-Mex, Cajun, Blues, Rhythm & Blues, Rockabilly

VOLUME: 33⅓ – 1,000
          45 – 200
          78 – 0
    Other – 0

STOCK: Domestic/New & Used

SEARCH: Not available

COLLECTIONS: Will buy collections of rare records

PAYMENTS: Bank Check, Money Order, Personal Check

MAIL ORDER: Air Mail, 4th Class, Parcel Post; Prepayment

DISCOUNTS: Available

PUBLICATIONS: Free quarterly catalog; Free quarterly auction list

TEXARKANA

ATKINS RECORDS (I)
1304 Rio Grande
Texarkana 75503
(214) 792-2946

SERVICES: Mail Order Only

SPECIALTIES: Contemporary Jazz, Traditional Jazz

VOLUME: 33⅓ – 275
         45 – 0
         78 – 0
      Other – 0

STOCK: Domestic & Import/New & Used

SEARCH: Not available

COLLECTIONS: Will buy collections of rare records

PAYMENTS: Money Order, Personal Check

MAIL ORDER: Air Mail, 4th Class; Prepayment

DISCOUNTS: Not available

PUBLICATIONS: I.N.A.

WACO

HALF-PRICE BOOKS, RECORDS, AND MAGA-	M–F	10:00–5:30
ZINES (I)	S	10:00–5:00
301 North 25th Street	S	Closed
Waco 76710		
(817) 754-1051		

SERVICES: Walk-in Store Only

SPECIALTIES: All Major Categories

VOLUME: 33⅓ – 4,000
         45 – 500
         78 – 1,000
      Other – 0

STOCK: Domestic & Import/Used

SEARCH: Not available

COLLECTIONS: Will buy collections of rare records

PAYMENTS: Master Charge, Personal Check, VISA/BankAmericard

MAIL ORDER: Not available

DISCOUNTS: Available

PUBLICATIONS: I.N.A.

UTAH

SALT LAKE CITY

COSMIC AEROPLANE RECORDS (I)   M–S   10:00–9:00
258 East 1st South   S   2:00–7:00
Salt Lake City 84111
  (801) 355-1445

SERVICES: Walk-in Store Only

SPECIALTIES: All Major Categories

VOLUME: 33⅓ – 98%
            45   – 1%
            78   – 1%
            Other – 0

STOCK: Domestic & Import/New & Used

SEARCH: Not available

COLLECTIONS: Will buy collections of rare records

PAYMENTS: Master Charge, Personal Check, VISA/BankAmericard

MAIL ORDER: Not available

DISCOUNTS: Not available

PUBLICATIONS: I.N.A.

VIRGINIA

ARLINGTON

JEFF BARR RECORDS (I)
P.O. Box 6046
Arlington 22206
  Telephone: I.N.A.

SERVICES: Mail Order Only

SPECIALTIES: Bop Jazz, Contemporary Jazz, Big Band, Vocal, Traditional Jazz

VOLUME: 33⅓ – 7,500
            45   – 0
            78   – 0
            Other – 0

STOCK: Domestic & Import/New & Used

SEARCH: Available with no service charge; Want lists maintained and requester notified when record comes in

COLLECTIONS: Will buy collections of rare records

PAYMENTS: Money Order, Personal Charge Account, Personal Check

MAIL ORDER: Air Mail, 1st Class, 4th Class, U.P.S., Whatever shipment method requested; Prepayment

DISCOUNTS: Not available

PUBLICATIONS: Free semiannual catalog; Free semiannual auction list

FALLS CHURCH

WALTER V. SAUNDERS RECORDS (I)
P.O. Box 3063
Falls Church 22043
 (703) 893-7828

SERVICES: Mail Order Only

SPECIALTIES: Bluegrass, Old-Time
Country, Country & Western

VOLUME: 33⅓ – 500
             45   – 0
             78   – 0
           Other – 0

STOCK: Import/New

SEARCH: Want lists maintained and
requester notified when record comes
in

COLLECTIONS: Will not buy collections of rare records

PAYMENTS: Money Order, Personal
Check

MAIL ORDER: 4th Class; Prepayment

DISCOUNTS: Not available

PUBLICATIONS: Free occasional catalog

FLOYD

DAVID FREEMAN'S RECORD BARN (I)
Main Street
Floyd 24091
 (703) 745-2002

SERVICES: Mail Order Only

SPECIALTIES: Country & Western,
Bluegrass, Old-Time Country, Hillbilly, Gospel/Sacred, Blues

VOLUME: 33⅓ – 20,000
             45   – 32,000
             78   – 15,000
           Other – 0

STOCK: Domestic/New & Used

SEARCH: Want lists maintained and
requester notified when record comes
in

COLLECTIONS: Will buy collections of
rare records

PAYMENTS: Money Order, Personal
Check

MAIL ORDER: U.P.S., Parcel Post;
Prepayment

DISCOUNTS: Not available

PUBLICATIONS: Free bimonthly auction list

FLOYD

RECORD DEPOT/COUNTY SALES (I)
P.O. Box 191
Floyd 24091
(703) 745-2922

SERVICES: Mail Order Only

SPECIALTIES: (Alphabetical)   Bluegrass, Country & Western, Hillbilly

VOLUME: 33⅓ – 5,000
           45 – 10,000
           78 – 20,000
           Other – 0

STOCK: Domestic/New & Used

SEARCH: Want lists maintained and
requester notified when record comes
in

COLLECTIONS: Will buy collections of
rare records

PAYMENTS: Money Order, Personal
Check

MAIL ORDER: 4th Class; Prepayment

DISCOUNTS: Not available

PUBLICATIONS: I.N.A.

NEWPORT NEWS

MEMORY LANE/MARANATHA RECORDS (I)	M	Closed
15394 Warwick Boulevard	T–F	10:00–9:00
Newport News 23602	S	10:00–5:00
(804) 877-6877	S	Closed

SERVICES: Walk-in Store/Mail Order

SPECIALTIES: (Alphabetical) Beatles,
Big Band, Broadway Shows, Easy Lis-
tening, Elvis, Rhythm & Blues, Rock,
Rock & Roll, Rockabilly, Sinatra

VOLUME: 33⅓ – 10,000
           45 – 80,000
           78 – 30,000
           Other – 0

STOCK: Domestic & Import/New &
Used

SEARCH: Want lists maintained and
requester notified when record comes
in

COLLECTIONS: Available for purchase;
Will buy collections of rare records

PAYMENTS: Master Charge, Money
Order, Personal Check, VISA/Bank-
Americard

MAIL ORDER: 4th Class, U.P.S.; Prepayment or C.O.D.

DISCOUNTS: Available

PUBLICATIONS: Free quarterly catalog
available; Free quarterly auction list
available

ROANOKE

ROANOKE'S RECORD ROOM (I)   M–S   Noon–6:00
P.O. Box 2445
Roanoke 24010
(703) 342-8155

SERVICES: Walk-in Store/Mail Order

SPECIALTIES: Rock & Roll, Rock, Rhythm & Blues, Rockabilly, Blues, Comedy, Elvis, Instrumental, Novelty, Promotional, Sinatra, Surfing

VOLUME: 33⅓ – 100%
             45 – 0
             78 – 0
             Other – 0

STOCK: Domestic & Import/New & Used

SEARCH: Available with no service charge; Want lists maintained and requester notified when record comes in

COLLECTIONS: Available for purchase; Will buy collections of rare records

PAYMENTS: Master Charge, Money Order, Personal Check, VISA/Bank-Americard

MAIL ORDER: Air Mail, 4th Class, Whatever shipment method requested; Prepayment

DISCOUNTS: Not available

PUBLICATIONS: Free bimonthly catalog

SPRINGFIELD

ROCKAWAY (I)
P.O. Box 708
Brookfield Station
Springfield 22150
Telephone: I.N.A.

SERVICES: Mail Order Only

SPECIALTIES: (Alphabetical) Bluegrass, Blues, Classical, Contemporary Jazz, Disco, Ethnic, Folk, Hillbilly, Punk Rock/New Wave, Reggae, Rhythm & Blues, Rock & Roll, Traditional Jazz

VOLUME: 33⅓ – 85%
             45 – 15%
             78 – 0
             Other – 0

STOCK: Domestic & Import/New

SEARCH: Not available

COLLECTIONS: Will not buy collections of rare records

PAYMENTS: Money Order, Personal Check

MAIL ORDER: U.P.S.; Prepayment

DISCOUNTS: Not available

PUBLICATIONS: Periodic catalog available for 50¢ per issue U.S.A. and $1.00 per issue non-U.S.A.

WASHINGTON

BELLINGHAM

CELLOPHANE SQUARE (I)   M–S 10:00 A.M.–mid.
207 East Holly   S   Noon–8:00
Bellingham 98225
(206) 676-1404

SERVICES: Walk-in Store/Mail Order   COLLECTIONS: Will buy collections of
                                            rare records
SPECIALTIES: All Major Categories
                                            PAYMENTS: Master Charge, Money
VOLUME: 33⅓ – 4,000   Order, Personal Check, VISA/Bank-
             45 – 100   Americard
             78 – 0
             Other – 0   MAIL ORDER: Air Mail, 1st Class; Pre-
                                            payment
STOCK: Domestic & Import/New &
Used   DISCOUNTS: Available

SEARCH: Available with no service   PUBLICATIONS: I.N.A.
charge; Want lists maintained and re-
quester notified when record comes in

LYNNWOOD

TOWER RECORDS (II)   M–S   9:00 A.M.–mid.
4601 200th Southwest
Lynnwood 98036
(206) 771-4141 or 4171

SERVICES: Walk-in Store/Mail Order   COLLECTIONS: Will not buy collec-
(Limited)   tions of rare records

SPECIALTIES: All Major Categories   PAYMENTS: Master Charge, Money
                                            Order, Personal Charge Account,
VOLUME: 33⅓ – 100%   VISA/BankAmericard
             45 – 0
             78 – 0   MAIL ORDER: 4th Class, U.P.S.; Pre-
             Other – 0   payment

STOCK: Domestic & Import/New   DISCOUNTS: Available

SEARCH: Not available   PUBLICATIONS: Not available

REDMOND

NOSTALGIA (I)
P.O. Box 82
Redmond 98052
(206) 883-9584

M–F	9:00–6:00
S	10:00–4:00
S	1:00–3:00

SERVICES: Walk-in Store (By Appointment)/Mail Order

SPECIALTIES: Nostalgia, Crosby, Jolson, Contemporary Jazz, Traditional Jazz, Big Band, Dixieland, Swing, Personalities, Historical, Radio Shows

VOLUME:
33⅓ – 100%
45 – 0
78 – 0
Other – 0

STOCK: Domestic & Import/New

SEARCH: Not available

COLLECTIONS: Will buy collections of rare records

PAYMENTS: Master Charge, Money Order, Personal Check, VISA/BankAmericard

MAIL ORDER: U.P.S.; Prepayment

DISCOUNTS: Not available

PUBLICATIONS: Annual catalog available for $1.00 per year

SEATTLE

ALLEY CAT RECORDS (I)
P.O. Box 17145
Seattle 98107
(206) 778-0993

M–S	7:00 P.M.–9:00 P.M.
S	10:00 A.M.–9:00 P.M.

SERVICES: Mail Order Only (Above Times for Telephone)

SPECIALTIES: Rock, Promotional, Obscure Rock, Sound Tracks, Rockabilly, Disco, Punk Rock/New Wave, Soul, Beatles, Contemporary Jazz

VOLUME:
33⅓ – 50%
45 – 50%
78 – 0
Other – 0

STOCK: Domestic & Import/New & Used

SEARCH: Want lists maintained and requester notified when record comes in

COLLECTIONS: Will buy collections of rare records

PAYMENTS: Money Order, Personal Check

MAIL ORDER: Whatever shipment method requested; Prepayment

DISCOUNTS: I.N.A.

PUBLICATIONS: Not available

SEATTLE

CELLOPHANE SQUARE (I)
1315 Northeast 42nd Street
Seattle 98105
(206) 634-2280

M–S 10:00 A.M.–mid.
S   Noon–8:00

SERVICES: Walk-in Store/Mail Order

SPECIALTIES: Rock, Rock & Roll, Contemporary Jazz, Bop Jazz, Punk Rock/New Wave, Beatles, Disco, Soul, Vocal, Blues, Promotional, Reggae

VOLUME: 33⅓ – 1,000
             45 – 250
             78 – 0
             Other – 0

STOCK: Domestic & Import/New & Used

SEARCH: Want lists maintained and requester notified when record comes in

COLLECTIONS: Will buy collections of rare records

PAYMENTS: Master Charge, Money Order, Personal Check, VISA/Bank-Americard

MAIL ORDER: 4th Class, Whatever shipment method requested; Prepayment

DISCOUNTS: Available

PUBLICATIONS: Planning an auction list for the future

SEATTLE

FILLIPI BOOK AND RECORD SHOP (I)
1351 East Olive Way
Seattle 98122
(206) 682-4266

M   Closed
T–S   10:00–5:30
S   Closed

SERVICES: Walk-in Store/Mail Order

SPECIALTIES: All Major Categories

VOLUME: 33⅓ – 10,000
             45 – 0
             78 – 20,000
             Other – 0

STOCK: Domestic & Import/Used

SEARCH: Not available

COLLECTIONS: Available for purchase

PAYMENTS: Money Order, Personal Check

MAIL ORDER: Whatever shipment method requested; Prepayment

DISCOUNTS: Not available

PUBLICATIONS: Not available

SEATTLE

GOLDEN OLDIES RECORDS (I)
4538 Roosevelt Way Northeast
Seattle 98105
(206) 634-0322

M	Closed
T–F	11:00–5:00
S	11:00–7:00
S	Closed

SERVICES: Walk-in Store/Mail Order

SPECIALTIES: Rock & Roll, Rhythm & Blues, Country & Western, Rockabilly, Elvis, Beatles, Instrumental, Novelty, Hillbilly, Blues

VOLUME:
- 33⅓ – 0
- 45 – 250,000
- 78 – 0
- Other – 0

STOCK: Domestic & Import/New & Used

SEARCH: Available with no service charge; Want lists maintained and requester notified when record comes in

COLLECTIONS: Available for purchase; Will buy collections of rare 45 r.p.m. records

PAYMENTS: Master Charge, Money Order, Personal Charge Account, Personal Check, VISA/BankAmericard

MAIL ORDER: 4th Class; Prepayment

DISCOUNTS: Available

PUBLICATIONS: Free biweekly catalog; Free biweekly auction list

SEATTLE

ROXY MUSIC (I)
4208 University Way Northeast
Seattle 98105
(206) 632-1695

M–S	10:00–8:00
S	Noon–6:00

SERVICES: Walk-in Store/Mail Order

SPECIALTIES: All Major Categories

VOLUME:
- 33⅓ – 25,000
- 45 – 5,000
- 78 – 2,000
- Other – 0

STOCK: Domestic & Import/New & Used

SEARCH: Want lists maintained and requester notified when record comes in

COLLECTIONS: Will buy collections of rare records

PAYMENTS: Master Charge, Money Order, Personal Check, VISA/BankAmericard

MAIL ORDER: Air Mail, 1st Class, 4th Class, U.P.S.; Prepayment

DISCOUNTS: Available

PUBLICATIONS: I.N.A.

SEATTLE

SECOND TIME RECORDS (I)   M–S   10:00–8:00
4141 University Way Northeast   S   Noon–6:00
Seattle 98105
   (206) 632-1698

SERVICES: Walk-in Store/Mail Order   COLLECTIONS: Will buy collections of
SPECIALTIES: All Major Categories   rare records

VOLUME: 33⅓ – 25,000   PAYMENTS: Master Charge, Money
             45 – 5,000   Order, Personal Check, VISA/Bank-
             78 – 2,000   Americard
             Other – 0   MAIL ORDER: Air Mail, 1st Class, 4th
STOCK: Domestic & Import/New &   Class, U.P.S.; Prepayment
Used   DISCOUNTS: Available

SEARCH: Want lists maintained and   PUBLICATIONS: I.N.A.
requester notified when record comes
in

SEATTLE

TOWER RECORDS (II)   M–S   9:00 A.M.–mid.
500 Mercer Street
Seattle 98109
   (206) 283-4456

SERVICES· Walk-in Store/Mail Order   COLLECTIONS: Will not buy collec-
(Limited)   tions of rare records
SPECIALTIES: All Major Categories   PAYMENTS: Master Charge, Money
VOLUME: 33⅓ – 100%   Order, Personal Charge Account,
             45 – 0   VISA/BankAmericard
             78 – 0   MAIL ORDER: 4th Class, U.P.S.; Pre-
             Other – 0   payment
STOCK: Domestic & Import/New   DISCOUNTS: Available
SEARCH: Not available   PUBLICATIONS: Not available

SEATTLE

TOWER RECORDS (II)   M–S   9:00 A.M.–mid.
4321 University Way Northeast
Seattle 98105
   (206) 632-1187

SERVICES: Walk-in Store/Mail Order   COLLECTIONS: Will not buy collec-
(Limited)   tions of rare records

SPECIALTIES: All Major Categories   PAYMENTS: Master Charge, Money
                                      Order, Personal Charge Account,
VOLUME: 33⅓ – 100%   VISA/BankAmericard
            45 – 0
            78 – 0   MAIL ORDER: 4th Class, U.P.S.; Pre-
         Other – 0   payment

STOCK: Domestic & Import/New   DISCOUNTS: Available

SEARCH: Not available   PUBLICATIONS: Not available

SEATTLE

YESTERDAY & TODAY RECORDS (I)   M–S   10:00–8:00
4311½ University Way Northeast   S   Noon–6:00
Seattle 98105
   (206) 632-1693

SERVICES: Walk-in Store/Mail Order   COLLECTIONS: Will buy collections of
                                      rare records
SPECIALTIES: All Major Categories
                                      PAYMENTS: Master Charge, Money
VOLUME: 33⅓ – 25,000   Order, Personal Check, VISA/Bank-
            45 – 5,000   Americard
            78 – 2,000
         Other – 0   MAIL ORDER: Air Mail, 1st Class, 4th
                                      Class, U.P.S.; Prepayment
STOCK: Domestic & Import/New &
Used   DISCOUNTS: Available

SEARCH: Want lists maintained and   PUBLICATIONS: I.N.A.
requester notified when record comes
in

SNOHOMISH

LARRY'S RECORD SHOP (II)   M–F   10:00–5:30
1108 1st Street   S–S   Closed
Snohomish 98290
(206) 568-3554

SERVICES: Walk-in Store/Mail Order

SPECIALTIES: (Alphabetical) Easy Listening, Rock, Rock & Roll, Soul

VOLUME: 33⅓ – I.N.A.
            45   – I.N.A.
            78   – I.N.A.
            Other – I.N.A.

STOCK: Domestic & Import/New & Used

SEARCH: Available with no service charge; Want lists maintained and requester notified when record comes in

COLLECTIONS: Will not buy collections of rare records

PAYMENTS: Money Order

MAIL ORDER: 1st Class, 4th Class; Prepayment

DISCOUNTS: Available

PUBLICATIONS: I.N.A.

TACOMA

WILLIAM O. ROHR SALES COMPANY (I)   M–F   10:00–7:00
10005 Pacific Avenue   S   10:00–6:00
Tacoma 98444   S   Closed
(206) 531-1868

SERVICES: Walk-in Store/Mail Order

SPECIALTIES: (Alphabetical) Bluegrass, Blues, Classical, Contemporary Jazz, Country & Western, Folk, Hillbilly, Rhythm & Blues, Rock, Rock & Roll, Traditional Jazz

VOLUME: 33⅓ – 3,000
            45   – 5,000
            78   – 3,000
            Other – 0

STOCK: Domestic & Import/New & Used

SEARCH: Available with no service charge

COLLECTIONS: Will buy collections of rare records

PAYMENTS: Money Order

MAIL ORDER: 4th Class; Prepayment

DISCOUNTS: Not available

PUBLICATIONS: I.N.A.

TACOMA

TOWER RECORDS (II)   M–S   9:00 A.M.–mid.
2941 South 38th Street
Tacoma 98408
  (206) 475-9222

SERVICES: Walk-in Store/Mail Order   COLLECTIONS: Will not buy collec-
(Limited)   tions of rare records

SPECIALTIES: All Major Categories   PAYMENTS: Master Charge, Money

VOLUME: 33⅓ – 100%   Order, Personal Charge Account,
               45 – 0   VISA/BankAmericard
               78 – 0   MAIL ORDER: 4th Class, U.P.S.; Pre-
            Other – 0   payment

STOCK: Domestic & Import/New   DISCOUNTS: Available

SEARCH: Not available   PUBLICATIONS: Not available

WISCONSIN

MADISON

G'S JAZZ (I)
P.O. Box 9164
Madison 53715
  (608) 274-3527

SERVICES: Mail Order Only   COLLECTIONS: Will buy collections of
                                         rare records
SPECIALTIES: Bop Jazz, Contempo-
rary Jazz, Vocal Jazz, Big Band, Tra-   PAYMENTS: Money Order
ditional Jazz, Dixieland, Swing   MAIL ORDER: Whatever shipment

VOLUME: 33⅓ – 8,500   method requested; Prepayment
               45 – 300   DISCOUNTS: Not available
               78 – 500
            Other – 0   PUBLICATIONS: Free semiannual auc-
                                         tion list
STOCK: Domestic/Used

SEARCH: Want lists maintained and
requester notified when record comes
in

MADISON

SOUND MEMORIES (I)
P.O. Box 2242
Madison 53701
  (608) 251-6035

SERVICES: Mail Order Only

SPECIALTIES: Vocal, Broadway Shows, Sound Tracks, Nostalgia, Television Shows

VOLUME: 33⅓ – 1,000
           45   – 0
           78   – 0
        Other   – 0

STOCK: Domestic/Used

SEARCH: Not available

COLLECTIONS: Will buy collections of rare records

PAYMENTS: Money Order, Personal Check

MAIL ORDER: Air Mail, 4th Class; Prepayment

DISCOUNTS: Not available

PUBLICATIONS: Free semiannual catalog

MILWAUKEE

RADIO DOCTORS AND RECORDS LIMITED (II)
240 West Wells Street
Milwaukee 53203
  (414) 276-6422 or 562-7607

M	9:00–7:00
T–W	9:00–5:30
T–F	9:00–7:00
S	9:00–5:30
S	Closed

SERVICES: Walk-in Store/Mail Order

SPECIALTIES: All Major Categories

VOLUME: 33⅓ – I.N.A.
           45   – I.N.A.
           78   – I.N.A.
        Other   – I.N.A.

STOCK: Domestic & Import/New

SEARCH: Available with no service charge

COLLECTIONS: Will not buy collections of rare records

PAYMENTS: Master Charge, Money Order, Personal Check, VISA/BankAmericard

MAIL ORDER: Air Mail, 3rd Class, U.P.S.; Prepayment or C.O.D.

DISCOUNTS: Available

PUBLICATIONS: I.N.A.

MILWAUKEE

YESTERDAY'S MEMORIES BOOK AND OLD   M–S   1:00–9:00
  RECORD SHOP (I)
5406 West Center Street
Milwaukee 53210
  (414) 444-6210

SERVICES: Walk-in Store/Mail Order

SPECIALTIES: (Alphabetical) Bluegrass, Blues, Classical, Contemporary Jazz, Country & Western, Easy Listening, Folk, Hillbilly, Opera, Religious, Rhythm & Blues, Rock & Roll, Soul, Traditional Jazz

VOLUME: 33⅓ – 3,000
          45   – 4,000
          78   – 10,000
      Other – 0

STOCK: Domestic/Used

SEARCH: Available with no service charge; Want lists maintained and requester notified when record comes in

COLLECTIONS: Will buy collections of rare records

PAYMENTS: Money Order

MAIL ORDER: 1st Class; Prepayment

DISCOUNTS: Available

PUBLICATIONS: I.N.A.

WYOMING

CHEYENNE

BUDGET TAPES AND RECORDS (II)   M–F   11:00–8:00
110 16th Street   S   11:00–6:00
Cheyenne 82001   S   Closed
  (307) 634-8347

SERVICES: Walk-in Store/Mail Order (Limited)

SPECIALTIES: (Alphabetical) Bluegrass, Blues, Comedy, Contemporary Jazz, Country & Western, Disco, Easy Listening, Folk, Rhythm & Blues, Rock & Roll, Soul, Traditional Jazz

VOLUME: 33⅓ – 250
          45   – 0
          78   – 0
      Other – 0

STOCK: Domestic & Import/New

SEARCH: Want lists maintained and requester notified when record comes in

COLLECTIONS: Will not buy collections of rare records

PAYMENTS: Money Order

MAIL ORDER: 4th Class, U.P.S.; Prepayment

DISCOUNTS: Available

PUBLICATIONS: I.N.A.

AUSTRALIAN RECORD DEALERS

VICTORIA

CARLTON

MONDO MUSIC (II)
304 Lygon Street
Carlton 3053
(03) 347-1030

M–T	9:00–6:00
F	9:00–9:00
S	8:30–1:00
S	Closed

SERVICES: Walk-in Store/Mail Order

SPECIALTIES: (Alphabetical) Blues, Classical, Country & Western, Disco, Ethnic, Folk, Opera, Reggae, Religious, Rhythm & Blues, Rock & Roll, Soul, Traditional Jazz

VOLUME:
33⅓ – 50%
45 – 50%
78 – 0
Other – 0

STOCK: Domestic & Import/New & Used

SEARCH: Available with no service charge; Want lists maintained and requester notified when record comes in

COLLECTIONS: Will not buy collections of rare records

PAYMENTS: Money Order, Personal Check

MAIL ORDER: Air Mail, 1st Class; C.O.D.

DISCOUNTS: Not available

PUBLICATIONS: I.N.A.

CARLTON

READINGS RECORDS AND BOOKS (I)
366 Lygon Street
Carlton 3053
(03) 347-7473

M–T	10:00–6:00
F	10:00–9:00
S	9:00–1:00
S	Closed

SERVICES: Walk-in Store/Mail Order

SPECIALTIES: Rock, Punk Rock/New Wave, British Musical Shows, Broadway Shows, Film Scores, Sound Tracks, Classical, Folk, Country & Western, Feminist, Blues, Reggae, Beatles

VOLUME:
33⅓ – 2,000
45 – 0
78 – 0
Other – 0

STOCK: Domestic & Import/New & Used

SEARCH: Available with no service charge; Want lists maintained and requester notified when record comes in

COLLECTIONS: Will buy collections of rare records

PAYMENTS: Money Order, Personal Check

MAIL ORDER: Whatever shipment method requested; Prepayment

DISCOUNTS: Not available

PUBLICATIONS: Free quarterly catalog

234

HAWTHORN

READINGS RECORDS AND BOOKS (I)	M–T	10:00–6:00
710 Glenferrie Road	F	10:00–9:00
Hawthorn	S	9:00–1:00
Telephone: (03) 819–1917	S	Closed

SERVICES: Walk-in Store/Mail Order

SPECIALTIES: Rock, Punk Rock/New Wave, British Musical Shows, Broadway Shows, Film Scores, Sound Tracks, Classical, Folk, Country & Western, Feminist, Blues, Reggae, Beatles

VOLUME: 33⅓ – 2,000
          45   – 0
          78   – 0
          Other – 0

STOCK: Domestic & Import/New & Used

SEARCH: Available with no service charge; Want lists maintained and requester notified when record comes in

COLLECTIONS: Will buy collections of rare records

PAYMENTS: Money Order, Personal Check

MAIL ORDER: Whatever shipment method requested; Prepayment

DISCOUNTS: Not available

PUBLICATIONS: Free quarterly catalog

SOUTH YARRA

READINGS RECORDS AND BOOKS (I)	M–T	10:00–6:00
Corner Toorak Road and Davis Avenue	F	10:00–9:00
South Yarra	S	9:00–1:00
Telephone: (03) 267–1885	S	Closed

SERVICES: Walk-in Store/Mail Order

SPECIALTIES: Rock, Punk Rock/New Wave, British Musical Shows, Broadway Shows, Film Scores, Sound Tracks, Classical, Folk, Country & Western, Feminist, Blues, Reggae, Beatles

VOLUME: 33⅓ – 2,000
          45   – 0
          78   – 0
          Other – 0

STOCK: Domestic & Import/New & Used

SEARCH: Available with no service charge; Want lists maintained and requester notified when record comes in

COLLECTIONS: Will buy collections of rare records

PAYMENTS: Money Order, Personal Check

MAIL ORDER: Whatever shipment method requested; Prepayment

DISCOUNTS: Not available

PUBLICATIONS: Free quarterly catalog

WESTERN AUSTRALIA

PERTH

78 RECORDS (II)	M–W	9:00–6:00
843 Hay Street	T	9:00–9:00
Perth 6000	F	9:00–6:00
(09) 322-6384	S	9:00–1:00
	S	Closed

SERVICES: Walk-in Store/Mail Order

SPECIALTIES: Rock, Contemporary Jazz, Traditional Jazz, Soul, Blues, Country & Western, Bluegrass, Folk, Ethnic, Disco, Reggae, Comedy

VOLUME: 33⅓ – 100%
            45 – 0
            78 – 0
         Other – 0

STOCK: Domestic & Import/New & Used

SEARCH: Available with no service charge

COLLECTIONS: I.N.A.

PAYMENTS: Bank Check, Money Order, Personal Check

MAIL ORDER: Air Mail, Whatever shipment method requested; Prepayment

DISCOUNTS: Not available

PUBLICATIONS: Not available

BRITISH RECORD DEALERS
ENGLAND

BEXHILL-ON-SEA

FLYRIGHT RECORDS (I)
c/o Swift Record Exports
20 Endwell Road
Bexhill-On-Sea
East Sussex
  (0424) 214-390
  Telex: 957082 Swift

SERVICES: Mail Order Only

SPECIALTIES: Contemporary Jazz, Bop Jazz, Rock & Roll, Rockabilly, Rhythm & Blues, Country & Western, Ethnic, Folk, Nostalgia, Sound Tracks, Vocal

VOLUME: 33⅓ – 28,000
            45   – 10,000
            78   – 0
            Other – 0

STOCK: Domestic & Import/New

SEARCH: Not available

COLLECTIONS: Not available for purchase

PAYMENTS: Consult for arrangements

MAIL ORDER: Air Mail, 1st Class, Sea Freight; Consult for arrangements

DISCOUNTS: I.N.A.

PUBLICATIONS: Free monthly catalog

BIRKENHEAD

SKELETON RECORDS (I)
46 Argyle Street
Birkenhead
Merseyside
  (051) 647-9650 or 4505

M–S	10:00–6:00
S	Closed

SERVICES: Walk-in Store/Mail Order

SPECIALTIES: (Alphabetical) Beatles, Bluegrass, Contemporary Jazz, Country & Western, Disco, Elvis, Punk Rock/New Wave, Reggae, Rhythm & Blues, Rock, Rock & Roll

VOLUME: 33⅓ – 10,000
            45   – 5,000
            78   – 0
            Other – 0

STOCK: Domestic & Import/New & Used

SEARCH: Available with no service charge; Want lists maintained and requester notified when record comes in

COLLECTIONS: Available for purchase; Will buy collections of rare records

PAYMENTS: Money Order, Personal Check

MAIL ORDER: Air Mail, 1st Class, 2nd Class; Prepayment

DISCOUNTS: Available

PUBLICATIONS: Free periodic catalog; Free quarterly set-sale list

237

BLACKPOOL

ALAN POWER RECORDS (I)
57 St. Heliers Road
Blackpool
Lancashire
  Telephone: I.N.A.

SERVICES: Mail Order Only

SPECIALTIES: (Alphabetical) Blue-
grass, Blues, Contemporary Jazz,
Country & Western, Hillbilly,
Rhythm & Blues, Rock & Roll

VOLUME: 33⅓ – 0
            45   – 5,000
            78   – 1,500
            Other – 0

STOCK: Domestic & Import/New &
Used

SEARCH: Not available; Want lists
maintained and requester notified
when record comes in

COLLECTIONS: Will buy collections of
rare records

PAYMENTS: Money Order, Personal
Check

MAIL ORDER: Air Mail, Parcel Post;
Prepayment

DISCOUNTS: Not available

PUBLICATIONS: I.N.A.

BRIGHTON

THE RECORD ALBUM (I)
34 North Road
Brighton BN1 1YB
Sussex
  (0273) 605-022

M–S	10:00–5:30
S	Closed

SERVICES: Walk-in Store/Mail Order

SPECIALTIES: Rock, Film Scores,
Sound Tracks, Standards, Bop Jazz,
Classical, Big Band, Rhythm & Blues,
Country & Western, Instrumental,
Bluegrass, Vocal

VOLUME: 33⅓ – 30,000
            45   – 1,000
            78   – 0
            Other – 0

STOCK: Domestic & Import/New &
Used

SEARCH: Not available; Want lists
maintained and requester notified
when record comes in

COLLECTIONS: Available for purchase

PAYMENTS: Personal Check

MAIL ORDER: Air Mail; Prepayment

DISCOUNTS: Not available

PUBLICATIONS: Not available

CHADDERTON

DALTON MAIL SALES (I)   M–F   9:30–6:00
65 Coalshawgreen Road   S   9:30–5:30
Chadderton   S   Closed
Oldham
Lancashire
  (061) 620-7279

SERVICES: Walk-in Store/Mail Order

SPECIALTIES: (Alphabetical) Classical, Country & Western, Disco, Easy Listening, Folk, Reggae, Rock, Rock & Roll, Soul

VOLUME: 33⅓ – 8,000
            45   – 5,000
            78   – 0
          Other – 0

STOCK: Domestic & Import/New

SEARCH: Want lists maintained and requester notified when record comes in

COLLECTIONS: Will not buy collections of rare records

PAYMENTS: Money Order, Personal Check

MAIL ORDER: 2nd Class; Prepayment

DISCOUNTS: Available

PUBLICATIONS: I.N.A.

CHIGWELL

M. J. G. MOIR RECORDS (I)
25 Manor Road
Chigwell
Essex
  (01) 504-1966

SERVICES: Walk-in Store (By Appointment)/Mail Order (By Special Arrangement)

SPECIALTIES: Classical, Instrumental, Opera, Vocal, English Singers, Military Bands, Royal, Fifties, Popular

VOLUME: 33⅓ – 4,000
            45   – 1,000
            78   – 20,000
          Other – 0

STOCK: Domestic & Import/Used

SEARCH: Available with no service charge (by special arrangement); Want lists maintained and requester notified when record comes in (by special arrangement)

COLLECTIONS: Will buy collections of rare records

PAYMENTS: Money Order, Personal Check

MAIL ORDER: By special arrangement only

DISCOUNTS: Not available

PUBLICATIONS: Not available

EPSOM

DISCO EPSOM LIMITED (I)
45 Burgh Heath Road
Epsom
Surrey
  (01) 940-1988

SERVICES: Mail Order Only

SPECIALTIES: Classical, Opera

VOLUME: 33⅓ – 5,000
             45   – 0
             78   – 100,000
             Other – 0

STOCK: Domestic & Import/New & Used

SEARCH: Available with service charge; Want lists maintained and requester notified when record comes in

COLLECTIONS: Will buy collections of rare records

PAYMENTS: Money Order, Personal Check

MAIL ORDER: Air Mail, Parcel Post; Prepayment

DISCOUNTS: Available

PUBLICATIONS: I.N.A.

HARROW

DON RECORDS (I)
100 Hindes Road
Harrow
Middlesex HA1 1RP
  Telephone: I.N.A.

SERVICES: Mail Order Only

SPECIALTIES: (Alphabetical) Country & Western, Hillbilly, Old-Time Country, Rhythm & Blues

VOLUME: 33⅓ – 0
             45   – 2,000
             78   – 300
             Other – 0

STOCK: Domestic & Import/New & Used

SEARCH: Want lists maintained and requester notified when record comes in

COLLECTIONS: Will buy collections of rare records

PAYMENTS: Money Order

MAIL ORDER: Whatever shipment method requested; Prepayment

DISCOUNTS: Not available

PUBLICATIONS: Free semiannual auction list

HIGH WYCOMBE

S. J. PARKER RECORDS (I)
19 Kingsley Crescent
High Wycombe HP11 2VL
Buckinghamshire
  (0494) 23528

SERVICES: Mail Order Only

SPECIALTIES: Rock & Roll, Rock-
abilly, Instrumental, Surfing, Country
& Western, Rhythm & Blues, Rock,
Soul, Elvis, Blues

VOLUME: 33⅓ – 5,000
           45 – 5,000
           78 – 0
           Other – 0

STOCK: Domestic & Import/New &
Used

SEARCH: Available with service
charge

COLLECTIONS: Will buy collections of
rare records

PAYMENTS: Money Order, Personal
Check

MAIL ORDER: Air Mail, 1st Class,
Whatever shipment method requested;
Prepayment

DISCOUNTS: Not available

PUBLICATIONS: Free occasional auction list

LIVERPOOL

E. J. BEATTIE RECORDS (I)
82 Vandyke Street
Liverpool L8 0RT
  Telephone: I.N.A.

SERVICES: Mail Order Only

SPECIALTIES: (Alphabetical) Country
& Western, Disco, Easy Listening,
Reggae, Rock, Rock & Roll

VOLUME: 33⅓ – 0
           45 – 30,000
           78 – 0
           Other – 0

STOCK: Domestic/Used

SEARCH: Want lists maintained and
requester notified when record comes
in

COLLECTIONS: Will buy collections of
rare records

PAYMENTS: Money Order, Personal
Check

MAIL ORDER: Air Mail, 2nd Class;
Prepayment

DISCOUNTS: Available

PUBLICATIONS: I.N.A.

LONDON

| CHARMDALE RECORD DISTRIBUTORS | M–S | 9:30–6:00 |
| LIMITED (II) | S | Closed |

182 Acton Lane
London NW 10
(01) 961-9331
Telex: 931-945 Hetrec

SERVICES: Walk-in Store Only

SPECIALTIES: (Alphabetical) Bluegrass, Blues, Contemporary Jazz, Country & Western, Disco, Easy Listening, Folk, Punk Rock/New Wave, Reggae, Rhythm & Blues, Rock & Roll, Soul

VOLUME: 33⅓ – 500,000
         45   – 250,000
         78   – 0
         Other – 0

STOCK: Domestic & Import/New & Used

SEARCH: Not available

COLLECTIONS: Will not buy collections of rare records

PAYMENTS: Money Order

MAIL ORDER: Not available

DISCOUNTS: Available

PUBLICATIONS: Free periodic catalog available

LONDON

COLLECTOR'S CORNER (I)	M–F	10:00–6:00
63 Monmouth Street	S	10:00–1:00
London WC 2	S	Closed

(01) 836-5614

SERVICES: Walk-in Store/Mail Order

SPECIALTIES: (Alphabetical) Classical, Nostalgia, Opera

VOLUME: 33⅓ – 4,000
         45   – 100
         78   – 2,500
         Other – 0

STOCK: Domestic & Import/New & Used

SEARCH: Not available

COLLECTIONS: Will buy collections of rare records

PAYMENTS: Money Order, Personal Check

MAIL ORDER: 1st Class; Prepayment

DISCOUNTS: Not available

PUBLICATIONS: I.N.A.

LONDON

COLLECTOR'S CORNER (I)
62 New Oxford Street
London WC 1
(01) 580-6155

M–F		10:00–6:00
S		10:00–1:00
S		Closed

SERVICES: Walk-in Store/Mail Order

SPECIALTIES: (Alphabetical) Classical, Nostalgia, Opera

VOLUME:
33⅓ – 4,000
45 – 100
78 – 2,500
Other – 0

STOCK: Domestic & Import/New & Used

SEARCH: Not available

COLLECTIONS: Will buy collections of rare records

PAYMENTS: Money Order, Personal Check

MAIL ORDER: 1st Class; Prepayment

DISCOUNTS: Not available

PUBLICATIONS: I.N.A.

LONDON

COLLETS RECORD SHOP (I)
180 Shaftesbury Avenue
London WC2H 8JS
(01) 240-3969

M–F		10:00–6:00
S		10:00–4:00
S		Closed

SERVICES: Walk-in Store/Mail Order

SPECIALTIES: Contemporary Jazz, Folk, Bop Jazz, Ethnic, Blues, Old-Time Country, Swing, Traditional Jazz, Bluegrass, Political

VOLUME:
33⅓ – 1,000
45 – 100
78 – 500
Other – 0

STOCK: Domestic & Import/New & Used

SEARCH: Occasionally available with no service charge

COLLECTIONS: Available for purchase

PAYMENTS: Money Order, Personal Check

MAIL ORDER: Whatever shipment method requested; Prepayment

DISCOUNTS: Not available

PUBLICATIONS: Not available

LONDON

JAMES H. CRAWLEY RECORDS (I)
246 Church Street
Edmonton
London N9 9HQ
  (01) 807-7760

SERVICES: Walk-in Store (By Appointment)/Mail Order

SPECIALTIES: (Alphabetical) Classical, Opera, Personalities

VOLUME: 33⅓ – 1,000
            45   – 0
            78   – 500,000
          Other – 0

STOCK: Domestic & Import/New & Used

SEARCH: Available with service charge

COLLECTIONS: Will buy collections of rare records

PAYMENTS: Money Order, Personal Check

MAIL ORDER: Air Mail, 1st Class; Prepayment

DISCOUNTS: Not available

PUBLICATIONS: I.N.A.

LONDON

CURIOS (I)   M–S   11:00–6:00
453 Edgware Road   S   Closed
London W 9

SERVICES: Walk-in Store/Mail Order

SPECIALTIES: Beat, Rock & Roll

VOLUME: 33⅓ – 650
            45   – 8,000
            78   – 0
          Other – 0

STOCK: Domestic/New

SEARCH: Available with no service charge; Want lists maintained and requester notified when record comes in

COLLECTIONS: Will buy collections of rare records

PAYMENTS: Money Order, Personal Check

MAIL ORDER: Air Mail, 2nd Class; Prepayment

DISCOUNTS: Not available

PUBLICATIONS: I.N.A.

LONDON

DOBELL'S JAZZ & BLUES RECORD   M–S   10:00–7:00
   SHOP LTD. (I)   S   Closed
75/77 Charing Cross Road
London WC2H OAA
   (01) 437-4197

SERVICES: Walk-in Store/Mail Order

SPECIALTIES: Contemporary Jazz, Mainstream Jazz, Jazz Reissues, Traditional Jazz, Blues, Folk, Dixieland, Bop Jazz, Big Band, Swing

VOLUME: 33⅓ – 10,000
          45   – 0
          78   – 500
     Other   – 0

STOCK: Domestic & Import/New & Used

SEARCH: Not available

COLLECTIONS: Not available for purchase

PAYMENTS: Bank check in pounds sterling; Personal Check

MAIL ORDER: Whatever shipment method requested; Prepayment

DISCOUNTS: Available

PUBLICATIONS: Free periodic catalogs available

LONDON

GRAMOPHONE EXCHANGE LIMITED (I)   M–F   9:30–5:30
80–82 Wardour Street   S   9:30–1:00
London W1V 43D   S   Closed
   (01) 437-5313 or 5314

SERVICES: Walk-in Store/Mail Order

SPECIALTIES: (Alphabetical) Classical, Opera, Religious, Spoken Word, Vocal

VOLUME: 33⅓ – 40%
          45   – 0
          78   – 60%
     Other   – 0

STOCK: Domestic & Import/New & Used

SEARCH: Not available

COLLECTIONS: Will buy collections of rare records

PAYMENTS: Money Order, Personal Check, VISA/BankAmericard

MAIL ORDER: Air Mail, 1st Class; Prepayment

DISCOUNTS: Available

PUBLICATIONS: Free monthly catalog; Free quarterly set-sale list

LONDON

M. J. G. MOIR RECORDS (I)
8 Phoenix House
104/110 Charing Cross Road
London WC2H 0JN
(01) 836-3264

SERVICES: Walk-in Store (By Appointment Only)/Mail Order (By Special Arrangement)

SPECIALTIES: Classical, Instrumental, Opera, Vocal, English Singers, Military Bands, Royal, Fifties, Popular

VOLUME: 33⅓ – 4,000
          45 – 1,000
          78 – 20,000
    Other – 0

STOCK: Domestic & Import/Used

SEARCH: Available with no service charge (by special arrangement); Want lists maintained and requester notified when record comes in (by special arrangement)

COLLECTIONS: Will buy collections of rare records

PAYMENTS: Money Order, Personal Check

MAIL ORDER: By special arrangement only

DISCOUNTS: Not available

PUBLICATIONS: Not available

LONDON

MOONDOGS RECORD STORE (I)
400–A High Street North
Manor Park
London E12
(01) 552-0809

M	Noon–6:00	F	Noon–6:00
T	Closed	S	11:00–6:00
W	Noon–6:00	S	Closed
T	Closed		

SERVICES: Walk-in Store/Mail Order

SPECIALTIES: Rock & Roll, Rhythm & Blues, Rockabilly, Elvis, Hillbilly, Country & Western, Soul, Blues, Rock, Beatles

VOLUME: 33⅓ – 10,000
          45 – 70,000
          78 – 5,000
    Other – 0

STOCK: Domestic & Import/New & Used

SEARCH: Want lists maintained and requester notified when record comes in

COLLECTIONS: Will buy collections of rare records

PAYMENTS: Money Order, Personal Check

MAIL ORDER: 2nd Class, Whatever shipment method requested; Prepayment or C.O.D.

DISCOUNTS: Available

PUBLICATIONS: Free quarterly catalog available

LONDON

OASIS RECORDS (I)
c/o Mr. Tim Oake
18 Newport Court
London WC2H 7JS
(01) 734-0795

M–S   11:00–7:00
S   Closed

SERVICES: Walk-in Store/Mail Order

SPECIALTIES: (Alphabetical) Bluegrass, Contemporary Jazz, Disco, Ethnic, Folk, Folk-Rock, Reggae, Rhythm & Blues, Rock, Soul

VOLUME: 33⅓ – 1,000
            45 – 150
            78 – 0
        Other – 0

STOCK: Domestic & Import/New & Used

SEARCH: Available with no service charge; Want lists maintained and requester notified when record comes in

COLLECTIONS: Will buy collections of rare records

PAYMENTS: Money Order, Personal Check

MAIL ORDER: Air Mail, 1st Class; Prepayment

DISCOUNTS: Available

PUBLICATIONS: I.N.A.

LONDON

OPERA RARA RECORD CLUB (I)
8 Haverstock Street
Islington
London N1
(01) 253-1618

SERVICES: Mail Order Only

SPECIALTIES: Rare Opera

VOLUME: 33⅓ – I.N.A.
            45 – I.N.A.
            78 – I.N.A.
        Other – 0

STOCK: Domestic/New

SEARCH: Not available

COLLECTIONS: I.N.A.

PAYMENTS: Money Order, Personal Check

MAIL ORDER: Whatever shipment method requested; Prepayment

DISCOUNTS: Available

PUBLICATIONS: Not available

LONDON

SAILOR VERNON RECORDS (I)
Ora-Nelle Villas
19 Brockenhurst Gardens
Mill Hill
London NW7 2JY
  (01) 959-5347

SERVICES: Walk-in Store (By Appointment)/Mail Order

SPECIALTIES: Blues, Rhythm & Blues, Pre-War Jazz 78's, Rock, Soul, Rock & Roll, Gospel/Sacred, Rockabilly, Old-Time Country, Hillbilly, Dance, Country & Western, Cajun

VOLUME: 33⅓ – 500
           45 – 5,000
           78 – 3,000
           Other – 0

STOCK: Domestic & Import/New & Used

SEARCH: Not available

COLLECTIONS: Will buy collections of rare records

PAYMENTS: Money Order, Personal Check

MAIL ORDER: Whatever shipment method requested; Prepayment

DISCOUNTS: Available

PUBLICATIONS: Quarterly catalog/ magazine; Quarterly auction list; Quarterly set-sale list; [Cost I.N.A.]

LONDON

S. P. & S. RECORDS (LONDON) LIMITED (II)   M–F   8:30–5:00
Hega House   S–S   Closed
Ullin Street
London E14 6PN
  (01) 987-3812 or 2386
  Telex: 8951427 Spsldn

SERVICES: Walk-in Store/Mail Order (Trade Enquiries Only)

SPECIALTIES: All Major Categories

VOLUME: 33⅓ – 1,500,000
           45 – 0
           78 – 0
           Other – 0

STOCK: Domestic & Import/New

SEARCH: Not available

COLLECTIONS: Will not buy collections of rare records

PAYMENTS: Consult for arrangements

MAIL ORDER: Consult for arrangements

DISCOUNTS: Consult for arrangements

PUBLICATIONS: I.N.A.

LONDON

HENRY STAVE AND COMPANY (I)
11 Great Marlborough Street
London W1
  (01) 734-2092
  Telex: 27950 Mono Ref 1006

M–S   10:00–6:00
S   Closed

SERVICES: Walk-in Store/Mail Order

SPECIALTIES: Classical, Opera

VOLUME: 33⅓ – 8,000
               45   – 0
               78   – 0
           Other   – 0

STOCK: Domestic & Import/New & Used

SEARCH: Available with no service charge

COLLECTIONS: Will buy collections of rare records

PAYMENTS: American Express, Diners Club, Master Charge, Personal Charge Account, Personal Check, VISA/BankAmericard

MAIL ORDER: Air Mail, Parcel Post; Prepayment

DISCOUNTS: Not available

PUBLICATIONS: I.N.A.

LONDON

SUMMIT RECORDS (I)
20 Baker Street
London W1
  Telephone: I.N.A.

M–S   10:30–6:30
S   Closed

SERVICES: Walk-in Store/Mail Order

SPECIALTIES: Rock, Promotional, Punk Rock/New Wave, Contemporary Jazz, Reggae, Rhythm & Blues, Traditional Jazz, Blues, Folk, Rock & Roll

VOLUME: 33⅓ – 1,000
               45   – 0
               78   – 0
           Other   – 0

STOCK: Domestic & Import/New & Used

SEARCH: Want lists maintained and requester notified when record comes in

COLLECTIONS: Available for purchase; Will buy collections of rare records

PAYMENTS: Money Order, Personal Check

MAIL ORDER: Whatever shipment method requested; Prepayment

DISCOUNTS: Not available

PUBLICATIONS: Not available

LONDON

SUPERDISC (II)   M–S   10:00–5:30
330 Norwood Road   S   Closed
West Norwood
London SE27 9AF
(01) 761-2292

SERVICES: Walk-in Store/Mail Order   COLLECTIONS: Not available for pur-
SPECIALTIES: All Major Categories   chase
VOLUME: 33⅓ – 75%   PAYMENTS: Money Order
           45 – 25%   MAIL ORDER: Whatever shipment
           78 – 0   method requested; Prepayment
           Other – 0   DISCOUNTS: Not available
STOCK: Domestic & Import/New   PUBLICATIONS: Free semiannual cata-
SEARCH: Not available   log; Free periodic auction list

LONDON

THE TALKING MACHINE (I)   M–F   2:30–6:00
30 Watford Way   S   11:00–5:30
Hendon   S   Closed
London NW4
(01) 202-3473

SERVICES: Walk-in Store Only   SEARCH: Not available
SPECIALTIES: All Major Categories   COLLECTIONS: Available for purchase;
VOLUME: 33⅓ – 0   Will buy collections of rare 78 r.p.m.
           45 – 0   records
           78 – 6,000   PAYMENTS: Money Order
           Other – Edison   MAIL ORDER: Not available
                   Diamond   DISCOUNTS: Not available
                   Discs/Cylinders   PUBLICATIONS: Not available
STOCK: Domestic & Import/Used

LONDON

THAT'S ENTERTAINMENT II (I)   M–S   10:00–7:00
11 Drury Lane   S   Closed
Drury Lane Hotel Precinct
London WC 2
  (01) 240-2227

SERVICES: Walk-in Store/Mail Order

SPECIALTIES: British Musical Shows, Broadway Shows, Sound Tracks, Film Scores, Vocal, Sinatra, Nostalgia, Personalities, Television Shows, Comedy

VOLUME: 33⅓ – 2,500
             45 – 0
             78 – 0
             Other – 0

STOCK: Domestic & Import/New & Used

SEARCH: Available with no service charge; Want lists maintained and requester notified when record comes in

COLLECTIONS: Will buy collections of rare records

PAYMENTS: American Express, Carte Blanche, Diners Club, Master Charge, Money Order, VISA/BankAmericard

MAIL ORDER: Air Mail, 1st Class, 2nd Class; Whatever shipment method requested; Prepayment

DISCOUNTS: Not available

PUBLICATIONS: Not available

LONDON

MICHAEL THOMAS RECORDS (I)   M–F   11:00–6:00
54 Lymington Road   S   11:00–4:00
London NW 6   S   Closed
  (01) 435-1476

SERVICES: Walk-in Store/Mail Order

SPECIALTIES: Classical Opera

VOLUME: 33⅓ – 100%
             45 – 0
             78 – 0
             Other – 0

STOCK: Domestic & Import/New & Used

SEARCH: Available with no service charge

COLLECTIONS: Will buy collections of rare records

PAYMENTS: Money Order, Personal Check

MAIL ORDER: Air Mail, 1st Class; Prepayment

DISCOUNTS: Not available

PUBLICATIONS: I.N.A.

LONDON

TUMBLEWEED CONNECTION (II)
5 (Basement) Picton Place
London W1
   Telephone: I.N.A.

M		Closed
T–S		10:30–6:30
S		Closed

SERVICES: Walk-in Store/Mail Order

SPECIALTIES: (Alphabetical) Blues, Disco, Easy Listening, Folk, Folk-Rock, Reggae, Rhythm & Blues, Rock, Rock & Roll, Soul

VOLUME: 33⅓ – 160
            45   – 180
            78   – 0
         Other – 0

STOCK: Domestic & Import/New & Used

SEARCH: Available with no service charge; Want lists maintained and requester notified when record comes in

COLLECTIONS: Will buy collections of rare records

PAYMENTS: Money Order, Personal Check

MAIL ORDER: Air Mail, 2nd Class; Prepayment

DISCOUNTS: Available

PUBLICATIONS: I.N.A.

MANCHESTER

RARE RECORDS LIMITED (I)
36 John Dalton Street
Manchester M2 6LE
   (061) 832-7344 or 7345

M–S		9:15–5:30
S		Closed

SERVICES: Walk-in Store/Mail Order

SPECIALTIES: All Major Categories

VOLUME: 33⅓ – 50%
            45   – 50%
            78   – 0
         Other – 0

STOCK: Domestic & Import/New & Used

SEARCH: Available with service charge

COLLECTIONS: Will not buy collections of rare records

PAYMENTS: Money Order, Personal Check

MAIL ORDER: Air Mail, 1st Class, 2nd Class; Prepayment

DISCOUNTS: Available

PUBLICATIONS: I.N.A.

SOUTHEND-ON-SEA

RECORD MART (I)
96–D Southchurch Road
Southend-On-Sea
Essex SS1 2LX
  Southend 611-856

M–T	10:00–6:00
W	Closed
T–S	10:00–6:00
S	Closed

SERVICES: Walk-in Store/Mail Order

SPECIALTIES: (Alphabetical) Elvis, Nostalgia, Rhythm & Blues, Rock & Roll, Rockabilly

VOLUME: 33⅓ – 25%
          45 – 50%
          78 – 25%
    Other – 0

STOCK: Domestic & Import/New & Used

SEARCH: Available with no service charge

COLLECTIONS: Will buy collections of rare records

PAYMENTS: Money Order, Personal Check

MAIL ORDER: Whatever shipment method requested; Prepayment

DISCOUNTS: Not available

PUBLICATIONS: Monthly catalog available for $11.00 per year

TWICKENHAM

THE OLD RECORD (I)
1–A May Road
Twickenham TW2 6QW
Middlesex
  (01) 894-7746

M–W	10:00–5:00
T	Closed
F–S	10:00–5:00
S	Closed

SERVICES: Walk-in Store/Mail Order

SPECIALTIES: (Alphabetical) Classical, Historical, Instrumental, Vocal

VOLUME: 33⅓ – 5,000
          45 – 0
          78 – 100,000
    Other – 0

STOCK: Domestic & Import/Used

SEARCH: Not available

COLLECTIONS: Will buy collections of rare records

PAYMENTS: Money Order, Personal Check

MAIL ORDER: Whatever shipment method requested; Prepayment

DISCOUNTS: Not available

PUBLICATIONS: Free annual catalog

YORK

SONGS AND STORIES (I)   M–S   9:00–5:30
2 & 2ᵃ Low Ousegate   S   Closed
York
  (0904) 31929

SERVICES: Walk-in Store Only

SPECIALTIES: (Alphabetical) Beatles, Chamber Music, Classical, Country & Western, Disco, Opera, Organ, Popular, Punk Rock/New Wave, Rock, Rock & Roll, Vocal

VOLUME: 33⅓ – 2,500
           45 – 0
           78 – 0
         Other – 0

STOCK: Domestic & Import/New & Used

SEARCH: Want lists maintained and requester notified when record comes in

COLLECTIONS: Will buy collections of rare records

PAYMENTS: Money Order, Personal Check, VISA/BankAmericard

MAIL ORDER: Not available

DISCOUNTS: I.N.A.

PUBLICATIONS: Not available

IRELAND

DUBLIN

DISC FINDER (I)   M–S   10:00–6:00
147 Lower Baggot Street   S   Closed
Dublin 2
  Dublin 760-429

SERVICES: Walk-in Store/Mail Order

SPECIALTIES: Popular, Rock, Classical, Easy Listening, Contemporary Jazz, Traditional Jazz, Opera, Punk Rock/New Wave, Sound Tracks, Comedy, Folk

VOLUME: 33⅓ – 100%
           45 – 0
           78 – 0
         Other – 0

STOCK: Domestic & Import/New

SEARCH: Available with no service charge; Want lists maintained and requester notified when record comes in

COLLECTIONS: Available for purchase

PAYMENTS: Will buy collections of rare records

MAIL ORDER: Whatever shipment method requested; Prepayment or C.O.D.

DISCOUNTS: Available

PUBLICATIONS: Not available

DUN LAOGHAIRE

MURRAYS RECORD CENTRE (II)   M–S   9:30–6:00
71 Upper Georges Street   S   Closed
Dun Laoghaire
County Dublin
(01) 801-402

SERVICES: Walk-in Store/Mail Order

SPECIALTIES: (Alphabetical) Blues, Classical, Contemporary Jazz, Country & Western, Disco, Folk, Opera, Religious, Rhythm & Blues, Rock & Roll, Soul, Traditional Jazz

VOLUME: 33⅓ – I.N.A.
             45 – I.N.A.
             78 – I.N.A.
             Other – I.N.A.

STOCK: Domestic & Import/New & Used

SEARCH: Available with no service charge; Want lists maintained and requester notified when record comes in

COLLECTIONS: Will buy collections of rare records

PAYMENTS: Money Order, Personal Check

MAIL ORDER: Air Mail, 1st Class; Prepayment

DISCOUNTS: Not available

PUBLICATIONS: I.N.A.

ISLE OF WIGHT

RYDE

D. HALL RECORDS (I)   M–S   9:00 A.M.–10:00 P.M.
Flat 5
Nelson House
Nelson Street
Ryde
 Ryde 66770

SERVICES: Walk-in Store/Mail Order

SPECIALTIES: (Alphabetical) Bluegrass, Country & Western, Easy Listening, Folk, Hillbilly, Reggae, Rhythm & Blues, Rock, Rock & Roll

VOLUME: 33⅓ – 100%
             45 – 0
             78 – 0
             Other – 0

STOCK: Domestic & Import/New & Used

SEARCH: Available with no service charge; Want lists maintained and requester notified when record comes in

COLLECTIONS: Will buy collections of rare records

PAYMENTS: American Express, Money Order, Personal Charge Account, Personal Check

MAIL ORDER: Whatever shipment method requested; Prepayment

DISCOUNTS: Available

PUBLICATIONS: Free periodic catalog

CANADIAN RECORD DEALERS
BRITISH COLUMBIA
NORTH VANCOUVER

FRIENDS RECORDS (I)
741 Lonsdale Avenue
North Vancouver V7M 2G9
(604) 980-6933

M–S   11:00–6:00
S   2:00–5:00

SERVICES: Walk-in Store/Mail Order

SPECIALTIES/: Rock & Roll, Punk Rock/NewWave, Contemporary Jazz, Rockabilly, Rock, Beatles, Blues, Instrumental, Rhythm & Blues, Soul

VOLUME: 33⅓ – 1,000
           45 – 0
           78 – 0
       Other – 0

STOCK: Domestic & Import/New & Used

SEARCH: Available with service charge; Want lists maintained and requester notified when record comes in

COLLECTIONS: Will buy collections of rare records

PAYMENTS: Money Order, Personal Check

MAIL ORDER: Whatever shipment method requested; Prepayment or C.O.D.

DISCOUNTS: I.N.A.

PUBLICATIONS: Not available

VANCOUVER

THE CHARLES BOGLE PHONOGRAPH DISPENSARY (I)
4430 West Tenth Avenue
Vancouver V6R 2H9
(604) 224-0232

M–T   11:00–6:00
F   11:00–9:00
S   10:00–600
S   Closed

SERVICES: Walk-in Store/Mail Order

SPECIALTIES: Rock, Punk Rock/New Wave, Beatles, Folk, Contemporary Jazz, Traditional Jazz, Sound Tracks, Blues, Rhythm & Blues

VOLUME: 33⅓ – 60%
           45 – 20%
           78 – 20%
       Other – 0

STOCK: Domestic & Import/New & Used

SEARCH: Available with service charge; Want lists maintained and requester notified when record comes in

COLLECTIONS: Will buy collections of rare records

PAYMENTS: Master Charge, Money Order, Personal Check, VISA/BankAmericard

MAIL ORDER: Whatever shipment method requested; Prepayment or C.O.D.

DISCOUNTS: Available

PUBLICATIONS: Not available

VANCOUVER

D & G COLLECTORS RECORDS LIMITED (I)	M–T	10:00–6:00
3580 East Hastings Street	F	10:00–9:00
Vancouver V5K 2A7	S	10:00–6:00
(604) 294-5737	S	Noon–6:00

SERVICES: Walk-in Store/Mail Order

SPECIALTIES:. Elvis, Rock & Roll, Rock, Country & Western, Rockabilly, Rhythm & Blues, Hillbilly, Blues, Surfing, Old-time Country

VOLUME:
33⅓ – 5,000
45 – 30,000
78 – 3,000
Other – Picture Discs

STOCK: Domestic & Import/New & Used

SEARCH: Want lists maintained and requester notified when record comes in

COLLECTIONS: Will buy collections of rare records

PAYMENTS: American Express, Carte Blanche, Diners Club, Master Charge, Money Order, Personal Check, VISA/BankAmericard

MAIL ORDER: Whatever shipment method requested; Prepayment or C.O.D.

DISCOUNTS: Not available

PUBLICATIONS: Free monthly general catalog; Free quarterly Elvis catalog; Free periodic auction list

VANCOUVER

ERNIE'S HOT WAX LIMITED (II)	M–S	10:00–9:00
1116 Denman Street	S	Noon–9:00
Vancouver V6G 2M8		
(604) 681-2929		

SERVICES: Walk-in Store/Mail Order

SPECIALTIES: Rock, Folk, Contemporary Jazz, Classical, Disco, Blues, Bluegrass, Traditional Jazz, Rockabilly, Big Band

VOLUME:
33⅓ – 100%
45 – 0
78 – 0
Other – 0

STOCK: Domestic & Import/New & Used

SEARCH: Want lists maintained and requester notified when record comes in

COLLECTIONS: Will buy collections of rare records

PAYMENTS: Money Order, Personal Charge Account, Personal Check, VISA/BankAmericard

MAIL ORDER: Whatever shipment method requested; Prepayment

DISCOUNTS: Available

PUBLICATIONS: Not available

VANCOUVER

| FRIENDS RECORDS (I) | M–S | 11:00–6:00 |
| 319 East Broadway | S | 2:00–5:00 |

319 East Broadway
Vancouver
(604) 879-3411

SERVICES: Walk-in Store/Mail Order

SPECIALTIES: Rock & Roll, Punk Rock/New Wave, Contemporary Jazz, Rockabilly, Rock, Beatles, Blues, Instrumental, Rhythm & Blues, Soul

VOLUME: 33⅓ – 1,000
           45   – 0
           78   – 0
           Other – 0

STOCK: Domestic & Import/New & Used

SEARCH: Available with service charge; Want lists maintained and requester notified when record comes in

COLLECTIONS: Will buy collections of rare records

PAYMENTS: Money Order, Personal Check

MAIL ORDER: Whatever shipment method requested; Prepayment or C.O.D.

DISCOUNTS: I.N.A.

PUBLICATIONS: Not available

VANCOUVER

MEMORY LANE RECORDS (I)
23 West Broadway
Vancouver V5Y 1P1
(604) 873-1413

M–T	Closed
W–F	1:00–8:00
S	1:00–6:00
S	4:00–8:00

SERVICES: Walk-in Store/Mail Order

SPECIALTIES: Rock, Rock & Roll, Doo Wop, Bop Jazz, Rockabilly, Soul, Rhythm & Blues, Swing, Big Band, Vocal, Punk Rock/New Wave

VOLUME: 33⅓ – 1,500
           45   – 600
           78   – 50
           Other – 0

STOCK: Domestic & Import/Used

SEARCH: Available with no service charge

COLLECTIONS: Will buy collections of rare records

PAYMENTS: Money Order

MAIL ORDER: Whatever shipment method requested; Prepayment or C.O.D.

DISCOUNTS: Available

PUBLICATIONS: Not available

VICTORIA

THE RECORD GALLERY (II)
574 Johnson Street
Victoria V8W 1M3
(604) 383-5131

M–T	10:00–5:30
F	10:00–9:00
S	10:00–5:30
S	Closed

SERVICES: Walk-in Store/Mail Order

SPECIALTIES: Classical, Contemporary Jazz, Traditional Jazz, Broadway Shows, O pera, Folk, Ethnic, Easy Listening, Documentary, Comedy, Childrens

VOLUME: 33⅓ – 100%
45   – 0
78   – 0
Other – 0

STOCK: Domestic & Import/New

SEARCH: Want lists maintained and requester notified when record comes in

COLLECTIONS: Will buy collections of rare records

PAYMENTS: Master Charge, Money Order, Personal Check, VISA/BankAmericard

MAIL ORDER: 1st Class, Whatever shipment method requested; Prepayment or C.O.D.

DISCOUNTS: Not available

PUBLICATIONS: Not available

MANITOBA

WINNIPEG

WINNIPEG FOLKLORE CENTRE (II)
107 Osborne Street South
Winnipeg
(204) 284-9833

M–T	10:00–6:00
F	10:00–9:00
S	10:00–6:00
S	Closed

SERVICES: Walk-in Store/Mail Order

SPECIALTIES: (Alphabetical) Bluegrass, Blues, Folk, Foreign Language, Hillbilly, Traditional Jazz

VOLUME: 33⅓ – 600
45   – 0
78   – 0
Other – 0

STOCK: Domestic & Import/New

SEARCH: Want lists maintained and requester notified when record comes in

COLLECTIONS: Will buy collections of rare records

PAYMENTS: Master Charge, Money Order, Personal Check, VISA/BankAmericard

MAIL ORDER: Air Mail, 1st Class, 4th Class; Prepayment or C.O.D.

DISCOUNTS: Not available

PUBLICATIONS: I.N.A.

ONTARIO

OTTAWA

RAW "OLDIE" RECORDS INCORPORATED (I)
P.O. Box 2222
Station D
Ottawa KIP 5W4
  Telephone: I.N.A.

SERVICES: Mail Order Only

SPECIALTIES: (Alphabetical) Country & Western, Disco, Easy Listening, Folk, Folk-Rock, Gospel, Rhythm & Blues, Rock, Rock & Roll, Soul

VOLUME: 33⅓ – 0
           45 – 345,000
           78 – 0
           Other – 0

STOCK: Domestic & Import/New

SEARCH: Available with service charge; Want lists maintained and requester notified when record comes in

COLLECTIONS: Will buy collections of rare records

PAYMENTS: Money Order, Personal check

MAIL ORDER: Air Mail, 1st Class, 3rd Class; Prepayment

DISCOUNTS: Available

PUBLICATIONS: I.N.A.

OTTAWA

RECORD WAREHOUSE (I)
P.O. Box 2391
Ottawa KIP 5W5
  Telephone: I.N.A.

SERVICES: Mail Order Only

SPECIALTIES: (Alphabetical) Country & Western, Disco, Easy Listening, Folk, Folk-Rock, Rhythm & Blues, Rock, Rock & Roll, Soul

VOLUME: 33⅓ – 0
           45 – 31,000
           78 – 0
           Other – 0

STOCK: Domestic & Import/New & Used

SEARCH: Available with no service charge; Want lists maintained and requester notified when record comes in

COLLECTIONS: Will buy collections of rare records

PAYMENTS: Money Order, Personal Check

MAIL ORDER: Air Mail, 3rd Class; Prepayment

DISCOUNTS: Available

PUBLICATIONS: I.N.A.

TORONTO

JAZZ AND BLUES RECORD CENTRE (I)   M–T   11:00–6:00
893 Yonge Street   F   11:00–7:00
Toronto M4W 2HZ   S   10:00–6:00
  (416) 929-5065   S   Closed

SERVICES: Walk-in Store/Mail Order

SPECIALTIES: (Alphabetical) Blues, Contemporary Jazz, Traditional Jazz

VOLUME: 33⅓ – 100%
           45 – 0
           78 – 0
         Other – 0

STOCK: Domestic & Import/New & Used

SEARCH: Available with no service charge; Want lists maintained and requester notified when record comes in

COLLECTIONS: Will buy collections of rare records

PAYMENTS: Money Order, Personal Check

MAIL ORDER: Parcel Post; Prepayment

DISCOUNTS: Not available

PUBLICATIONS: I.N.A.

TORONTO

JAZZ HOUSE (I)
P.O. Box 455
Adelaide Street East Post Office
Toronto M5C 1J6
  Telephone: I.N.A.

SERVICES: Mail Order Only

SPECIALTIES: (Alphabetical) Blues, Contemporary Jazz, Traditional Jazz

VOLUME: 33⅓ – 5,500
           45 – 0
           78 – 0
         Other – 0

STOCK: Domestic & Import/New

SEARCH: Not available

COLLECTIONS: Will not buy collections of rare records

PAYMENTS: Money Order, Personal Check

MAIL ORDER: Air Mail, Parcel Post; Prepayment

DISCOUNTS: Available

PUBLICATIONS: I.N.A.

TORONTO

ONE MORE TIME (I)
293 King Street West
Toronto M5U 1V5
  (416) 368-2853

M–W	Closed
T–F	Noon–9:00
S	10:00–6:00
S	Closed

SERVICES: Walk-in Store/Mail Order

SPECIALTIES: Canadiana, Historical, Edison Discs/Cylinders, Classical, Opera, Hit Parade, Dixieland, Personality, Ragtime, Big Band, Swing, Vaudeville

VOLUME: 33⅓ – 1,000
                   45 – 1,000
                   78 – 50,000
                   Other – Edison
                            Diamond
                            Discs/Cylinders

STOCK: Domestic & Import/New & Used

SEARCH: Available with service charge; Want lists maintained and requester notified when record comes in

COLLECTIONS: Will buy collections of rare records

PAYMENTS: Master Charge, VISA/BankAmericard

MAIL ORDER: Parcel Post; Prepayment

DISCOUNTS: Not available

PUBLICATIONS: Free quarterly auction list

QUEBEC

BEACONSFIELD

DISC HYSTERIA (I)
P.O. Box 152–D
186 Sutton House
Beaconsfield H9W 5T7
  (514) 695-9810
  Telex: 822505 (NISSCO MTL)

M–F	9:00–6:00
S–S	Closed

SERVICES: Walk-in Store (By Appointment Only)/Mail Order

SPECIALTIES: Rock, Punk Rock/New Wave, Rock & Roll, Beatles, Disco, Elvis, Blues, Promotional, Reggae

VOLUME: 33⅓ – 5,000
                   45 – 5,000
                   78 – 0
                   Other – 0

STOCK: Domestic & Import/New
SEARCH: I.N.A.

COLLECTIONS: Will buy collections of rare records

PAYMENTS: Master Charge, Money Order, Personal Check, VISA/BankAmericard

MAIL ORDER: Whatever shipment method requested; Prepayment; C.O.D. (Canada Only)

DISCOUNTS: Available

PUBLICATIONS: Monthly catalog available for $1.00 per year

MONTREAL

HERKA (I)
2122 Fullum
Montreal
   Telephone: I.N.A.

M–W	11:00–6:00
T–F	11:00–9:00
S	11:00–5:00
S	Closed

SERVICES: Walk-in Store/Mail Order

SPECIALTIES: All Major Categories

VOLUME: 33⅓ – 2,000
           45 – 1,000
           78 – 0
    Other – 0

STOCK: Domestic & Import/Used

SEARCH: Available with no service charge; Want lists maintained and requester notified when record comes in

COLLECTIONS: Will buy collections of rare records

PAYMENTS: Money Order

MAIL ORDER: Whatever shipment method requested; Prepayment

DISCOUNTS: I.N.A.

PUBLICATIONS: I.N.A.

MONTREAL

MAISON DU DISQUES (I)
4000 Hochelaca Street
Montreal
   (514) 255-0312

M–W	9:00–6:00
T–F	9:00–9:00
S	9:00–5:00
S	Closed

SERVICES: Walk-in Store/Mail Order

SPECIALTIES: (Alphabetical)   Blues, Bossa Nova, Country & Western, Disco, Easy Listening, Folk, Reggae, Rhythm & Blues, Rock, Rock & Roll, Soul

VOLUME: 33⅓ – 50%
           45 – 50%
           78 – 0
    Other – 0

STOCK: Domestic & Import/New

SEARCH: Available with no service charge; Want lists maintained and requester notified when record comes in

COLLECTIONS: Will not buy collections of rare records

PAYMENTS: American Express, Master Charge, Money Order, VISA/Bank-Americard

MAIL ORDER: Air Mail, 3rd Class; Prepayment or C.O.D.

DISCOUNTS: Available

PUBLICATIONS: Periodic catalog available for $2.00 per issue

MISCELLANEOUS INTERNATIONAL RECORD DEALERS

ARGENTINA

BUENOS AIRES

COLON RECORDS S.R.L. (I)
Treinta y Tres Orientales 955/57
1236 Buenos Aires
922–5323
CABLE CODE: Colonrec

SERVICES: Walk-in Store (By Appointment Only)/Mail Order

SPECIALTIES: Opera, Instrumental, Classical, Tango, Edison Discs/Cylinders, Historical, Spoken Word, Military, Political, Traditional Jazz

VOLUME: 33⅓ – 7,000
45 – 0
78 – 40,000
Other – Edison
Discs/Cylinders

STOCK: Domestic & Import/New & Used

SEARCH: Available with no service charge; Want lists maintained and requester notified when record comes in

COLLECTIONS: Available for purchase; Will buy collections of rare records

PAYMENTS: Money Order, Personal Check

MAIL ORDER: Whatever shipment method requested; Prepayment or C.O.D.

DISCOUNTS: Not available

PUBLICATIONS: Free quarterly catalog

BRAZIL

SAO PAULO

A & R DISCOS LTDA. (I)
Rua Barao de Itapetininga 255 LJ 25
01042 Sao Paulo
Telephone: I.N.A.

SERVICES: Walk-in Store (By Appointment Only)/Mail Order

SPECIALTIES: Rock, Brazilian Music, Punk Rock/New Wave, Elvis, Beatles, Rock & Roll

VOLUME: 33⅓ – I.N.A.
45 – I.N.A.
78 – I.N.A.
Other – I.N.A.

STOCK: Domestic & Import/New & Used

SEARCH: Available with no service charge

COLLECTIONS: I.N.A.

PAYMENTS: Money Order, Personal Check

MAIL ORDER: Air Mail; Prepayment

DISCOUNTS: Not available

PUBLICATIONS: Free quarterly catalog

264

FRANCE

PARIS

COLLECTOR'S RECORD SHOP (I)   M–S   11:00–7:30
22 bis, rue de Bellefond   S   Closed
75009 Paris
  (1) 526-6084

SERVICES: Walk-in Store/Mail Order

SPECIALTIES: (Alphabetical) Blues, Contemporary Jazz, Country & Western, Hillbilly, Rhythm & Blues, Rock & Roll, Soul, Traditional Jazz

VOLUME: 33⅓ – 3,000
              45   – 300
              78   – 50
          Other – 0

STOCK: Domestic & Import/New & Used

SEARCH: Available with no service charge; Want lists maintained and requester notified when record comes in

COLLECTIONS: Will buy collections of rare records

PAYMENTS: Money Order, Personal Check

MAIL ORDER: Air Mail, 4th Class; Prepayment or C.O.D.

DISCOUNTS: Available

PUBLICATIONS: I.N.A.

ITALY

BOLOGNA

F. BONGIOVANNI RECORDS (I)   M–W 8:30–12:30/3:30–7:30
Via Rizzoli 28/E   T   8:30–12:30
40125 Bologna   F–S 8:30–12:30/3:30–7:30
  (051) 225-722   S   Closed

SERVICES: Walk-in Store/Mail Order

SPECIALTIES: Opera, Classical, Sound Tracks, Film Scores, Historical, Folk, Vocal

VOLUME: 33⅓ – 100%
              45   – 0
              78   – 0
          Other – 0

STOCK: Domestic & Import/New

SEARCH: Want lists maintained and requester notified when record comes in

COLLECTIONS: Will not buy collections of rare records

PAYMENTS: Money Order, Personal Check

MAIL ORDER: Air Mail, 1st Class, 2nd Class; Prepayment

DISCOUNTS: Available

PUBLICATIONS: Free semiannual auction list; Free semiannual set-sale list

THE NETHERLANDS

AP HENGELO OV.

DIWA RECORDS (I)   M–F   8:30–5:30
P.O. Box 612   S–S   Closed
Ap Hengelo Ov. 7550
 (074) 424-762

SERVICES: Mail Order Only (Above Times for Telephone)

SPECIALTIES: Rock & Roll, Rockabilly, Country & Western, Elvis, Blues, Rhythm & Blues, Instrumental, Boogie-Woogie, Mersey Beat, Surfing

VOLUME: 33⅓ – 2,500
           45 – 400
           78 – 0
           Other – 0

STOCK: Domestic & Import/New

SEARCH: Not available

COLLECTIONS: Not available for purchase

PAYMENTS: Money Order, Personal Check

MAIL ORDER: 1st Class, Whatever shipment method requested; Prepayment or C.O.D.

DISCOUNTS: Available

PUBLICATIONS: Free monthly catalog

DEN HAAG

PAUL VANDERKOOY RECORDS (I)
Baambruggestrasse 49
Den Haag
 Telephone: I.N.A.

SERVICES: Mail Order Only

SPECIALTIES: (Alphabetical) Country & Western, Instrumental, Rhythm & Blues, Rock, Rock & Roll, Rockabilly, Surfing

VOLUME: 33⅓ – 1,000
           45 – 10,000
           78 – 0
           Other – 0

STOCK: Domestic & Import/New & Used

SEARCH: Available with no service charge; Want lists maintained and requester notified when record comes in

COLLECTIONS: Will buy collections of rare records

PAYMENTS: Money Order

MAIL ORDER: Air Mail, 2nd Class; Prepayment

DISCOUNTS: I.N.A.

PUBLICATIONS: I.N.A.

TILBURG

HENK VAN BROEKHOVEN RECORDS (I)   M–S   10:00–10:00
Donizettistraat 33
5049 KK–Tilburg
   (013) 554021

SERVICES: Mail Order Only (Above Times for Telephone)

SPECIALTIES: All Major Categories

VOLUME: 33⅓ – 50%
            45 – 50%
            78 – 0
            Other – 0

STOCK: Domestic & Import/New & Used

SEARCH: Want lists maintained and requester notified when record comes in

COLLECTIONS: Will buy collections of rare records

PAYMENTS: Money Order

MAIL ORDER: Registered

DISCOUNTS: Not available

PUBLICATIONS: Free periodic auction list

SWEDEN

SOLLENTUNA

OVE JOHANNISSON RECORDS (I)
Ribbingsvag 16A¹
19152 Sollentuna
   Telephone: I.N.A.

SERVICES: Mail Order Only

SPECIALTIES: Rock & Roll, Rockabilly, Elvis, Beatles, Surfing, Rhythm & Blues, Comedy, Country & Western, Blues

VOLUME: 33⅓ – 500
            45 – 1,000
            78 – 200
            Other – 0

STOCK: Domestic & Import/New & Used

SEARCH: Available with service charge; Want lists maintained and requester notified when record comes in

COLLECTIONS: Available for purchase; Will buy collections of rare records

PAYMENTS: American Express, Master Charge, Money Order, Personal Charge Account, Personal Check

MAIL ORDER: Air Mail, 1st Class, 2nd Class, Whatever shipment method requested; Prepayment

DISCOUNTS: Not available

PUBLICATIONS: Free semiannual catalog; Free semiannual auction list

STOCKHOLM

JONAS "MR. R & B" BERNHOLM (I)
Halsingegatan 14–A
113 23 Stockholm
(08) 334-620

SERVICES: Mail Order Only

SPECIALTIES: Rhythm & Blues, Blues, Rockabilly, Elvis, Beatles, Rock & Roll, Cajun, Hillbilly, Old-Time Country, Soul

VOLUME: 33⅓ – 10,000
           45 – 2,500
           78 – 500
           Other – 0

STOCK: Domestic & Import/New & Used

SEARCH: Not available

COLLECTIONS: Not available for purchase; Will buy collections of rare records

PAYMENTS: Money Order

MAIL ORDER: Whatever shipment method requested; Prepayment or C.O.D.

DISCOUNTS: Not available

PUBLICATIONS: Free quarterly catalog; Free semiannual auction list

SWITZERLAND

ECHANDENS

CLAUDE SUMI RECORDS (I)
Route de Bremblens 8
1026 Echandens
(021) 894-161

SERVICES: Walk-in Store (By Appointment)/Mail Order

SPECIALTIES: (Alphabetical) Country & Western, Rock, Rock & Roll

VOLUME: 33⅓ – 200
           45 – 100
           78 – 0
           Other – 0

STOCK: Domestic & Import/New & Used

SEARCH: Available with service charge; Want lists maintained and requester notified when record comes in

COLLECTIONS: Will buy collections of rare records

PAYMENTS: Money Order

MAIL ORDER: Air Mail, 1st Class; Prepayment

DISCOUNTS: Not available

PUBLICATIONS: I.N.A.

KILCHBERG

BUSCHOR BALTHASAR (I)
Neuwaidstrasse 7
8802 Kilchberg
Kt. Zurich
  (01) 715-4552

M–S   9:00–5:00
S   Closed

SERVICES: Walk-in Store/Mail Order

SPECIALTIES: (Alphabetical) Beat,
Punk Rock/New Wave, Rock & Roll

VOLUME: 33⅓ – 50%
            45   – 50%
            78   – 0
          Other – 0

STOCK: Domestic & Import/New & Used

SEARCH: Available with service charge; Want lists maintained and requester notified when record comes in

COLLECTIONS: Will buy collections of rare records

PAYMENTS: American Express, Diners Club, Money Order, Personal Check

MAIL ORDER: Air Mail, Parcel Post; Prepayment

DISCOUNTS: Available

PUBLICATIONS: I.N.A.

WEST GERMANY

POST SULZHEIM

CATTLE RECORDS (I)
c/o Reimar Binge
Siedlung 67
D–8722 Monchstockheim
Post Sulzheim
  Telephone: I.N.A.

SERVICES: Mail Order Only

SPECIALTIES: (Alphabetical) Bluegrass, Cajun, Country & Western, Hillbilly, Old-time Country

VOLUME: 33⅓ – 1,500
            45   – 0
            78   – 0
          Other – 0

STOCK: Domestic & Import/New & Used

SEARCH: Not available

COLLECTIONS: Will buy collections of rare records

PAYMENTS: Money Order

MAIL ORDER: Air Mail, 4th Class; Prepayment

DISCOUNTS: Available to dealers only

PUBLICATIONS: Free quarterly catalog available; Free annual auction list available

Part II

RECORD
DEALERS

**ADDITIONAL NAMES AND
ADDRESSES ONLY**

AMERICAN RECORD DEALERS

This section is a listing of over four hundred names and addresses of dealers who it is *known* are rare record carriers or who it is *strongly believed* are rare record carriers. For varying reasons, these people did not return a completed questionnaire.

ALABAMA

Norman Rogers Records
408½ South Broad Street
Albertville, Alabama 35950

ARIZONA

Angie's Record Shop
1640 East McDowell Road
Phoenix, Arizona 85006

Merrill Hammond Records
P.O. Box 602
Cave Creek, Arizona 85331

Jellyroll Productions Records
P.O. Box 3017
Scottsdale, Arizona 85257

Reichart Records
1256 West Devonshire Street
Mesa, Arizona 85201

CALIFORNIA

Andrews Records
P.O. Box 700
Redondo Beach, California 90277

Arcade Music
650 F Street
San Diego, California 92410

Arcade Music
4904 Voltaire
San Diego, California 92107

Big Band Sounds Records
P.O. Box 1
Norco, California 91760

Bob's Jazz Disc Auctions
P.O. Box 16318
San Francisco, California 94116

Bressen Records
P.O. Box 1154
San Francisco, California 94101

Caledonia Records
44 Bolinas Road
Fairfax, California 94930

California Music Company
2933 West Pico Boulevard
Los Angeles, California 90006

Celebrity Records
426½ La Cienega Boulevard
Los Angeles, California 90069

Classical Records
P.O. Box 99412
San Francisco, California 94109

Bill Cook Records
P.O. Box 19108
Los Angeles, California 90019

Dial Records
190 West J Street
Benicia, California 94510

Discount Classics Records
6642 Vista Del Mar
Playa Del Rey, California 90291

Dufault Records
294 Union
San Rafael, California 94901

El Camino Record Center
4037 El Camino Way
Palo Alto, California 94306

Elvis Rare Records
P.O. Box 4213
Glendale, California 91202

Encore Records
4593 El Cajon Boulevard
San Diego, California 92115

The Experience Record Stop
11835 Braddock Drive
Culver City, California 90230

Festival Records
2769 West Pico Boulevard
Los Angeles, California 90006

Flash Record Shop
1861 West Adams Boulevard
Los Angeles, California 90018

Geof Galetti Records
P.O. Box 73
West Covina, California 91793

Ed Harkins Records
617 Canyon Place
Solana Beach, California 92075

Hearne Records
1047 West 97th Street
Los Angeles, California 90044

Ideal Music Company
11514 Wilmington
Los Angeles, California 90059

Jack's Records
P.O. Box 14068
San Francisco, California 94114

Kearne Records
P.O. Box 99332
San Diego, California 92109

Kuhn Records
P.O. Box 46266
Los Angeles, California 90046

Long Live Rock Records
5500 Sandburg Drive
Sacramento, California 95819

Lynn-Art Records
1771 Lake Street
San Mateo, California 94403

Mills Records
903 28th Street
San Pedro, California 90731

Music & Memories
10850 Ventura Boulevard
Studio City, California 91604

Music Barn
144 Del Amo Fashion Square
Torrance, California 90503

Musical Grafitti
316 South Gaffey Street
San Pedro, California 90731

Jack Nelson Records
557 Duboce Avenue
San Francisco, California 94117

Nostalgia Records
3580 Main
Riverside, California 92501

Off the Record
6136 El Cajon Boulevard
San Diego, California 92115

Off the Record
2621 Wilshire Boulevard
Santa Monica, California 90403

Paradox Music
23703 Madison Street
Torrance, California 90505

Platter Palace Record Shop
2739 San Bruno Avenue
San Francisco, California 94134

Record Collector's Haven
P.O. Box 37215
Los Angeles, California 90037

Record Collector's Studio
2240 Main Street
Chula Vista, California 92011

Record World
1533 North Hacienda Boulevard
La Puente, California 91744

Recorded Treasures
P.O. Box 5872
Buena Park, California 90622

Records
P.O. Box 668
Yucaipa, California 92399

Records International
P.O. Box 1904
Los Angeles, California 90028

Recycled Records
P.O. Box 5223
Stockton, California 95205

Rooks and Becords
2222 Polk Street
San Francisco, California 94109

Lainie Rotter Records
10061 Whispering Pine Circle
Westminster, California 92683

Sounds of Music, II
131 Union Square Mall
Union City, California 94587

Tape and Record Room
205 East 3rd
Long Beach, California 90802

Thunder Road Records
P.O. Box 1774
Lakewood, California 90716

Ronny Weiser Records
6918 Peach Avenue
Van Nuys, California 91406

Whalon Records
2321 Hill Lane
Redondo Beach, California 90278

Al Winter Records
P.O. Box 188
Big Pine, California 93513

COLORADO

Duke of Discs
P.O. Box 26544
Denver, Colorado 80226

Frank Haskett Records
8563 East Davies Avenue
Englewood, Colorado 80112

Independent Records
6646 West Colfax
Denver, Colorado 80214

David Origlio Records
17 Lansing Street
Aurora, Colorado 80010

Recycled Records
219 North Union Boulevard
Colorado Springs, Colorado 80909

Villa Music Company
6911 South University Boulevard
Denver, Colorado 80210

CONNECTICUT

Alto Music Company
860 Howard Avenue
Bridgeport, Connecticut 06605

Cutler's Record Shop
33 Broadway
New Haven, Connecticut 06511

Earport Records and Tapes
2270 Black Rock Turnpike
Fairfield, Connecticut 06430

Elmwood Records
P.O. Box 10232
Elmwood, Connecticut 06110

Lee's Records
25 Amaryllis Avenue
Waterbury, Connecticut 06710

Mar-Jim Record Shop
1125 New Britain Avenue
West Hartford, Connecticut 06110

Sporties Records
858 Albany Avenue
Hartford, Connecticut 06112

DELAWARE

The Finishing Touch Record Shop
Bay Road
Dover, Delaware 19901

David Martens Records
7 Constitution Boulevard
New Castle, Delaware 19720

Record Museum
Concord Mall
Wilmington, Delaware 19802

Record Music, Incorporated
Blue Hen Mall
Dover, Delaware 19901

DISTRICT OF COLUMBIA

Libra Sounds, Unlimited
P.O. Box 54129
Washington, D.C. 20032

Modern Language Book/Record
Store
3160 O Street Northwest
Washington, D.C. 20001

Sam K Records
731 11th Street Northwest
Washington, D.C. 20001

Sam K Records
1839 7th Street Northwest
Washington, D.C. 20001

FLORIDA

Bird Westchester Music Mart
9256 Bird Road
Miami, Florida 33165

Charlotte's Old Record Gallery
2920 Harbor View Avenue
Tampa, Florida 33611

Collector's Paradise and Museum
P.O. Box 505
Intercession City, Florida 33848

D.J. Record Shop
2999 Edison Avenue
Jacksonville, Florida 32205

W. Patrick Ernst Records
7720 Atlanta Street
Hollywood, Florida 33024

Everything Audio
16756 Northeast 4th Court
North Miami Beach, Florida
33162

Steve Gronda Records
222 Forty-second Avenue
St. Petersburg, Florida 33706

Robert Hiott Records
P.O. Box 440471
Miami, Florida 33144

John Miller Records
P.O. Box 640116
Miami, Florida 33164

Old Records
2920 Harbor View Road
Tampa, Florida 33611

Madeline Passantino Records
P.O. Box 17161
Plantation, Florida 33318

P.D.Q. Promotions
11700 Northwest Thirty-sixth Avenue
Miami, Florida 33167

Record Bar of Jacksonville, Incorporated
Regency Square
Jacksonville, Florida 32211

Record Bar of Jacksonville, Incorporated
40 West Forsyth Street
Jacksonville, Florida 32202

Ross Records
P.O. Box 391824
Miami Beach, Florida 33139

Ford Ross Records
510 Northwest 93rd Terrace
Pembroke Pines, Florida 33024

Rouchaleau Records
326 Southwest 27th Street
Gainesville, Florida 32607

GEORGIA
Robert Chittenden Records
2960 Pearl Street
East Point, Georgia 30344

Clark Music
115 Sycamore
Decatur, Georgia 30030

Record Haven
1046 North Highland Avenue
Atlanta, Georgia 30312

Earl Ross Records
919 Crosby Street
Savannah, Georgia 31401

HAWAII
Collector's Paradise
Rural Route 1
P.O. Box 261-B
Kapaa, Hawaii 96746

ILLINOIS
V.H. Anderson Record Center
1614 North Pulaski
Chicago, Illinois 60639

The Boogie Shop
5607 West Chicago Avenue
Chicago, Illinois 60651

Bwana Disc Records
1921 North Keystone Avenue
Chicago, Illinois 60639

The Collector's Record Shop
5849 West Irving Park Road
Chicago, Illinois 60634

Robert Crain Records
1106 East Fairview Street
Peoria, Illinois 61615

Jim Hawkins Records
815 Hardin–#64
Jacksonville, Illinois 62650

Hollander Music Shop
2624 West North Avenue
Chicago, Illinois 60647

Jemm's Records
P.O. Box 157
Glenview, Illinois 60025

Ken Kotal Records
P.O. Box 549
Berwyn, Illinois 60402

Midwest Rare Records
1803 Glenview Road
Glenview, Illinois 60025

Frank Queen Records
2153 West Cuyler Avenue
Chicago, Illinois 60618

Monroe Sands Records
308 South Ellen Street
Homer, Illinois 61849

Sounds Good
4821 West Irving Park Road
Chicago, Illinois 60641

Tom's Records
5124 South Kedzie Avenue
Chicago, Illinois 60632

Vinyl Visions Records
P.O. Box 6029
Chicago, Illinois 60680

V. L. Walsh Records
619 East 2nd
Centralia, Illinois 62801

Steven Yates Records
Rural Route 1
Camden, Illinois 62319

INDIANA

John V. Beck Records
906–D Maxwell Terrace
Bloomington, Indiana 47401

J. T.'s Record Shop
662 East 38th Street
Indianapolis, Indiana 46205

J. Lindsey Records
1820 Bauer Road
Indianapolis, Indiana 46218

Jerry Williams Records
1736 North Berwick Avenue
Indianapolis, Indiana 46222

IOWA

Astroid Records
1007 Main Street
Dubuque, Iowa 52001

Leo Hirtz Records
P.O. Box 6
Bernard, Iowa 52032

KANSAS

Gene Joslin Records
P.O. Box 213
Parsons, Kansas 67357

Midwest Records
P.O. Box 3716
Lawrence, Kansas 66044

KENTUCKY

Larry Stidom Records
Route 5
P.O. Box 336
Morehead, Kentucky 40351

LOUISIANA

Richard Harrison Records
311 Park Avenue
Monroe, Louisiana 71201

Van's Record Shop
200 East Judge Perez Drive
Chalmette, Louisiana 70043

MAINE

Shellac Stack Records
P.O. Box 252
Friendship, Maine 04547

The Wax Museum Shop
372 Fore Street
Portland, Maine 04101

MARYLAND

Joseph Bussard Records
Route 7
Cherry Hill
Frederick, Maryland 21701

Philip Guntner Records
1847 Loch Shiel Road
Baltimore, Maryland 21234

Jack Miller Records
P.O. Box 222
Randallstown, Maryland 21133

Music World
7851 Eastpoint Mall
Eastpoint, Maryland 21224

Music World
5801 Westview Mall
Westview, Maryland 21228

O'Neil's Music Center
Route 301 North
Waldorf, Maryland 20601

Record and Tape Collector
Parkside Shopping Center
5120 Sinclair Lane
Baltimore, Maryland, 21206

Record and Tape Collector
409 West Cold Spring Lane
Baltimore, Maryland 21210

Record and Tape Collector
Danville Square Shopping Center
1543 Merritt Boulevard
Dundalk, Maryland 21222

Record and Tape Collector
Jumpers–The Mall and More
8148 Ritchie Highway
Pasadena, Maryland 21122

Records Unlimited, Incorporated
Petty Hill Shopping Center
7968 Belair Road
Baltimore, Maryland 21236

Riffle Records
9109 Forty-ninth Avenue
College Park, Maryland 20740

Luther Sies Records
1011 Fowler Road
Westminster, Maryland 21157

Sound Shack
2307 East Monument Street
Baltimore, Maryland 21205

MASSACHUSETTS

Baron Records
11 Dell Avenue
Melrose, Massachusetts 02176

The Big Wopper
P.O. Box 1113
Lawrence, Massachusetts 01842

Bill's Records
4 Cross Street
Natick, Massachusetts 01760

Jack Bradley Records
24 Skippers Drive
Harwich, Massachusetts 02645

Buchman Records
18–A Aborn Avenue
Wakefield, Massachusetts 01880

C & S Talking Machine Company
864 Massachusetts Avenue
Cambridge, Massachusetts 02139

Dynamite Sounds
8 Belmont Street
Lowell, Massachusetts 01851

Globe Record Shop
1514 South Main Street
Fall River, Massachusetts 02724

Mike Michel Records
P.O. Box 505–Kenmore Station
Boston, Massachusetts 02215

NERT Records
P.O. Box 268
Lawrence, Massachusetts 01842

Music Sales, Incorporated
6 Gill Street
Building 8
Woburn, Massachusetts 01801

The Music Smith
591 Memorial Drive
Chicopee, Massachusetts 01020

Music Suppliers, Incorporated
77 Wexford Street
Needham, Massachusetts 02192

Northeast Music City
829 Boylston
Boston, Massachusetts 02116

David Osepowicz Records
43 Orchard Street
Northampton, Massachusetts
  01060

Records
P.O. Box 154
Astor Station
Boston, Massachusetts 02123

W. Sarill Records
143 Pearl Street
Cambridge, Massachusetts 02139

Soundtrack Records
P.O. Box 3895
Springfield, Massachusetts 01101

Waltham Record Shop
20 Lexington Street
Waltham, Massachusetts 02154

MICHIGAN

Arnold's Archive
1106 Eastwood Southeast
East Grand Rapids, Michigan
  49506

Ellen Brown Records
4240 Oakland Drive
Kalamazoo, Michigan 49008

Cappy's Record Mart
12575 Gratiot Avenue
Detroit, Michigan 48205

Dearborn Music
22000 Michigan Avenue
Dearborn, Michigan 48124

Fenkell Record Shop
3712 Fenkell
Detroit, Michigan 48238

Herbert Grimm Records
25075 Orchid Street
Mt. Clemens, Michigan 48043

Glenn Harder Records
2554 Haverford Road
Troy, Michigan 48098

Cynthia Hunter Records
P.O. Box 1144
Midland, Michigan 48640

International Record Shop
23400 Michigan Avenue
Dearborn, Michigan 48124

Liberty Music Shop
417 East Liberty Street
Ann Arbor, Michigan 48108

Richard Miller Records
1713 West Farnum Avenue
Royal Oak, Michigan 48067

Jim Peace Records
316 Stuart–#1
Kalamazoo, Michigan 49007

Record Recovery Room
P.O. Box 37113
Oak Park, Michigan 48237

Relic Rack Records
23150 Van Dyke Street
Warren, Michigan 48089

Doug Smith Records
P.O. Box 266
Linden, Michigan 48451

Trevor Thor Records
711 West Street
Three Rivers, Michigan 49093

MINNESOTA

Bluestein Records
2844 Georgia Avenue South
Minneapolis, Minnesota 55426

Disk Records
2931 Gettysburg Avenue South
Minneapolis, Minnesota 55426

Dored Records
1508 West Broadway
Minneapolis, Minnesota 55411

Electric Fetus
2010 Fourth Avenue South
Minneapolis, Minnesota 55404

Oar Folkjokeopus
2557 Lyndale Avenue South
Minneapolis, Minnesota 55405

MISSISSIPPI

Bennett's Records Distributor
3247 Delta Drive
Jackson, Mississippi 39213

Bennett's Records Distributor
1064 Forest Avenue
Jackson, Mississippi 39206

Ray Bishop Records
P.O. Box 433
Philadelphia, Mississippi 39350

MISSOURI

Krieger Records
520 Bryan Avenue
Kirkwood, Missouri 63122

Leisure Days, Incorporated
P.O. Box 51
Mexico, Missouri 65265

Music Systems
34 North Gore Avenue
St. Louis, Missouri 63119

Rockdom
8104 McGee–#4
Kansas City, Missouri 64114

Rockin' Records
P.O. Box 6012
Kansas City, Missouri 64110

Sanders Soundtracks
P.O. Box 715
Florissant, Missouri 63032

NEBRASKA

Dirt Cheap Record Shop
227 North 11th Street
Lincoln, Nebraska 68508

Dirt Discs
217 North 11th
Lincoln, Nebraska 68508

Trade-A-Tape and Records and
the Comic Center
1127 P Street
Lincoln, Nebraska 68508

NEVADA

Nite City Records
P.O. Box 11395
Reno, Nevada 89510

NEW HAMPSHIRE

Ayer's Records
P.O. Box 96
Newton Junction, New Hampshire 03859

John Banks Records
P.O. Box 697
Danville, New Hampshire 03819

Beijer Archives of Recorded
Sound
Harkness Road
Jaffrey, New Hampshire 03452

Pitchfork Records
146 North Main
Concord, New Hampshire 03300

NEW JERSEY

Aartsma Records
P.O. Box 1132
Paterson, New Jersey 07509

Clifton Music Center
1135 Main Street
Clifton, New Jersey 07011

Crazy Rhythms Records
4 Newman Avenue
Verona, New Jersey 07044

Don T. Fonshill Records
P.O. Box 223
Cranford, New Jersey 07016

George's Golden Oldies
135 Genesee Avenue
Paterson, New Jersey 07503

Hackensack Record King
304 Main Street
Hackensack, New Jersey 07601

Irene Locantre
623 Newton Avenue
Camden, New Jersey 08103

Mike's Records
4619 Cottage Avenue
North Bergen, New Jersey 07047

Jay Monroe Records
25 Plymouth Road
Summit, New Jersey 07901

Olde Tyme Music Scene
917 Main Street
Boonton, New Jersey 07005

Park Records
134 Washington
Paterson, New Jersey 07050

Platter World
P.O. Box 234
Garfield, New Jersey 07026

Recollections
P.O. Box 197
Roselle Park, New Jersey 07204

Record Arcade
419 Broad
Bloomfield, New Jersey 07003

Record Finders
336 West Lincoln Avenue
Roselle Park, New Jersey 07204

Records
P.O. Box 764
Hillside, New Jersey 07205

Relic Rack Records
136 Main Street
Hackensack, New Jersey 07601

Sicignano Records
29 Columbia Avenue
Nutley, New Jersey 07110

Floyd Silver Records
Vincentown Pemberton Road
Vincentown, New Jersey 08088

Thibault Records
P.O. Box 42
Cedar Brook, New Jersey 08018

Rudolph Villegas Records
63 Melody Hill Road
Clifton, New Jersey 07013

Walton Records
4 Wexford Road
Gibbsboro, New Jersey 08026

NEW YORK

Academy Book Store
10 West 18th Street
New York, New York 10011

The Antique Phonograph Shop
320 Jerico Turnpike
Floral Park, New York 11001

A R G Records
341 Cooper Station
New York, New York 10003

Biograph Records
P.O. Box 109
Canaan, New York 12029

Tim Brooks Records
1940 80th Street
Jackson Heights, New York 11370

Amy Carraro Records
25 Aberdeen Street
Malverne, New York 11565

Cohawk Records
278 West 19th Street
New York, New York 10011

C. Cohn Records
250 Brevoort Lane
Rye, New York 10580

Coppernoll's Records
P.O. Box 6
Palatine Bridge, New York 13428

Direct Discount Records
1546 Broadway
New York, New York 10036

Disco-Disc
71–59 Austin Street
Forest Hills, New York 11375

Disques Du Monde
P.O. Box 836
Madison Square Station
New York, New York 10010

Dusty Discs
P.O. Box 174
Bay Ridge Station
Brooklyn, New York 11220

Fell Records
733 West Park
Long Beach, New York 11561

Fiorino Records
P.O. Box 153
Brooklyn, New York 11209

Flashback Records
412 East 9th Street
New York, New York 10009

Footlight Records
94 Third Avenue
New York, New York 10003

Frankevich Records
388 Warburton Avenue
Hastings-On-Hudson, New York
10706

Lenny Fry's Record Cellar
936 Nostrand Avenue
Brooklyn, New York 11225

Geordie Records
Rural Delivery #2
P.O. Box 367
Mechanicville, New York 12118

Charles Goldman Records
855 East 19th Street
Brooklyn, New York 11230

Basil Gramatan Records
21 Wildcliff Road
New Rochelle, New York 10805

The Gramophone
32 Saint Marks Place
New York, New York 10003

John Greco Records
P.O. Box 176
Staten Island, New York 10312

Hanson Records
2110 Plaza
Schenectady, New York 12309

Hobbyville
433 West 34th Street
New York, New York 10001

Jackson Records
P.O. Box 724
Farmingdale, New York 11735

Jazz Record Exchange
P.O. Box 125
Jamaica, New York 11415

G. Kaplan Records
P.O. Box 214
Valley Stream, New York 11582

Kelway Records
22 Duchess Avenue
Staten Island, New York 10304

Kirschenbaum Records
236 Union Street
Schenectady, New York 12305

Bob Kruse Records
P.O. Box 334–2RD, Number 1
Geneva, New York 14456

Fred Lang Records
1 Margo Place
Huntington, New York 11743

Lawalt Records
P.O. Box 201
Oriskany, New York 13424

Liberman Records
1397 East 2nd Street
Brooklyn, New York 11230

Lincoln Square Music Company
  Incorporated
2109 Broadway
New York, New York 10023

Richard Lynch Records
1 Christopher Street
New York, New York 10014

Manny's Books and Records
114 Fourth Avenue
New York, New York 10003

The Memory Bank
259–18 Hillside Avenue
Floral Park, New York 11004

The Mole Records
204 East 11th Street
Huntington Station, New York
11746

Music Masters Uptown Incorporated
25 West 43rd Street
New York, New York 10036

Musique Records
129 Howell Street
Canandaigua, New York 14424

Nipper Records
P.O. Box 4
Woodstock, New York 12498

Nostalgia and All That Jazz
248 Lark
Albany, New York 12210

Nostalgia and All That Jazz
55 West 27th Street
New York, New York 10001

Openheim Records
161–31 Normal Road
Jamaica, New York 11432

Joseph Pierson Records
1125 Fifth Avenue
New York, New York 10028

Rare Impressions
123 Greenwich Avenue
New York, New York 10014

Rare Records
P.O. Box 254
Getzville, New York 14068

The Record Album
254 West 81st Street
New York, New York 10024

Record Baron
1404 Forest Avenue
Staten Island, New York 10302

Record City
734 Broadway
New York, New York 10003

The Record Exchange
842 Seventh Avenue
New York, New York 10019

The Record Exchange Limited
72–05 Austin Street
Forest Hills, New York 11375

Records
Department HF6
P.O. Box 125
Jamaica, New York 11415

Records
P.O. Box 547
Rifton, New York 12471

Records Revisited
34 West 33rd Street
New York, New York 10001

The Ripe Record
P.O. Box 182
Pratt Station
Brooklyn, New York 11205

Rick Rosen Records
P.O. Box 42
Homecrest Station
Brooklyn, New York 11229

Sample, Incorporated
1631 Hertel Avenue
Buffalo, New York 14216

Second Coming Records Incorporated
235 Sullivan Street
New York, New York 10012

Skolnick Parkside Records
25 Parade Place
Brooklyn, New York 11226

Spin-A-Disc Records
410 North Goodman Street
Rochester, New York 14609

Stan's Record Shop
651 Elton Avenue
Bronx, New York 10455

Tager Records
79 Wall Street
Suite 501
New York, New York 10010

Tamburino Records
1039 Calhoun Avenue
Bronx, New York 10465

Treasure House Record Shop
2 High Street
Fairport, New York 14450

Tunemaster Records
100 Westchester Avenue
White Plains, New York 10601

Vail Records
209 North Avenue
New Rochelle, New York 10801

Valentine Oldies Bop Shop
5 Bay 25th Street
Brooklyn, New York 11214

Venus Records
P.O. Box 86
Cooper Station
New York, New York 10003

Village Oldies
179 MacDougal Street
New York, New York 10011

John Wilson Records
1679 81st Street
Brooklyn, New York 11214

D. Wiur Records
41 Locust Avenue
Bethpage, New York 11714

Zig Zag Records, Incorporated
2301 Avenue U
Brooklyn, New York 11229

NORTH CAROLINA

Ernie's Record Shop
Park Road Shopping Center
Charlotte, North Carolina 28209

Powell Records
P.O. Box 10863
Raleigh, North Carolina 27605

Rare Records
P.O. Box 2027
Chapel Hill, North Carolina 27514

John Swain Records
P.O. Box 383
Raleigh, North Carolina 27060

NORTH DAKOTA

Dave Baker Records
1102 East 4th
West Fargo, North Dakota 58078

OHIO

Akron's Records Unlimited
35 South Union
Akron, Ohio 44304

J.B. Records
322 Briarwood
Columbus, Ohio 43213

Lenny's Records
205 West 58th Street
Ashtabula, Ohio 44004

Don Mack Records
P.O. Box 33451
Royalton, Ohio 44133

Frank Merrill Records
P.O. Box 5693
Toledo, Ohio 43613

Music Box
155 2nd Street
Akron, Ohio 44314

Rockhouse Records
349 East Cooke Road
Columbus, Ohio 43214

Ken Stone Records
2037–D Guildhall Drive
Columbus, Ohio 43209

Jim Tartal Records
2156 Green Acres Drive
Parma, Ohio 44134

Traditional Jazzland
P.O. Box 366
Dayton, Ohio 45405

OKLAHOMA

Jack Jones Records
Route 2
Overlook Road
Ponca City, Oklahoma 74601

OREGON

Steve Bates Records
P.O. Box 3176
Sunriver, Oregon 97701

Book and Record Shop
3638 Southeast Hawthorne Boulevard
Portland, Oregon 97214

Chrystalship
164 West Broadway
Eugene, Oregon 97401

Park Avenue Records
P.O. Box 14913
Portland, Oregon 97214

Rainy Day Records
1269 Bay Street
Florence, Oregon 97439

Yesterday Records
3822 Northeast Sandy Boulevard
Portland, Oregon 97232

PENNSYLVANIA

Be-Bop Records
P.O. Box 372
Upper Darby, Pennsylvania 19082

Bonanni Records
2340 Ripley Street
Philadelphia, Pennsylvania 19152

Bothy Press Records
320 East New Street
Lancaster, Pennsylvania 17602

Cohn Records
2205 Marylane
Broomall, Pennsylvania 19008

Collectors' Records
8313 Shawnee Street
Philadelphia, Pennsylvania 19118

Colosseum Records
134 South 20th Street
Philadelphia, Pennsylvania 19103

Tim Doyle Records
892 Millville Road
Altoona, Pennsylvania 16601

Flo's Records
116 Bouquet Street
Pittsburgh, Pennsylvania 15213

45's Unlimited
6325 Greene
Philadelphia, Pennsylvania 19144

Gallagher Records
3 Logan Avenue
Lock Haven, Pennsylvania 17745

Hanusey Music Company
244 West Girard Avenue
Philadelphia, Pennsylvania 19123

Hatboro Music Shop
11 South York Road
Hatboro, Pennsylvania 19040

Heller's Records and Tapes
3149 Kensington Avenue
Philadelphia, Pennsylvania 19134

Knights of the Turntable
335 Phoenix Street
McKees Rocks, Pennsylvania
   15136

Dave Kressley Records
P.O. Box 463
New Tripoli, Pennsylvania 18066

Lou's Records and Tapes
1000 Greentree Road
Pittsburgh, Pennsylvania 15220

Anthony Navarro Records
P.O. Box 4791
Pittsburgh, Pennsylvania 15206

Nineteen Sixty Five Records
P.O. Box 17156
Philadelphia, Pennsylvania 19105

R & B Records
P.O. Box B
Havertown, Pennsylvania 19083

Record Museum
2216 Cottman Avenue
Philadelphia, Pennsylvania 19149

Charles Reinhart Records
1616 Robert Road
Lancaster, Pennsylvania 17601

Roseman Records
P.O. Box 16083
Philadelphia, Pennsylvania 19114

Rotman Records
8134 Cadwalader Avenue
Elkins Park, Pennsylvania 19117

Phil Schwartz Records
P.O. Box 1516
Lancaster, Pennsylvania 17604

Stak-O-Wax Records
P.O. Box 11412
Philadelphia, Pennsylvania 19111

Vault of Memories
P.O. Box 9542
Pittsburgh, Pennsylvania 15223

Weber Records
8508 Torresdale Avenue
Philadelphia, Pennsylvania 19136

RHODE ISLAND

Domart Records
128 5th Street
Providence, Rhode Island 02906

TENNESSEE

Bojangles Records
P.O. Box 4511
Nashville, Tennessee 37216

Recordland
P.O. Box 16786
Memphis, Tennessee 38116

Doug Seroff Records
P.O. Box 506
Route 3
Goodletsville, Tennessee 37072

TEXAS

Boudreaux Records
2914 Westerland
Houston, Texas 77063

Collector's Records
P.O. Box 3603
Temple, Texas 76501

Collectors Records
608 South Bryan
Bryan, Texas 77801

Half-Price Books, Records, and Magazines
3306 Fairfield
Ridglea Shopping Center
Fort Worth, Texas 76116

Half-Price Books, Records, and Magazines
3207 Broadway
San Antonio, Texas 78209

Half-Price Books, Records, and Magazines
Towne & Country Mall
Temple, Texas 76501

Howell Records
P.O. Box 179
Nome, Texas 77629

The Record Box
2907 West Avenue
San Antonio, Texas 78201

Record Junction
6116 Southwest Freeway
Houston, Texas 77057

Richardson's Record Shop
4511 Mowery Road
Houston, Texas 77047

Joe Salerno Records
9407 Westheimer
Houston, Texas 77063

Ed Smith Records
P.O. Box 3380
El Paso, Texas 79923

VERMONT

Martin Bryan Records
37 Caledonia Street
St. Johnsbury, Vermont 05819

VIRGINIA

Comix Record Shop
P.O. Box 2037
Springfield, Virginia 22152

Jan Garris Records
2422 Winchester Circle
Vienna, Virginia 22180

Gramophone
944 West Grace Street
Richmond, Virginia 23220

Lynn McCutcheon Records
753 Old Waterloo Road
Warrenton, Virginia 22186

Don Riswick Records
1105 Gaston Court
Chesapeake, Virginia 23323

Bill Vernon Records
P.O. Box 472
Rock Mount, Virginia 24151

WASHINGTON

Collector's Nook
213 North I Street
Tacoma, Washington 98403

Czardas Records
211 West Yakima Avenue
Yakima, Washington 98902

Larry J. Long Records
11504 20th Northeast
Lake Stevens, Washington 98258

Standard Records and Hi-Fi Company
1028 Northeast 65th Street
Seattle, Washington 98115

Ticket to Ryde, Ltd.
P.O. Box 3393
Lacey, Washington 98503

WISCONSIN

Brynd Records
12 Langdon Street
Madison, Wisconsin 53703

Establishment Records
P.O. Box 5645
Milwaukee, Wisconsin 53205

Dennis Finn Records
2305 East Bennet
Milwaukee, Wisconsin 53207

Grendysa Records
9708 Caddy Lane
Caledonia, Wisconsin 53108

Mean Mountain Music
P.O. Box 04352
Milwaukee, Wisconsin 53204

Mel Music
Route 2
P.O. Box 315
Marinette, Wisconsin 54143

Record Head
7418 West Hampton Avenue
Milwaukee, Wisconsin 53218

Record Head
6766 West Lincoln Avenue
Milwaukee, Wisconsin 53219

Schroeder Books & Records
708 West Wisconsin Avenue
Milwaukee, Wisconsin 53233

Seitz Records
423 Center Avenue
Sheboygan, Wisconsin 53081

Jim Van Records
908 Christiana Street
Green Bay, Wisconsin 54303

AUSTRALIAN RECORD DEALERS

NEW SOUTH WALES

Ashwood Party Limited
376 Pitt Street
Sydney, New South Wales

Gravino Records
82 Sutherland Street
Paddington
Sydney, New South Wales

QUEENSLAND

The Record Market
117 Queen Street
Brisbane, Queensland

The Record Market
Redcliffe Arcade
Redcliffe, Queensland

SOUTH AUSTRALIA

Southern Record Exchange
1140a South Road
Clovly Park
Adelaide, South Australia

VICTORIA

Import Record Kollectors
49 Peel
North Melbourne, Victoria

BRITISH RECORD DEALERS

ENGLAND

A•C•A Records
42 Great Cambridge Road
Tottenham
London, England N 17

All Change Jazz Records
20 Baker Street
London, England W1

Allerton Records
7 Caldervale Road
London, England SW4

John Beecher Records
236 Hook Road
Chessington
Surrey, England KT9 1PL

The Blake Head Bookshop
104 Middlegate
York, England YO1 1JX

Dave Carey's Swing Shop
1-B Mitcham Lane
Streatham
London, England SW 16

Central Radio
15 Langney Road
Eastbourne
Sussex, England BN21 3QB

Childs Records
29 Wycombe End
Beaconsfield
Buckinghamshire, England

The Cottage Record Shop
111 Church Street
Brighton
Sussex, England

Dead Wax Records
37 Watcombe Circus
Nottingham, England NG5 2DU

Discurio Records
9 Shepherd Street
London, England W1Y 7LG

Farringdon Records
42 Cheapside
London, England EC2

Farringdon Records
3 Greville Street
London, England EC1 SPQ

Feaver Records
47 Mount Road
Dover, England

George Fraser Records
7 Sondes Street
Walworth
London, England SE17

Gray & Butt Ltd.
45 King Street
Stanford-Le-Hope
Essex
England

Heathrow Records
3 Sandringham Mews
Ealing
London, England W5 3DG

House of Music
761 Stockport Road
Manchester, England

House of Wax
238 Kentish Town Road
London, England NW 5

George Ingram Records
107 Ribchester Road
Salesbury
Blackburn, England BBL 9HQ

Jones Records
114 Allcroft Road
Hall Green
Birmingham, England

Kaleidoscope Records
Hega House
Ullin Street
London, England E 14

Mole Jazz
374 Grays Inn Road
London, England WC 1

Opus Record Shop
65 Old Church Road
Chingford
London, England E4 6ST

Poulton Records
61 The Deansway
Kidderminster
Worcester
Worcestershire, England

Record Cellar
Rye Lane
Peckham
London, England SE 15

The Record Shop
Adderley Street
Uppingham
Leicestershire, England

Record & Tape Exchange
38 Notting Hill Gate
London, England W 11

Rock On Records
3 Kentish Town Road
London, England NW 1

Rockin' Records
146 Maple Road
Penge
London, England SE 20 8JB

78 Record Exchange
9 Lower Hillgate
Stockport
Cheshire, England

S.P. & S. Records Limited
Glampor House
47 Bengal Street
Manchester, England M4 6AF

Henry Stave and Company
29 King William Street
London, England EC4

Henry Stave and Company
9 Dean Street
London, England W1

Stevens Records
48 Eversley Avenue
Barnehurst
Kent, England

John Stoten Records
78 Watermead House
Kingsmead Estate
Homerton
London, England EQ 5RT

That's Entertainment
42 Leaside Avenue
London, England N10

Vintage Record Centre, Ltd.
91 Roman Way
London, England N7 8UN

IRELAND

Walton's Musical Galleries
2 North Frederick Street
Dublin, Ireland 1

SCOTLAND

Allan's Record Shop
104 Portobello High Street
Edinburgh, Scotland EH15 1AL

The Black Disc
201 Gordie Road
Edinburgh, Scotland 11

J.D. Cuthbertson & Company
21 Cambridge Street
Glasgow, Scotland 2

E.M.I. Record Shops, Limited
72–74 St. James Center
Edinburgh, Scotland EH1 3SL

Gloria's Record Bar Limited
234–236 Battlefield Road
Glasgow, Scotland G42 9HN

The Gramophone Shop
1017 Argyle Street
Glasgow, Scotland G3 8NA

H.M.V., Limited
72 Union Street
Glasgow, Scotland C1

James Kerr & Company
98–110 Woodlands Road
Glasgow, Scotland G3 6HB

Rae Macintosh Limited
6–7–8 Queensferry Street
Edinburgh, Scotland EH2 4PA

Milngavie Record Center
Douglas Street
Milngavie, Scotland

Mike's Country Music Room
18 Hilton Avenue
Aberdeen, Scotland

Ritchie Records
24 Claypotts Place
Broughty Ferry, Scotland

WALES

Ken Smith Records
Hendy
Ynysfor
Llanfrothen
Gwynedd, North Wales

CANADIAN RECORD DEALERS

ALBERTA

Collectables, Comics, and Records
1225–A Ninth Avenue Southeast
Calgary, Alberta

Kelly's Records
110 Eighth Avenue Northwest
Calgary, Alberta

BRITISH COLUMBIA

A & B Sound
556 Seymour Street
Vancouver, British Columbia

A & B Sound
641 Yates Street
Victoria, British Columbia

Collectors R.P.M.
4470 Main Street
Vancouver, British Columbia

Frank's Records
3712 West Tenth Avenue
Vancouver, British Columbia V6R
2G4

Ken Lindgren Records
476 East Fifty-ninth Avenue
Vancouver, British Columbia V5X
1Y1

Quintessence Records
1869 West 4th
Vancouver, British Columbia

Record Search
1294 Gladwin
North Vancouver, British Columbia V7R 1A3

Record Search
1529 West 64th
Vancouver, British Columbia

MANITOBA

Charles Ward Records
409 Southall Drive
Winnipeg, Manitoba

ONTARIO

Atchison Records
32 Westleigh Crescent
Toronto, Ontario M8W 3Z7

Gramps & Britisher's Recordrama
844 Danforth Avenue
Toronto, Ontario

Jeff Hannusch Records
69 Cyprus
Kitchener, Ontario

The Record Hunter
P.O. Box 738
Scarborough, Ontario

Record Runner
214 Rideau
Ottawa, Ontario

Showler Records
1440 Lawrence Avenue West

Apartment 809
Toronto, Ontario M6L 1B4

Spicer Records
3283 Lonefeather Crescent
Mississauga, Ontario L4Y 3G6

PRINCE EDWARD ISLAND

William MacEwen Records
R.R. 2
Cornwall, Prince Edward Island

QUEBEC

Discorama Limited
Metro Level
Alexis Hihon Plaza
Montreal, Quebec

Disques Yvon
3207 Beaubien East
Montreal, Quebec

Freddy Imports and Exports
2130 Cote Vertu
Montreal, Quebec

Bob Fuller Records
1421 Gohier Street
St. Laurent, Quebec

Les Galeries Charlesbourg
Charlesbourg, Quebec

Jazz House
P.O. Box 455
Adelaide Street
Toronto, Ontario

Pierre Leblanc Musique
1222 Mont Royal East
Montreal, Quebec

Royaume de Disque ENR
Centre d'Achat la Canardiere
Quebec, Quebec

MISCELLANEOUS INTERNATIONAL RECORD DEALERS

ARGENTINA

Rudi Sazunic Records
Virrey Liniers 577
Buenos Aires, Argentina

BELGIUM

Mac Records
P.O. Box 8
Lanaken, Belgium 3760

Robert Van Den Hove Records
Postbus 328
B 9000 Gent, Belgium

DENMARK

Host Records
Norrekaer 99
Rodovre, Denmark 2610

FRANCE

Dumazert Records
54 rue Blanche
Paris, France 75009

Phonographe Disques
73 rue Blanche
Paris, France 75009

Au Vieux Phono
6 rue Vintimille
Paris, France 75009

ITALY

Anselmo Records
Via Principe Eugenio 90
Rome, Italy 00185

MEXICO

Joe Thomas Records
Moscu 44-4
Guadalajara
Jalisco, Mexico

THE NETHERLANDS

Caminada Records
73 Leidsestrasse
Amsterdam, Netherlands

Concerto Records B.V.
60 Utrechtstrasse
Amsterdam, Netherlands

NEW ZEALAND

Cornelius Records
16 Jubilee Avenue
Devonport
Auckland, New Zealand

Delta Trading Company
Classic Editions Limited
96 Courtenay Place 1
Wellington, New Zealand

Milford Sound and Music Center
113 Kitchener Road
Milford
Auckland, New Zealand

NORWAY

Elysium Records
Ebellsgate 4
Oslo, Norway

SWEDEN

Gustof Bartoll Records
Egnahemsvagen 2
Sundbyberg, Sweden 4

Lundgren Records
Stora Mossens Backe 10
Bromma, Sweden S–161 37

Ronny's Music
P.O. Box 4297
Malmo, Sweden S–203 14

Jorn Wounlund Records
Brusewitzg 6
Gothenburg, Sweden S–411 40

WEST GERMANY

Reimar Binge Records
D–4006 Erkrath 1
Muehlenstrasse, West Germany 12

Hot Wax Records
Postfach 34
D–2880 Brake/Utw.
West Germany

Josef Lange Records
Ossietzkyring 16–3
Hannover 91, West Germany

W. Metzmacher Records
Weierstrasse 31
D–5030 Hurth
West Germany

Ulrich Neuert Records
Vossheide 7A
Werther, West Germany 4806

Richard Weize Records
2871 Harmenhausen
Hohe Seite, West Germany

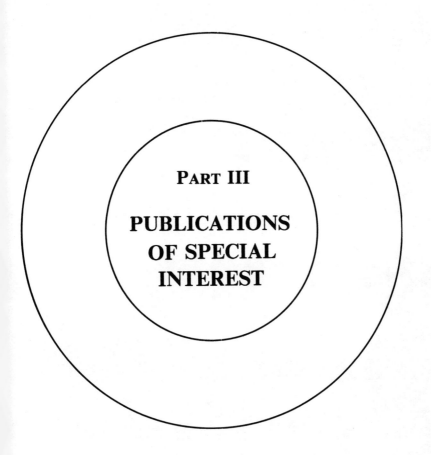

PART III

**PUBLICATIONS
OF SPECIAL
INTEREST**

The following section of the book consists of two parts. First is a compilation of major magazines, journals, newsletters, and fanzines (fan club magazines) of special interest to record collectors. Although in most cases these publications are devoted primarily or exclusively to the particular concerns of record collectors, as with the world's largest such magazine *Goldmine,* there are a few instances in which the relevant concern may be only classified advertising about rare records.

For each publication, the following information has been provided: name of the publication, address to which subscription or other inquiries are to be directed, the number of issues per year, the 1980 single-issue price, the categories of music/recording featured, and what the primary concerns of the publication are. This basic information will enable you to pursue any of these publications which may relate to your own interest or needs.

In several instances publishers did not respond by the given deadline to inquiries about their publication(s) and thus current and/or verified price and other information cannot be included here. In these cases, the name only has been listed alphabetically at the end of this first part of this section of the book.

It should be remembered that, as in any specialized field of publishing, magazines come and go, so it is possible that within a year or so some of these publications may no longer be in business. Generally this tends to be true more often with fanzines.

As with the listing of stores/dealers in the main body of this book, there are bound to be publications which are not included here. Where this has occurred, it is through lack of knowledge of the specific publication.

The second part of this section provides a representative sampling of directories, books, and guides of various types which have proved useful and of interest to most collectors of records. It must be understood that these are only a smattering of literally hundreds of such publications which could have been listed here.

MAGAZINES / JOURNALS / NEWSLETTERS / FANZINES

Add Some Music
P.O. Box 10405
Elmwood, Connecticut 06110
(4 issues per year) (USA: $1.00;
   Non-USA: $2.00)
Categories: Rock & Roll,
   Popular [Specializing: Beach
   Boys, Phil Spector, Jan &
   Dean]
Focus: Columns highlighting
   collectable Beach Boy records;
   Classified ads with multiple
   records for set sale; News of
   forthcoming collections,
   bootlegs, etc.

Afta
c/o Bill-Dale Marcinko
47 Crater Avenue
Wharton, New Jersey 07885
(2 issues per year) (USA: $1.50;
   Non-USA: $2.00)
Categories: Rock & Roll
Focus: Book reviews; Music
   articles; Film articles;
   Television articles

American Phonograph Journal
c/o Tim Christen
P.O. Box 265
Belmont, California 94002
(4 issues per year) (USA: $2.00;
   Non-USA: $3.00)
Categories: Discs and Cylinders
Focus: All aspects of disc and
   cylinder phonograph and
   record research

American Record Guide
1 Windsor Place
Melville, New York 11747
(12 issues per year) (USA: $1.00;
   Non-USA: $2.00)
Categories: Musical Theater,

Jazz, Classical
Focus: Reviews of classical
   recordings and books on
   music; Feature articles;
   Discographies; Classified
   advertising

Antique Phonograph Monthly
c/o Allen Koenigsberg, Editor
650 Ocean Avenue
Brooklyn, New York 11226
(10 issues per year) (USA: $.80;
   Non-USA: $1.00)
Categories: Classical, Jazz,
   Documentary, Acoustic,
   Popular, Cylinders, Discs
   [Mainly from period
   1877–1929]
Focus: Feature articles; Reviews;
   History; Advertisements;
   Auctions; Interviews;
   Discographies

**Association for Recorded Sound
Collections Journal**
P.O. Box 1643
Manassas, Virginia 22110
(3 issues per year) (USA: $4.00;
   Non-USA: $4.00)
Categories: Classical (primarily),
   Jazz, Documentary, Rock
Focus: Articles on scholarly
   subjects; Discographies;
   Reviews; Bibliographic
   features; Collector's column

The Atlantic
Atlantic Subscription Processing
   Center
P.O. Box 1857
Greenwich, Connecticut 06830
(12 issues per year) (USA: $1.50;
   Non-USA: $1.75)
Categories: Classified Advertising

Focus: Classified Advertising

Audio
c/o North American Publishing
  Company
401 North Broad Street
Philadelphia, Pennsylvania 19108
(12 issues per year) (USA: $1.25;
  Non-USA: $1.50)
Categories: Rock, Jazz, Blues,
  Classical, Folk, Theater,
  Audiophile
Focus: Feature articles on
  records and recording
  methods; Primary emphasis on
  high-end audio equipment
  reviews, and audio theory and
  technology

Back Door Man
c/o Phast Phreddie
P.O. Box 6726
Torrance, California 90504
(6 issues per year) (USA: $1.00;
  Non-USA: $1.50)
Categories: Rock & Roll
Focus: Feature articles;
  Interviews; Record reviews

Ballet News
c/o Metropolitan Opera Guild,
  Inc.
1865 Broadway
New York, New York 10023
(18 issues per year) (USA: $1.00;
  Non-USA: $2.00)
Categories: Classical
Focus: Feature articles; Record
  reviews

Bam Balam
c/o Brian Hogg
Flat 1
Castellau

Dunbar
East Lothian, Scotland
(2 issues per year) (USA: $1.50;
  Non-USA:$1.50)
Categories: Rock, Rock & Roll,
  Popular
Focus: Feature articles; Artist
  profiles; Discographies

**BAM–The California Music
  Magazine**
901 Ventura Avenue
Albany, California 94706
(12 issues per year) (USA: Free;
  Non-USA: $1.50)
Categories: Rock, Rock & Roll,
  Popular, Jazz, Crossover
Focus: Feature articles; Record
  reviews; Book reviews;
  Classified advertising;
  Interviews; Profiles

Beatlefan
c/o The Goody Press
P.O. Box 33515
Decatur, Georgia 30033
(6 issues per year) (USA: $1.00;
  Non-USA: $1.50)
Categories: Beatles
Focus: Profiles; Feature articles;
  Reprints; Interviews; Current
  happenings

Beatles Unlimited
P.O. Box 259
2400 AG Alphen aan de Rijn,
  Holland
(6 issues per year) (USA: $2.00;
  Non-USA: $1.75)
Categories: Beatles
Focus: Profiles; Feature articles;
  Reprints; Interviews; Current
  doings

Beggars Banquets
2718 Mills Avenue
Brooklyn, New York 11234
(12 issues per year) (USA: $.50;
    Non-USA: $.75)
Categories: Rock, Rock & Roll
Focus: Gossip; Feature articles;
    Artist profiles

Berlin
c/o B. Moore
Flat 3
No. 1 Mossley Hill Drive
Liverpool 17, England
(2 issues per year) (USA: $2.00;
    Non-USA: $1.75)
Categories: New Wave
Focus: Feature articles; Imagery;
    Graphics related to music

Biff! Bang! Pow!
c/o Lisa Fancher
7826 Cleon Avenue
Sun Valley, California 91352
(2 issues per year) (USA: $.65;
    Non-USA: $1.00)
Categories: Rock, Rock & Roll,
    New Wave
Focus: Feature articles; Profiles

The Big Bandwagon
3055 Hull Avenue
Bronx, New York 10467
(6 issues per year) (USA: $1.50;
    Non-USA: $2.50)
Categories: Jazz, Big Band,
    Thirties and Forties Vocalist
    and Musician, Sound Tracks
Focus: Biographies on jazz/big
    band leaders, musicians, and
    vocalists; Discographies;
    Current record reviews;
    Classified ads; Names of
    collectors; Auctions

Big Beat
8 rue Ferrer
42650 St. Jean Bonnefonds,
    France
(6 issues per year) (USA: $5.00;
    Non-USA: $5.00)
Categories: Rock & Roll,
    Country & Western, Blues
Focus: Articles; Reviews;
    Biographies; Discographies

Biohazard
1301 North Magnum Street
Durham, North Carolina 27701
(6 issues per year) (USA: $.75;
    Non-USA: $1.25)
Categories: Rock, Rock & Roll,
    New Wave, Punk Rock
Focus: Interviews: Discographies;
    Record reviews

Black Music & Jazz Review
c/o Napfield Limited
153 Praed Street
London, England W2
(12 issues per year) (USA: $1.75;
    Non-USA: $1.10)
Categories: Soul, Funk, Jazz,
    Reggae
Focus: Feature articles;
    Interviews; Record reviews;
    Classified ads

Blank Space
c/o Pete Stone
32 Avon Trading Estate
Avonmore Road
London, England W14
(6 issues per year) (USA: $1.50;
    Non-USA: $1.00)
Categories: Rock, Rock & Roll,
    Popular, Jazz
Focus: Profiles; Feature articles;
    Book reviews

Blitz
P.O. Box 279
Dearborn Heights, Michigan
48127
(6 issues per year) (USA: $.75;
Non-USA: $1.50)
Categories: New Wave, Popular,
Rock, Rock & Roll, Detroit
Sound
Focus: Interviews; Research/
history articles; Feature
articles

Block [Dutch Language]
P.O. Box 244
7900 Aimelo, Holland
(6 issues per year) (USA: $1.50;
Non-USA: $1.00)
Categories: Blues, Rock & Roll,
Boogie Woogie, Cajun-Zydeco,
Rockabilly, Rhythm & Blues
Focus: Articles; Interviews,
Concert information; Record
reviews; Film reviews;
Classified ads; Book reviews;
Information about newly
released records

Bluebeat
c/o Wolfgang Metzmacher
Esserstrasse 5
D-5030 Hurth, West Germany
(6 issues per year) (USA: $2.00;
Non-USA: $1.50)
Categories: Rock, Rock & Roll
Focus: Discographies; Feature
articles

Bluegrass Unlimited
P.O. Box 111
Broad Run, Virginia 22014
(12 issues per year) (USA: $1.25;
Non-USA: $2.00)
Categories: Bluegrass, Old-time

Country
Focus: Feature articles; Record
reviews; Classified ads;
Discographies; Auctions;
Profiles; Book reviews; Notes
and queries

Blues Research
65 Grand Avenue
Brooklyn, New York 11205
(1 issue per year) (USA: $.50;
Non-USA: $.50)
Categories: Contemporary Blues
Focus: Feature articles;
Research/history

Blues & Soul
P.O. Box 41745
Atlanta, Georgia 30331
(6 issues per year) (USA: $1.25;
Non-USA: $2.00)
Categories: Soul, Blues
Focus: News items; Short
features; Reviews of
performances; Historical
perspectives

Blues Unlimited
36 Belmont Park
Lewisham
London, England SE13 5DB
(6 issues per year) (USA: $2.00;
Non-USA: $1.75)
Categories: Blues, Rhythm &
Blues
Focus: Feature articles;
Discographies; Record reviews;
Classified ads

BOMP! Magazine
P.O. Box 7112
Burbank, California 91510
(6 issues per year) (USA: $1.50;
Non-USA: $2.00)

Categories: Rock & Roll,
Popular, British Invasion, New
Wave, Punk Rock
Focus: Feature articles; Record
reviews; Classified ads;
Discographies; Want lists;
Historical perspectives

Buygone Record Sales
30 Radcliffe Road
West Bridgford
Nottingham, England
(12 issues per year) (USA: $2.00;
Non-USA: $1.10)
Categories: All
Focus: Listings of rare records
for sale/auction

**Cadence: Monthly Review of
Jazz & Blues**
Route 1
P.O. Box 345
Redwood, New York 13679
(12 issues per year) (USA: $1.25;
Non-USA: $2.00)
Categories: Jazz, Blues, Rhythm
& Blues
Focus: Record reviews;
Collector's column;
Discographies; Classified ads;
Set-sale lists; Feature articles;
Interviews; Book reviews

California Music
2 Kentwell Avenue
Concord 2137, Australia
(12 issues per year) (USA: $2.00;
Non-USA: $1.75)
Categories: Surfing, Hot Rod
[Specializing: Beach Boys, Jan
& Dean]
Focus: Feature articles; Current
events; Gossip column

Cass d'Neon
1610 Chapel Street
New Haven, Connecticut 06511
(2 issues per year) (USA: $1.00;
Non-USA: $2.00)
Categories: Rock, Rock & Roll,
New Wave
Focus: Feature articles; Poetry;
Classified ads; Profiles; Record
reviews

Cat Talk
c/o Nick Garrad
6 Elizabeth Way
Hanworth
Feltham
Middlesex, England TW13 7PH
(4 issues per year) (USA: $1.50;
Non-USA: $1.10)
Categories: Rock & Roll,
Rockabilly
Focus: Feature articles; Profiles;
Current happenings; Record
reviews

Circus
115 East 57th Street
New York, New York 10022
(26 issues per year) (USA: $1.25;
Non-USA: $2.00)
Categories: Rock & Roll,
Popular
Focus: Feature articles; Profiles;
Articles on musical
instruments; Record reviews;
Classified ads

Clavier
1418 Lake Street
Evanston, Illinois 60204
(9 issues per year) (USA: $1.50;
Non-USA: $2.50)
Categories: Classical piano

Focus: Feature articles; Profiles; Interviews; Record reviews

Cle
c/o James Ellis
585 Walnut Drive
Cleveland, Ohio 44132
(4 issues per year) (USA: $.94; Non-USA: $1.50)
Categories: Rock & Roll, New Wave
Focus: Interviews; Feature articles; Profiles; Film articles

Coda: The Jazz Magazine
P.O. Box 87
Station J
Toronto
Ontario, Canada M4J 4X8
(6 issues per year) (USA: $1.75; Non-USA: $2.00)
Categories: Jazz, Blues
Focus: Feature articles; Record reviews; Classified ads

Contemporary Keyboard Magazine
P.O. Box 615
Saratoga, California 95070
(12 issues per year) (USA: $1.25; Non-USA: $2.00)
Categories: All
Focus: Feature articles on keyboard recording artists; Record reviews

Cool Press
The Mews
101 Templeogue Road
Dublin 6, Ireland
(4 issues per year) (USA: $1.00; Non-USA: $2.00)
Categories: All

Focus: Feature articles

Country Music Magazine
P.O. Box 2560
Boulder, Colorado 80302
(12 issues per year) (USA: $1.50; Non-USA: $2.50)
Categories: Country
Focus: Feature articles; Record reviews

Country Music News
P.O. Box 17068
Pittsburgh, Pennsylvania 15235
(12 issues per year) (USA: $1.00; Non-USA: $1.50)
Categories: Country & Western
Focus: Feature articles; Profiles; Record reviews; Classified ads

Country Music People
Powerscroft Road
Footscray
Sidcup
Kent, England
(12 issues per year) (USA: $2.00; Non-USA: $1.50)
Categories: Country & Western
Focus: Artist profiles; Feature articles

Country Style
11058 West Addison
Franklin Park, Illinois 60131
(12 issues per year) (USA: $1.00; Non-USA: $2.00)
Categories: Country, Country-Rock, Rockabilly, Bluegrass
Focus: Feature articles; Record reviews; Industry news; Interviews; Fan club information; Gossip column

County Sales Newsletter
P.O. Box 191
Floyd, Virginia 24091
(8 issues per year) (USA: Free;
Non-USA: Free)
Categories: Country & Western,
Bluegrass, Old-time Country
Focus: Record reviews; Auctions;
Feature articles

Cowabunga
c/o John M. Koenig
P.O. Box 1023
Midland, Michigan 48640
(Back Issues Only) (USA: $1.00;
Non-USA: $1.50)
Categories: Rock & Roll, Rock,
Punk Rock
Focus: Record reviews; Feature
articles; Fanzine reviews;
Artist profiles

Crazy Alligator News
c/o M. Claude Thillay
36 rue Jules Valles
3 Livry Gargan, France
(2 issues per year) (USA: $1.00;
Non-USA: $1.00)
Categories: Bill Haley Music
Focus: Feature articles;
Information about Bill Haley;
News from the Bill Haley
Appreciation Society

Creem
Creem Magazine, Inc.
187 South Woodward
Birmingham, Michigan 48011
(12 issues per year) (USA: $1.25;
Non-USA: $2.00)
Categories: Rock, Rock & Roll,
New Wave

Focus: Record reviews; Feature
articles; Profiles; Classified ads

Deeper and Deeper
c/o K. Murray
18 Stretton Close
Helmlands Estate
Prenton
Birkenhead
Merseyside, England
(4 issues per year) (USA: $.75;
Non-USA: $.75)
Categories: Soul
Focus: Discography; Record
reviews; Feature articles

Descenes
5018 8th Road
South Arlington, Virginia 22204
(4 issues per year) (USA: $.25;
Non-USA: $1.00)
Categories: Various
Focus: Reviews of live
performances; Feature articles
on the Washington, D.C.
bands

Disc Collector Newsletter
P.O. Box 169
Cheswold, Delaware 19936
(6 issues per year) (USA: $.25;
Non-USA: $.35)
Categories: Bluegrass, Old-time
Country, Country & Western
Focus: Record reviews; Book
reviews; Feature articles

Downbeat
c/o Maher Publications
222 West Adams Street
Chicago, Illinois 60606
(12 issues per year) (USA: $1.25;
Non-USA: $2.00)

Categories: Jazz, Contemporary
Music
Focus: Feature articles; Record
reviews; Profiles; Book
reviews; Classified ads

Elvis Monthly
41-47 Derby Road
Heanor
Derbyshire, England DE7 7QH
(12 issues per year) (USA: $1.00;
Non-USA: $1.00)
Categories: Elvis Music
Focus: Feature articles; Record
reviews; Photographs

Elvis World
P.O. Box 388
Bound Brook, New Jersey 08805
(4 issues per year) (USA: $5.00;
Non-USA: $7.00)
Categories: Elvis Music
Focus: Feature articles;
Photographs; Interviews;
Profiles

Every Little Thing
c/o Ticket To Ryde, Ltd.
P.O. Box 3393
Lacey, Washington 98503
(1 issue per year) (USA: $5.00;
Non-USA: $5.00)
Categories: Beatles, Solo Beatles
Focus: Complete listing of all the
Beatles mono/stereo and song
variations from 1962 to 1979

Fanfare
P.O. Box 720
Tenafly, New Jersey 07670
(4 issues per year) (USA: $2.50;
Non-USA: $2.50)
Categories: Classical

Focus: Reviews; Feature articles;
Interviews; Discographies;
Classified ads

Feanzeen
c/o Robert Barry Francos
P.O. Box 109
Parkville Station
Brooklyn, New York 11204
(2 issues per year) (USA: $1.00;
Non-USA: $2.00)
Categories: Rock, Rock & Roll
Focus: Interviews; Feature
articles; Record reviews;
Fanzine reviews

Folkscene Publication
P.O. Box 64545
Los Angeles, California 90064
(6 issues per year) (USA: $1.00;
Non-USA: $1.00)
Categories: Folk
Focus: Columns on old-timey
music; Current bluegrass
releases; Instrument columns;
Folklore; Feature articles on
American and British
traditional music; Record
reviews; Book reviews; Concert
reviews; Women's music;
Women artists

Footnote Magazine
c/o Terry Dash
44 High Street
Meldreth
Royston
Hertfordshire, England SG8 6JU
(8 issues per year) (USA: $1.00;
Non-USA: $1.00)
Categories: New Orleans Jazz
Focus: Feature articles; Record

reviews; Recent record releases; Classified ads; Set-sale lists

Gabba Gabba Gazette
6101 West Fletcher
Chicago, Illinois 60634
(6 issues per year) (USA: $.75; Non-USA: $1.50)
Categories: Punk Rock
Focus: Feature articles on the Chicago sound; Profiles; Reviews

Get Up And Go
c/o Rough Trade
202 Kensington Park Road
London, England W11
(6 issues per year) (USA: $1.00; Non-USA: $1.00)
Categories: Mod-Rock-Soul
Focus: Feature articles

Goldmine: The Record Collector's Marketplace
P.O. Box 187
Fraser, Michigan 48026
(12 issues per year) (USA: $1.50; Non-USA: $1.75)
Categories: Rock, Rock & Roll, Jazz, Blues, Folk, Country & Western, Rhythm & Blues, Bootlegs, Promotional Items
Focus: Set-sale lists; Auction lists; Feature articles; Profiles; Discographies; Record reviews; Book reviews; Concert reviews; Trading lists; Want lists; Classified ads; Display ads

Gorilla Beat
c/o Hans Jurgen Klitsch
Kuhlendahl 94

Mulheim, Germany
(4 issues per year) (USA: $2.00; Non-USA: $2.00)
Categories: Rock, Rock & Roll, Mersey, New Wave
Focus: Photographs; Interviews; News updates; Discographies; Feature articles

The GRACKLE: Improvised Music In Transition
c/o Ron Welburn
P.O. Box 244
Vanderveer Station
Brooklyn, New York 11210
(4 issues per year) (USA: $1.50; Non-USA: $2.50)
Categories: Contemporary Jazz, Classical, International
Focus: Interviews; Essays; Feature articles; Profiles

Gramophone
177–179 Kenton Road
Harrow
Middlesex, England HA3 OHA
(12 issues per year) (USA: $2.00; Non-USA: $1.10)
Categories: Classical, Popular, Jazz, Documentary
Focus: Reviews of classical releases; Artist interviews; Feature articles; Classified ads; Release lists

The Gunn Report
15 Lynton Road
Hadleigh
Benfleet
Essex, England SS7 2QG
(6 issues per year) (USA: $1.10; Non-USA: $1.10)
Categories: 78's of Jazz, Dance

Band, Personality,
Instrumental
Focus: Discographies; Technical
advice; Book reviews; Reissue
reviews; Record research;
Feature articles; Want lists;
Auctions

Harpers Magazine
1255 Portland Place
Boulder, Colorado 80323
(12 issues per year) (USA: $1.50;
Non-USA: $2.00)
Categories: Classified Advertising
Focus: Classified Advertising

Hi-Fi Stereo Buyer's Guide
P.O. Box 1855
General Post Office
New York, New York 10001
(6 issues per year) (USA: $1.50;
Non-USA: $2.50)
Categories: Classified Advertising
Focus: Classified Advertising

High Fidelity/Musical America
1 Sound Avenue
Marion, Ohio 43302
(12 issues per year) (USA: $1.50;
Non-USA: $2.50)
Categories: Classified Advertising
Focus: Classified Advertising

**Hillandale News: Journal of the
City of London Phonograph &
Gramophone Society**
157 Childwall Valley Road
Liverpool, England L16 1LA
(6 issues per year) (USA: $2.50;
Non-USA: $1.50)
Categories: Early Recording
History
Focus: Feature articles; Classified
ads; Sales lists

**Hobbies: The Magazine for
Collectors**
Lightner Publishing Corporation
1006 South Michigan Avenue
Chicago, Illinois 60605
(12 issues per year) (USA: $1.50;
Non-USA: $2.00)
Categories: All
Focus: Profiles; Historical
recordings; Classified ads;
Feature articles

Hoopla
c/o Jon Ginoli
210 East Morningside Drive
Peoria. Illinois 61614
(6 issues per year) (USA: $.50;
Non-USA: $1.00)
Categories: Rock, Rock & Roll,
New Wave
Focus: Reviews of performances;
Record reviews; Profiles;
Feature articles

**Hot Wacks [With Supplemental
Hot Wacks Newsletter to
Subscribers]**
c/o Bert Muirhead
16 Almondbank Terrace
Edinburgh, England EH11 LSS
(5 issues per year) (USA: $1.50;
Non-USA: $1.00)
Categories: Rock, New Wave,
Rock & Roll, Blues
Focus: Interviews; Reviews;
Classified ads; Auction lists;
Historical overviews;
Discographies; Label listings

Image
c/o Ric Menck
114 Fox Hunt Trail
Barrington, Illinois 60010
(6 issues per year) (USA: $1.00;

Non-USA: $1.50)
Categories: New Wave
Focus: Feature articles on the
Chicago New Wave sound

Imagine
c/o Gorman Bechard
P.O. Box 2715
Waterbury, Connecticut 06720
(6 issues per year) (USA: $1.25;
Non-USA: $1.75)
Categories: Rock, Rock & Roll,
Country & Western, Jazz
Focus: Feature articles; Record
reviews; Book reviews; Profiles

Invasion
c/o Bill Patrick
P.O. Box 426
Trexlertown, Pennsylvania 18086
(12 issues per year) (USA: $1.00;
Non-USA: $1.50)
Categories: Rock, Rock & Roll,
Popular
Focus: Record reviews; Reviews
of live performances; Feature
articles

It Will Stand
1505 Elizabeth Avenue
Charlotte, North Carolina 28204
(12 issues per year) (USA: $1.00;
Non-USA: $1.50)
Categories: Rock & Roll, Rock,
Popular
Focus: Artist interviews;
Information on dance contests;
Record reviews; Concert
reviews; Puzzles

It's Only Rock 'n' Roll
P.O. Box 5629
San Antonio, Texas 78201

(12 issues per year) (USA: $.50;
Non-USA: $1.00)
Categories: Rock & Roll, Rock
Focus: Feature articles; Profiles;
Concert reviews; Record
reviews

Jazz Americana
c/o The Delaware Valley Jazz
Society
P.O. Box 276
Bellmawr, New Jersey 08031
(4 issues per year) (USA $1.00;
Non-USA: $1.25)
Categories: Traditional Jazz,
Mainstream, Swing
Focus: Biographies;
Discographies of traditional
jazz people; Record reviews;
Book reviews; News of jazz
festivals; Classified ads;
Feature articles

Jazz, Blues & Co. [French
Language]
1 rue Dalloz
75013 Paris, France
(6 issues per year) (USA: $1.00;
Non-USA: $1.75)
Categories: Blues, Jazz
Focus: Profiles; Feature articles;
Record reviews

Jazz Echo
P.O. Box 671
Vienna, Austria
(6 issues per year) (USA: $1.00;
Non-USA: $1.50)
Categories: Jazz, Blues
Focus: Feature articles for
collectors; Record reviews;

Book reviews; Magazine reviews; Classified ads; Listings of collectors

Jazz Forum [English, German, and Polish Languages]
P.O. Box 671
Vienna, Austria
(6 issues per year) (USA: $2.50; Non-USA: $3.00)
Categories: Jazz, Blues
Focus: Feature articles for collectors; Record reviews; Book reviews; Magazine reviews; Classified ads; Listings of collectors

Jazz Journal International
Pitman Periodicals Ltd.
41 Parker Street
London, England WC2B 5PB
(12 issues per year) (USA: $1.50; Non-USA: $1.35)
Categories: Jazz
Focus: Jazz news; Profiles; Artist interviews; Jazz information; Feature articles; Record reviews; Jazz diary; Concert reviews

Jazz Magazine
P.O. Box 212
Northport, New York 11768
(4 issues per year) (USA: $2.50; Non-USA: $4.00)
Categories: Jazz
Focus: Feature articles, Jazz news; Record reviews; Profiles

JEMF Quarterly
c/o John Edwards Memorial Foundation

University of California at Los Angeles
Los Angeles, California 90024
(4 issues per year) (USA: $2.50; Non-USA: $2.50)
Categories: Folk, Country & Western, Bluegrass, Cowboy, Old-time Country, Sacred, Blues, Gospel, Documentary, Rock & Roll
Focus: Feature articles; Bibliographical articles; Biographical articles; Historical articles; Discographies; Book reviews; Record reviews

Jettset
c/o Goldie Acorn
975 Garfield Street
Winnipeg
Manitoba, Canada R3E 2N5
(1 issue per year) (USA: $1.00; Non-USA: $1.50)
Categories: Rock, Rock & Roll
Focus: Feature articles

Journal of Country Music
Country Music Foundation
4 Music Square East
Nashville, Tennessee 37203
(3 issues per year) (USA: $4.98; Non-USA: $4.98)
Categories: Country & Western, Old-time Country
Focus: Feature articles; Profiles; Interviews; Discographies; Historical articles

Journal of Jazz Studies
Institute of Jazz Studies
Transactions Periodicals Consortium

Rutgers University
116 College Avenue
New Brunswick, New Jersey
 08903
(2 issues per year) (USA: $5.00;
 Non-USA: $5.50)
Categories: Jazz, Blues, Ragtime
Focus: Discographies; Scholarly
 articles on music; Performers;
 Social history articles;
 Recording labels articles;
 Record reviews; Book reviews

**The Kastlemusick Monthly
 Bulletin**
901 Washington Street
Wilmington, Delaware 19801
(12 issues per year) (USA: $1.50;
 Non-USA: $2.00)
Categories: All
Focus: Feature articles;
 Discographies; Profiles;
 Classified ads

Kicks
c/o Miriam Linna-Billy Miller
P.O. Box 646
Cooper Station
New York, New York 10003
(6 issues per year) (USA: $1.50;
 Non-USA: $2.00)
Categories: Rock, Rock & Roll
Focus: Feature articles; Profiles;
 Interviews

Kids Stuff
17 Willcocks Close
Chessington
Surrey, England
(4 issues per year) (USA: $1.00;
 Non-USA: $.75)
Categories: Punk Rock, Rock,
 Rock & Roll

Focus: Feature articles;
 Interviews; Profiles

Killer Children
82 Norwood Avenue
Newtonville, Massachusetts
 02160
(4 issues per year) (USA: $1.00;
 Non-USA: $1.50)
Categories: New Wave, Rock &
 Roll
Focus: Feature articles on the
 Boston sound; Profiles;
 Interviews

The L.A. Weekly
5325 Sunset Boulevard
Los Angeles, California 90027
(12 issues per year) (USA: $.35;
 Non-USA: $1.00)
Categories: Popular, Rock, Rock
 & Roll, Jazz
Focus: Feature articles on club
 and music information

**Larry's Oldies But Goodies
 Newsletter**
P.O. Box 694
Morehead, Kentucky 40351
(2 issues per year) (USA: $1.00;
 Non-USA: $1.50)
Categories: Rock, Rock & Roll,
 Rockabilly
Focus: Interviews; Feature
 articles

Lightnin' Strikes
c/o Harry Young
5107 South Blackstone–#603
Chicago, Illinois 60615
(2 issues per year) (USA: $1.00;
 Non-USA: $1.50)
Categories: Lou Christie Music

Focus: Artist profile; Feature articles; Interviews; Everything Lou Christie

Living Blues Magazine
2615 North Wilton Avenue
Chicago, Illinois 60614
(4 issues per year) (USA: $1.50; Non-USA: $2.00)
Categories: Blues
Focus: Feature articles; Record reviews; News of new releases; Classified ads

Living in Paradise
241–08 140th Avenue
Rosedale, New York 11422
(6 issues per year) (USA: $.90; Non-USA: $1.50)
Categories: Rock, Rock & Roll, New Wave
Focus: Interviews; Artist profiles; Feature articles

Lost Music Network
P.O. Box 2391
Olympia, Washington 98507
(6 issues per year) (USA: $1.00; Non-USA: $2.00)
Categories: Rock & Roll, New Wave, Rock
Focus: Feature articles; Interviews; Reviews of live performances

Maximum Speed
40 Sidlaw House
Portland Avenue
Stamford Hill
London, England N 16
(4 issues per year) (USA: $1.00; Non-USA: $.75)
Categories: Rock, Mod, New Wave

Focus: Feature articles; Interviews

Mean Mountain Music
P.O. Box 04352
Milwaukee, Wisconsin 53204
(6 issues per year) (USA: $2.00; Non-USA: $2.50)
Categories: Rockabilly
Focus: Feature articles; Interviews; Discographies; Photographs

Media Review Digest
Pierian Press
P.O. Box 1808
Ann Arbor, Michigan 48106
(1 issue per year) (USA: $120.00; Non-USA: $120.00)
Categories: All
Focus: The most complete annual index to and digest of reviews, evaluations, and descriptions of records and tapes

Melody Maker
Surrey House
1 Throwley Way
Sutton
Surrey, England
(52 issues per year) (USA: $1.25; Non-USA: $1.00)
Categories: All
Focus: Feature articles; Interviews; Profiles; Record reviews

Memory Lane
40 Merryfield Approach
Leigh on Sea
Essex, England SS9 4HJ
(6 issues per year) (USA: $.90; Non-USA: $.90)

Categories: Dance Music, Jazz and Vocalists of the 78 r.p.m. era

Focus: Feature articles; Photographs; Discographies; Record reviews; Book reviews; Classified ads

Michigan Musician
P.O. Box 724
Detroit, Michigan 48232
(12 issues per year) (USA: $.50; Non-USA: $1.00)
Categories: Rock, Jazz, Blues, Opera, Classical, Electronic
Focus: Feature articles; Profiles; Interviews; Information about the Detroit jazz scene

Micrography
Stevinstraat 14
Alpen aan den Rijn, Holland
(4 issues per year) (USA: $1.30; Non-USA: $1.30)
Categories: Jazz and Blues to the 1950s
Focus: Information about new releases in jazz up to 1960

The Mississippi Rag
5644 Morgan Avenue South
Minneapolis, Minnesota 55419
(6 issues per year) (USA: $.75; Non-USA: $1.25)
Categories: Traditional Jazz, Ragtime
Focus: Record reviews; Concert photographs; Feature articles

Modern Recording Magazine
14 Vanderventer Avenue
Port Washington, New York 11050
(12 issues per year) (USA: $1.50; Non-USA: $1.50)
Categories: Rock & Roll, Jazz, Blues, Classical, Shows, Sound Tracks, Progressive Music
Focus: Artist profiles; Interviews; Record reviews; Producer profiles; Engineer profiles; Feature articles

Mom 'N' Pops Records Newsletter
2915 Kapiolani Boulevard
Honolulu, Hawaii 96814
(12 issues per year) (USA: $1.00; Non-USA: $1.50)
Categories: Rock, Rock & Roll, Popular
Focus: Feature articles; Record reviews; Set-sale lists; Auction lists

Mongoloid
P.O. Box 17388
Cleveland, Ohio 44117
(4 issues per year) (USA: $.50; Non-USA: $1.00)
Categories: Popular, Rock, Rock & Roll
Focus: Feature articles; Readers' polls; Interviews; Profiles; Current information about the Cleveland music scene

Moods for Moderns
c/o Gwynne Garfunkle
14127 Margate Street
Van Nuys, California 91401
(6 issues per year) (USA: $1.00; Non-USA: $1.50)
Categories: Elvis Costello

Focus: Tour information; Live
photographs; Feature articles;
Interviews

Music and Letters
c/o Journals Manager
Oxford University Press
Press Road
Neasden
London, England NW10 ODD
(4 issues per year) (USA: $1.50;
Non-USA: $1.50)
Categories: Classical
Focus: Reviews of music and
books on music

Music Phaze
P.O. Box 951
Fair Oaks, California 95628
(12 issues per year) (USA: $.75;
Non-USA: $1.25)
Categories: Popular, Rock, Rock
& Roll
Focus: Feature articles;
Information about the
Sacramento music scene;
Classified ads; Interviews;
Profiles

New Age
2505 Circle Pine Crescent
Greensboro, North Carolina
27407
(12 issues per year) (USA: $1.00;
Non-USA: $1.50)
Categories: Rock, Rock & Roll,
Popular
Focus: Feature articles; Profiles;
Interviews

The New Amberola Graphic
37 Caledonia Street
St. Johnsbury, Vermont 05819

(4 issues per year) (USA: $.50;
Non-USA: $.50)
Categories: All
Focus: Recorded sound from
1895 to 1935; Feature articles
on all phases of early
recordings and phonographs;
Discographies; Book reviews;
Information about record
collecting; Classified ads

New Kommotion
c/o Shazam Promotions
3 Bowrons Avenue
Wembley
Middlesex, England HAO 4QS
(4 issues per year) (USA: $3.00;
Non-USA: $2.00)
Categories: Rock & Roll,
Rockabilly
Focus: Feature articles; Session
discographies; Record reviews;
Classified ads; Profiles

New Kountry Korral Magazine
P.O. Box 5004
S-720 05 Vasteras, Sweden
(4 issues per year) (USA: $2.50;
Non-USA: $2.50)
Categories: Country & Western,
Rockabilly
Focus: Feature articles; Record
reviews; Book reviews;
Classified ads; Auction lists;
Set-sale lists; Charts

The New Music
P.O. Box 430
Postal Station A
Toronto
Ontario, Canada M5W 1C2

(12 issues per year) (USA: $1.00;
  Non-USA: $1.00)
Categories: New Wave, Punk
  Rock, Rock, Rock & Roll
Focus: Feature articles;
  Information on the Toronto
  music scene; Interviews;
  Profiles

New Musical Express
Third Floor
5-7 Carnaby Street
London, England W1V 1PG
(52 issues per year) (USA: $1.25;
  Non-USA: $1.00)
Categories: Rock, Rock & Roll,
  Popular, Jazz
Focus: Feature articles;
  Interviews; Profiles; Record
  reviews; Book reviews

The New Records
2019 Walnut Street
Philadelphia, Pennsylvania 19103
(12 issues per year) (USA: $8.00;
  Non-USA: $9.00 [Subscription
  Only])
Categories: Classical
Focus: Reviews of new classical
  recordings from throughout
  the world

New West Magazine
New West Magazine Subscription
  Department
P.O. Box 2965
Boulder, Colorado 80322
(26 issues per year) (USA: $1.00;
  Non-USA: $1.50)
Categories: Classified Advertising
Focus: Classified Advertising

New York Rocker
166 Fifth Avenue
New York, New York 10010
(12 issues per year) (USA: $1.25;
  Non-USA: $1.75)
Categories: Rock, Rock & Roll,
  New Wave, Punk Rock
Focus: Feature articles; Profiles;
  Interviews

New York Rocker Pix
166 Fifth Avenue
New York, New York 10010
(2 issues per year) (USA: $1.00;
  Non-USA: $1.50)
Categories: Rock, Rock & Roll,
  Popular, New Wave, Punk
  Rock
Focus: Photographs only

The Next Big Thing
60 Hamilton Road
Grangemouth
Stirlingshire, Scotland
(6 issues per year) (USA: $1.50;
  Non-USA: $1.00)
Categories: Popular, Rock, Rock
  & Roll
Focus: Feature articles;
  Interviews; Profiles

Not Fade Away
Vintage Rock 'N' Roll
  Appreciation Society
16 Coniston Avenue
Prescot
Merseyside, England L34 2SW
(4 issues per year) (USA: $4.00;
  Non-USA: $2.75)
Categories: 1950s Rock & Roll,
  Rockabilly, Rhythm & Blues,
  Blues

Focus: Record reviews; Feature articles; Want lists; Classified ads; Interviews; Profiles

Not Fade Away: The Texas Music Magazine
1316 Kenwood
Austin, Texas 78704
(6 issues per year) (USA: $1.50; Non-USA: $2.00)
Categories: Texas Music
Focus: Feature articles on Texas music 1950–1970; Interviews; Discographies; Record reviews; Profiles

Not Right
412 West Lovett
Charlotte, Michigan 48813
(2 issues per year) (USA: $1.00; Non-USA: $1.50)
Categories: Rock, Rock & Roll
Focus: Feature articles

Nuggets
1 Melville Road
Edgbaston
Birmingham, England B16 9LN
(5 issues per year) (USA: $1.50; Non-USA: $1.00)
Categories: Country & Western, Rock, Rock & Roll, Rockabilly
Focus: Record reviews; Profiles; Feature articles; Interviews

Old Time Music
33 Brunswick Gardens
London, England W8 4AW
(5 issues per year) (USA: $1.50; Non-USA: $1.00)
Categories: Pure Country Music

Focus: Feature articles; Record reviews; Discographies; Profiles

Omaha Rainbow
c/o Peter O'Brien
10 Lesley Court
Harcourt Road
Wallington
Surrey, England SM6 8AZ
(4 issues per year) (USA: $1.50; Non-USA: $1.00)
Categories: Rock, Rock & Roll, New Wave
Focus: Feature articles; Interviews; Profiles

Opera News
c/o Metropolitan Opera Guild, Inc.
1865 Broadway
New York, New York 10023
(18 issues per year) (USA: $1.50; Non-USA: $2.00)
Categories: Classical
Focus: Record reviews; Feature articles

Outlet
c/o Trev Faull
33 Aintree Crescent
Barkingside
Ilford, England IG6 2HD
(6 issues per year) (USA: $1.50; Non-USA: $1.00)
Categories: Rock, Rock & Roll, New Wave, Punk Rock
Focus: Gossip; Discographies; Feature articles; Record reviews

Paperback Writer
P.O. Box 7801
Fort Worth, Texas 76111

(6 issues per year) (USA: $1.50; Non-USA: $1.75)
Categories: Beatles
Focus: Feature articles; Profiles; Record reviews

Paul's Record Magazine
P.O. Box 14241
Hartford, Connecticut 06114
(6 issues per year) (USA: $2.00; Non-USA: $2.50)
Categories: Popular music of the 1950s and 1960s; Rock & Roll; Rhythm & Blues; Soul
Focus: Feature articles; Research articles; Artist profiles

Pet Sounds
Peter Reum
P.O. Box 1523
Greeley, Colorado 80632
(Back Issues Only) (USA: Write for Information; Non-USA: Write for Information)
Categories: California Music; Beach Boys, Jan & Dean
Focus: Interviews; Rare photographs; Discographies; Classified ads; Feature articles; Record reviews

The Phonographic News
P.O. Box 253
Prospect
South Australia, Australia 5082
(6 issues per year) (USA: $1.75; Non-USA: $1.75)
Categories: Feature articles; Book reviews; Record reviews; Classified ads; Special concern is Australia's contribution to recorded sound as deemed by

the Phonograph Society of South Australia

Pickin'
North American Building
401 North Broad Street
Philadelphia, Pennsylvania 19108
(12 issues per year) (USA: $1.50; Non-USA: $2.00)
Categories: Guitar Music
Focus: Feature articles; Record reviews; Information articles

Pig Paper
c/o Gary Pig
70 Cotton Drive
Mississauga
Ontario, Canada L5G 1Z9
(6 issues per year) (USA: $1.00; Non-USA: $1.00)
Categories: Rock & Roll, Punk Rock, New Wave
Focus: Feature articles; Interviews; Profiles

Piping Press News
P.O. Box 162
Hazel Park, Michigan 48030
(4 issues per year) (USA: $1.75; Non-USA: $1.75)
Categories: All
Focus: Feature articles; Reprints; Classified ads

Pop Top Magazine: The Record Buyer's Guide
909 Beacon Street
Boston, Massachusetts 02215
(12 issues per year) (USA: Free; Non-USA: $.50)
Categories: All
Focus: Record reviews; Information about new

releases; Feature articles;
Discographies; Collector's
reviews

Popular Music & Society
c/o R. Serge Denisoff
Department of Sociology
Bowling Green State University
Bowling Green, Ohio 43403
(2 issues per year) (USA: $3.00;
   Non-USA: $4.00)
Categories: All
Focus: Feature articles; Book
   reviews; Record reviews

**PTA (Pittsburgh's Top
   Alternatives)**
c/o Mark Pfeifer
No. 204
601 Clyde Street
Pittsburgh, Pennsylvania 15213
(6 issues per year) (USA: $1.00;
   Non-USA: $1.25)
Categories: Rock & Roll, Rock,
   New Wave
Focus: Feature articles; Profiles

Punk
P.O. Box 675
New York, New York 10009
(6 issues per year) (USA: $1.25;
   Non-USA: $1.50)
Categories: Punk Rock, New
   Wave
Focus: Interviews; Feature
   articles

Pure Blues
c/o Claudia Chapman
P.O. Box 388
Wolcottville, Indiana 46795
(6 issues per year) (USA: $.75;
   Non-USA: $1.00)

Categories: Led Zeppelin
Focus: Reviews of live
   performances; Feature articles;
   Photographs

Radio Free Jazz
3212 Pennsylvania Avenue, S.E.
Washington, D.C. 20020
(12 issues per year) (USA: $1.00;
   Non-USA: $2.00)
Categories: Jazz
Focus: Record reviews; Listings
   of new releases; Book reviews;
   Interviews; Feature articles

The Rag Times
c/o The Maple Leaf Club
5560 West 62nd Street
Los Angeles, California 90056
(6 issues per year) (USA: $1.00;
   Non-USA: $1.25)
Categories: Ragtime
Focus: Record reviews; Feature
   articles; Historical articles
   about ragtime music; Artist
   profiles

The Record Collector
503 Norwich Road
Ipswich, England IP1 6JT
(6 issues per year) (USA:
   Subscription Only; Non-USA:
   Subscription Only)
Categories: Classical Vocal
Focus: Artist biographies;
   Discographies; Feature articles;
   Book reviews; Record reviews

Record Digest
Groom Creek
Prescott, Arizona 86301
(24 issues per year) (USA: $1.00;
   Non-USA: $1.00)

Categories: Record information;
Records for sale; Feature
articles; Artist profiles

Record Exchanger
P.O. Box 6144
Orange, California 92667
(6 issues per year) (USA: $1.50;
Non-USA: $1.50)
Categories: Rock & Roll,
Rhythm & Blues, Blues, Elvis,
Rockabilly
Focus: Feature articles on the
Rock & Roll of the 1950s and
1960s; Discographies; Record
reviews

Record Mart
16 London Hill
Rayleigh
Essex, England SS6 7HP
(12 issues per year) (USA: $2.00;
Non-USA: $2.00)
Categories: Rock & Roll,
Rockabilly, Rhythm & Blues,
Boogie, Soul, Blues, Doo Wop,
Popular, Country & Western
Focus: Artist profiles; Classified
ads; Set-sale lists; Auction
lists; Photographs

Record Research Magazine
65 Grand Avenue
Brooklyn, New York 11205
(10 issues per year) (USA: $1.00;
Non-USA: $1.25)
Categories: Rock & Roll, Jazz,
Classical, Blues, Documentary
Focus: Feature articles; Record
reviews; Book reviews;
Auction lists

Record Review Magazine
c/o Ashley Communications
P.O. Box 91878
Los Angeles, California 90049
(6 issues per year) (USA: $1.25;
Non-USA: $1.50)
Categories: All
Focus: Interviews; Record
reviews; Feature articles

Recorded Sound
c/o The British Institute of
Recorded Sound
29 Exhibition Road
London, England SW 7
(4 issues per year) (USA: $8.00;
Non-USA: $5.75)
Categories: All
Focus: Feature articles; Artist
profiles; Record reviews; Book
reviews; Discographies;
Technical articles

Recycler
2898 Rowena Avenue
Los Angeles, California 90039
(52 issues per year) (USA: $.50;
Non-USA: $1.00)
Categories: Classified Advertising
Focus: Classified Advertising

Reggae News
P.O. Box 31125
San Francisco, California 94131
(6 issues per year) (USA: $.50;
Non-USA: $1.00)
Categories: Reggae Music
Focus: Feature articles;
Information articles; Classified
ads

Relix Magazine
P.O. Box 94
Brooklyn, New York 11229
(6 issues per year) (USA: $1.75;
Non-USA: $2.50)
Categories: Rock & Roll
Focus: Feature articles; Record
reviews; Classified ads;
Auction lists; Set-sale lists

Reviewsit
c/o Tom Luba
614½ North Oneida Street
Appleton, Wisconsin 54911
(6 issues per year) (USA: $1.25;
Non-USA: $1.50)
Categories: All
Focus: Record reviews; Artist
profiles

Revival
c/o Golden Oldies Club of Great
Britain
P.O. Box 142
London, England E17 4JW
(12 issues per year) (USA: $1.25;
Non-USA: $.90)
Categories: Rock & Roll, Rock,
Rockabilly
Focus: Artist profiles; Record
reviews; Classified ads; Feature
articles

R-O-C-K
P.O. Box 48
Hovseter
Oslo 7, Norway
(6 issues per year) (USA: $2.00;
Non-USA: $2.00)
Categories: Rock & Roll,
Rockabilly, Country &

Western, Rhythm & Blues,
Blues
Focus: Interviews; Biographies;
Discographies; Concert
reviews; Original photographs;
Record reviews; Want lists;
Set-sale lists

**Rock and Roll International
Magazine**
c/o John Garodkin
Snesere Torpvej 7
Snesere
4733 Tappernøje, Denmark
(6 issues per year) (USA: $1.85;
Non-USA: $1.50)
Categories: Rock & Roll,
Rockabilly, Rhythm & Blues
Focus: Biographies;
Discographies; Record reviews;
Rare photographs

**Rockages Collectors Club
Official Newsletter**
P.O. Box 27
Philadelphia, Pennsylvania 19105
(6 issues per year) (USA: $1.00;
Non-USA: $1.25)
Categories: New Wave, Rock,
Rock & Roll
Focus: Feature articles; Articles
on newly issued collectables;
Convention news; Classified
ads

Rockin' In the Fourth Estate
c/o Suzanne Newman
P.O. Box 96
Scarsdale, New York 10583
(6 issues per year) (USA: $1.75;
Non-USA: $2.00)

Categories: Rock, Rock & Roll, New Wave

Focus: Feature articles; Fan club information; Gossip; Artist profiles

Rockin' With Aware Research Magazine
P.O. Box 242
Gravesend Station
Brooklyn, New York 11223
(6 issues per year) (USA: $2.00; Non-USA: $3.00)
Categories: Rock & Roll; Beatles
Focus: Biographies; Discographies; Record reviews of reissues

Rocking Chair
P.O. Box 27
Philadelphia, Pennsylvania 19105
(6 issues per year) (USA: $1.00; Non-USA: $1.00)
Categories: Rock, Rock & Roll
Focus: Record reviews; Feature articles

Rocking Regards [German Language]
c/o Gotz Alsmann
Strassburger Weg 66
4400 Munster, West Germany
(5 issues per year) (USA: Subscription Only; Non-USA: Subscription Only)
Categories: Rock & Roll, Rhythm & Blues, Western Swing, Rockabilly, Black Swing, European Rock & Roll
Focus: Feature articles; Artist profiles; Record label articles; Record reviews; Interviews;

Classified ads; Set-sale lists

Rollin' Rock
6918 Peach Avenue
Van Nuys, California 91406
(6 issues per year) (USA: $2.00; Non-USA: $3.50)
Categories: Rock & Roll of the 1950s, Rockabilly, Rhythm & Blues
Focus: Reviews; Interviews; Biographies; Feature articles; Classified ads

Rolling Stone Magazine
745 Fifth Avenue
New York, New York 10022
(26 issues per year) (USA: $1.95; Non-USA: $2.50)
Categories: All
Focus: Feature articles; Artist profiles; Interviews; Record reviews; Book reviews; Biographies; Classified ads

Safe As Milk
45 Greenvale Road
London, England SE9 1PB
(6 issues per year) (USA: $2.00; Non-USA: $1.50)
Categories: Rock, Rock & Roll, New Wave, Punk Rock
Focus: Feature articles; Artist profiles; Concert reviews; Interviews

Saturday Review
P.O. Box 10010
Des Moines, Iowa 50340
(24 issues per year) (USA: $1.00; Non-USA: $1.75)
Categories: Classified Advertising
Focus: Classified Advertising

Scene
1314 Huron Road
Cleveland, Ohio 44115
(52 issues per year) (USA: $.30;
Non-USA: $.75)
Categories: Rock & Roll
Focus: Feature articles; Artist
profiles; Information about the
mid-Ohio Rock & Roll scene

Scone (Soundtrack Collectors of New England)
P.O. Box 813
Conway, New Hampshire 03818
(6 issues per year) (USA: $.50;
Non-USA: $1.50)
Categories: Movie Sound Tracks,
Original Cast, Personality
Focus: Feature articles; Market
values of albums; Record
reviews; News of new releases;
Information on obscure titles;
Classified ads; Auction lists;
Set-sale lists

Shades
c/o Sheila Wawanash
P.O. Box 310
Station B
Toronto
Ontario, Canada M5T 2W2
(12 issues per year) (USA: $1.00;
Non-USA: $1.50)
Categories: Rock & Roll
Focus: Feature articles; Artist
profiles; Information about the
Toronto Rock & Roll scene

Simple Visions
c/o Anne Steichen
2008 Emerson–#2
Berkeley, California 94703

(6 issues per year) (USA: $.50;
Non-USA: $1.00)
Categories: Rock, Rock & Roll,
Strawbs Music
Focus: Feature articles; Reviews
of live performances;
Interviews; Artist profiles

Sing Out! The Folk Song Magazine
505 Eighth Avenue
New York, New York 10018
(6 issues per year) (USA: $1.50;
Non-USA: $2.00)
Categories: Folk Music of all
types
Focus: Feature articles; Record
reviews; Book reviews;
Discographies; Information
about new releases; Songfinder
column

Slash
P.O. Box 48888
Los Angeles, California 90048
(12 issues per year) (USA: $1.00;
Non-USA: $1.50)
Categories: Rock & Roll, New
Wave, Punk Rock
Focus: Feature articles; Artist
profiles; Interviews; Record
reviews

Sniffin Glue
c/o Danny Baker
27 Dryden Chambers
119 Oxford Street
London, England W1
(6 issues per year) (USA: $1.25;
Non-USA: $1.00)
Categories: Punk Rock

Focus: Feature articles; Artist
profiles; Interviews; Concert
reviews

Soundtrack Collector's Quarterly
[Formerly: **SCN: Soundtrack
Collector's Newsletter**]
P.O. Box 3895
Springfield, Massachusetts 01101
(4 issues per year) (USA:
Subscription Only; Non-USA:
Subscription Only)
Categories: Film Music
Focus: Interviews; Record
reviews; Feature articles;
Filmographies; Discographies;
Classified ads

Spider
P.O. Box AP
Ventura, California 93001
(6 issues per year) (USA: $1.00;
Non-USA: $1.25)
Categories: Rock & Roll
Focus: Feature articles; Artist
profiles; Interviews;
Photographs

Stereo Magazine
The Publishing House
Great Barrington, Massachusetts
01230
(4 issues per year) (USA: $1.95;
Non-USA: $3.95)
Categories: All
Focus: Record reviews of
"audiophile" discs

Stereo Review [Formerly: **Hi Fi
Stereo Review**]
P.O. Box 2771
Boulder, Colorado 80323

(12 issues per year) (USA: $1.50;
Non-USA: $2.00)
Categories: Popular, Jazz, Rock,
Classical
Focus: Record reviews; Feature
articles; Technical information;
Classified ads

Story Untold
c/o Arcade Records
P.O. Box 18
Bayside, New York 11361
(4 issues per year) (USA: $2.00;
Non-USA: $2.50)
Categories: Rock & Roll,
Rhythm & Blues, Rock
Focus: Feature articles; Artist
profiles; Discographies; Record
reviews; Radio surveys

Strangled
40 Woodyates Road
London, England SE 12
(6 issues per year) (USA: $1.25;
Non-USA: $1.00)
Categories: Rock, New Wave,
Punk Rock
Focus: Interviews; Feature
articles

Strawberry Fields Forever
310 Franklin Street–#117
Boston, Massachusetts 02110
(6 issues per year) (USA: $1.00;
Non-USA: $1.50)
Categories: Beatles
Focus: Everything Beatles

Subway News
P.O. Box 149
118 Massachusetts Avenue
Boston, Massachusetts 02115

(6 issues per year) (USA: $1.00; Non-USA: $1.50)
Categories: Rock & Roll, New Wave
Focus: Feature articles; Record reviews; Artist profiles

Sunshine Music
c/o Doc Rock
P.O. Box 1166
Lawrence, Kansas 66044
(4 issues per year) (USA: $1.00; Non-USA: $1.50)
Categories: Jan & Dean Music
Focus: Feature articles; Artist profiles; Official Jan & Dean Authorized International Fan Club newsletter

Survivors
35 Burnside Road
Dagenham
Essex, England
(4 issues per year) (USA: $2.00; Non-USA: $1.50)
Categories: Kinks Music
Focus: Feature Articles; Artist profiles; Discographies

Swing Journal [Japanese and English Language]
c/o Swing Journal Company Limited
3-6-24 Shibakoen
Minato-ku
Tokyo, Japan
(12 issues per year) (USA: $6.00; Non-USA: $6.00)
Categories: Jazz, Popular, Rock
Focus: Feature articles; Record reviews; Artist profiles; Interviews; Concert reviews;

Technical information; New releases listed

Talking Machine Review
19 Glendale Road
Bournemouth, England BH6 4JA
(6 issues per year) (USA: Subscription Only; Non-USA: Subscription Only)
Categories: Any type of music or speech recorded on cylinders or 78 r.p.m. discs or reissued since
Focus: History of recording on cylinders and 78 r.p.m. discs; Feature articles; Artist profiles; History of recording companies; Record reviews; Classified ads; Want lists; Book listings

TB Sheets
c/o Bob Stremel
5632 North El Monte Avenue
Temple City, California 91780
(4 issues per year) (USA: $.50; Non-USA: $1.00)
Categories: Rock, Rock & Roll, New Wave
Focus: Record reviews; Feature articles; Artist profiles; Interviews

Teenage Depression
9 Reddlife Close
Old Brompton Road
London, England SW5 9HK
(6 issues per year) (USA: $2.00; Non-USA: $1.50)
Categories: Rock, New Wave, Punk Rock, Rock & Roll
Focus: Feature articles; Artist profiles; Interviews

Third Wave
218 Shelley Avenue
Elizabeth, New Jersey 07208
(4 issues per year) (USA: $1.00;
   Non-USA: $1.50)
Categories: Rock, Rock & Roll,
   New Wave
Focus: Interviews; Short feature
   articles; Reviews of live
   performances; Artist profiles

Thunder Road
P.O. Box 861
Cypress, California 90630 [West
   Coast]
or
P.O. Box 171
Bogota, New Jersey 07603 [East
   Coast]
(4 issues per year) (USA: $1.25;
   Non-USA: $1.50)
Categories: Bruce Springsteen
   Music, Rock & Roll
Focus: Interviews; Artist profiles

**Time Barrier Express: The Rock
& Roll History Magazine**
P.O. Box 206
Yonkers, New York 10710
(6 issues per year) (USA: $2.00;
   Non-USA: $2.50)
Categories: Classic American
   Rock & Roll with special
   attention given to the 1950s
   and 1960s
Focus: Feature articles; Artist
   profiles; Producer profiles;
   Record label histories;
   Discographies; Collector's
   column; Classified ads; Record
   reviews; Book reviews; Film
   reviews; Fanzine reviews;
   Events of interest to collectors

Top Rankin'
c/o Walt Taylor
P.O. Box 570
Havertown, Pennsylvania 19083
(4 issues per year) (USA: $.50;
   Non-USA: $.75)
Categories: Reggae
Focus: Feature articles

Top of the Rockpile
P.O. Box 1623
Ventura, California 93001
(4 issues per year) (USA: $1.00;
   Non-USA: $1.00)
Categories: Rock, Rock & Roll,
   New Wave
Focus: Feature articles; Artist
   profiles

Trouser Press
P.O. Box B
Old Chelsea Station
New York, New York 10011
(12 issues per year) (USA: $1.50;
   Non-USA: $2.00)
Categories: Rock, Rock & Roll,
   New Wave, Punk Rock
Focus: Feature articles; Artist
   profiles; Interviews; Concert
   reviews

**Trouser Press Collectors'
   Magazine**
P.O. Box 2450
Grand Central Station
New York, New York 10017
(6 issues per year) (USA: $.75;
   Non-USA: $1.25)
Categories: Rock, Rock & Roll,
   New Wave, Punk Rock
Focus: Auction listings; Set-sale
   listings; Collector-oriented
   feature articles; Discographies

Twisted
c/o Ajax
8045 Brooklyn Northeast
Seattle, Washington 98115
(4 issues per year) (USA: $.60;
Non-USA: $1.00)
Categories: Punk Rock
Focus: Party reviews; Artist
profiles; Feature articles;
Information about the
Northwest Punk Rock scene

Two Headed Dog
1222 Rucker
Everett, Washington 98201
(4 issues per year) (USA: $.50;
Non-USA: $.75)
Categories: Rock, Rock & Roll
Focus: Feature articles; Record
reviews; Artist profiles

Vintage Jazz Mart
4 Hillcrest Gardens
Dollis Hill
London, England NW2
(12 issues per year) (USA: $1.00;
Non-USA: $1.00)
Categories: Jazz, Blues, Pre-War
Dance Music
Focus: Auction lists; Set-sale
lists; Primary concern is 78
r.p.m. discs

Vintage Record Mart
16 London Hill
Rayleigh
Essex, England SS6 7HP
(6 issues per year) (USA: $2.00;
Non-USA: $2.00)
Categories: All
Focus: Auction lists; Set-sale
lists; Primary concern is 78
r.p.m. discs; Classified ads;
Photographs

Vocal Art
c/o James Crawley
246 Church Street
Edmonton
London, England N9 9HQ
(6 issues per year) (USA: $2.00;
Non-USA: $2.00)
Categories: Classical, Musical
Comedy, Music Hall
Focus: Feature articles; Listings
of records; Regular listings of
rare operatic records

What Goes On
c/o Philip Milstein
6 Wildwood Lane
Amherst, Massachusetts 01002
(2 issues per year) (USA: $1.00;
Non-USA: $1.50)
Categories: Rock
Focus: Feature articles; Artist
profiles

Whiskey, Women, and ...
c/o Daniel Kochakian
39 Pine Avenue
Haverhill, Massachusetts 01830
(6 issues per year) (USA: $1.00;
Non-USA: $1.25)
Categories: Specifically concerned
with 1940s and 1950s urban
and jump style blues
Focus: Interviews; Discographies;
Rare-record photographs;
Feature articles

White Noise
15865 Fielding
Detroit, Michigan 48223
(6 issues per year) (USA: $1.00;
Non-USA: $1.25)
Categories: Rock & Roll, Punk
Rock, New Wave

Focus: Feature articles; Satirical articles; Artist profiles; Information about the Detroit music scene

The Write Thing
c/o Barb Fenick
1792 Sunny Slope Lane
St. Paul, Minnesota 55116
(6 issues per year) (USA: $1.50; Non-USA: $2.00)
Categories: Beatles
Focus: Feature articles; Photographs; Contests; Set-sale listings; Everything Beatles

Young, Fast, and Scientific
c/o Todd Abramson

P.O. Box 185
Gillette, New Jersey 07933
(2 issues per year) (USA: $1.00; Non-USA: $1.50)
Categories: Rock, Rock & Roll
Focus: Feature articles; Artist reviews; Record reviews

ZigZag
118 Talbot Road
London, England W11
(12 issues per year) (USA: $1.50; Non-USA: $1.50)
Categories: New Wave, Popular, Rock, Rock & Roll, Reggae
Focus: Feature articles; Artist profiles; Interviews

Known Magazines, Journals, Newsletters, and Fanzines Not Responding to Inquiries Seeking Information

The Audio Advisor
Audiophile Directory
Ballroom Blitz
Bells
Big Town Review
Black Box
Blues Friends Worldwide
Blues Magazine
Country Music Explorer
Crazy Music
Creative Guitar International
Dead Relix
Devil's Box
Dig It
Disc
Discographer
Discographical Forum
Eurock
Full Blast
Graphic
Gulcher Magazine
Jazz Down Under
Jazz Report Magazine
Jazz, Rhythm & Blues
Jellyroll Productions
Keep-A-Rockin' International
Make It In The Business World
Matrix
Monthly Detroit
Music Gazette
Music Maker
Music Memories
Music & Musicians
Music Paper Oor

Music World
Musical Newsletter
New Gandy Dancer
No
Nostalgia Journal
Notes
Opera
Penniman News
Piano Quarterly
Ragtimer
Rare Record Review
Raunchy
The Record Finder
The Record Special
Red Hot
Rockpile
RSVP
Rundbrief
Shout
Soul Cargo
Sounds
Sounds Fine
Spooee
Stagione Lirica
Storyville
Sunrise
Synapse
Tempo
Traditional Music
Voices From The Mountains
Way Ahead
Whole Lotta Rockin'
The World of Yesterday

REPRESENTATIVE SAMPLING OF DIRECTORIES, BOOKS, AND GUIDES

DIRECTORIES

APM [Antique Phonograph Monthly] Directory of Phonograph and Record Collectors. Brooklyn, New York: Antique Phonograph Publications, 1979. Allen Koenigsberg, Editor. Lists over 250 collectors. $3.50. Address: 650 Ocean Avenue, Brooklyn, New York, 11226.

The Complete Hard Core of Continental European Record Collectors. Mannheim, West Germany: Rock-Pop Information Service, 1980. Lists over 3,000 names and addresses of European Rock & Roll, Beat, Rock, and New Wave collectors. $1,475.00. Address: c/o Goldmann Verlags GMBH, Hebelstrasse 9 (P.O. Box 907), 6800 Mannheim, West Germany. For dealers only.

Directory of Australian Music Organisations. Sydney, New South Wales, Australia: Australia Music Centre Ltd., 1979. Lists all organizations relevant to the collecting of records. $10.00. Address: Australia Music Centre Ltd., P.O. Box N9, Grosvenor Street, Sydney, New South Wales, Australia 2000.

Jazzman's International Reference Book. New York, New York: International Jazz Federation, Inc., 1980. A handy guide listing thousands of addresses of jazz organizations, clubs, festivals, promoters, radio and television producers, critics, etc. $25.00. Address: International Jazz Federation, Inc., 1697 Broadway, #1203, New York, New York 10019. [Available free with membership.]

Kastlemusick Directory for Collectors of Recordings: Part One. Wilmington, Delaware: Kastlemusick, Inc., 1979. Lists stores, auction and set-sale dealers, recording companies, distributors, importers, exporters, related products, antique phonographs, and relevant publications. $12.95. Address: Kastlemusick, Inc., 901 Washington Street, Wilmington, Delaware 19801. [See Part Two, below; price includes both.]

Kastlemusick Directory for Collectors of Recordings: Part Two. Wilmington, Delaware: Kastlemusick, Inc., 1979. Lists societies, clubs, associations which accept members and publish newsletters and lists private collectors with whom to correspond regarding buying, selling, or trading. $12.95. Address: Kastlemusick, Inc., 901 Washington Street, Wilmington, Delaware 19801. [See Part One, above; price includes both.]

The Record/Tape Collector's Directory, 2nd Edition. Santa Monica, California: Record/Tape Collector's Press, 1978–1979. Lists over 250 record and tape dealers and sellers of all kinds of music in the United

States and Europe as well as publications of potential interest to record and tape collectors. $4.95. Address: Record/Tape Collector's Press, 550 East Rustic Road, Santa Monica, California 90402.

Reference Directory of the Recording Institute of America, Inc. New York, New York: Recording Institute of America Inc., 1979. Lists thousands of names, addresses, and phone numbers of record manufacturers, independent production companies, music publishers, personal managers, and booking agents. $4.95. Address: Recording Institute of America, Inc., 15 Columbus Circle, New York, New York 10023.

The World Jazz Calendar. New York, New York: International Jazz Federation, Inc., 1980. The most comprehensive international jazz festivals directory available; includes names of the events as well as addresses, dates, principal officers, phone numbers, and descriptions; available for June 1980 through June 1981. $15.00. Address: International Jazz Federation, Inc., 1697 Broadway, #1203, New York, New York 10019. [Available free with membership.]

GUIDES AND BOOKS

American Premium Record Guide. By L. R. Docks. Florence, Alabama: Books Americana, 1980. This comprehensive guide includes approximately 45,000 recordings representing over 6,200 artists. Includes listings and values of jazz, dance band, big band, swing band, celebrity, blues, rhythm & blues, country & western, hillbilly, string band, fiddling, rock & roll, rockabilily, and blues records collectively from 1915 through the early 1960s. Also has large selection of label illustrations, complete alphabetical artist index, condition and grading of records. $10.95. Address: Books Americana, P.O. Box 2326, Florence, Alabama 35630.

The Collector's Guide to the American Musical Theatre, 2nd Edition. By David Hummel. Grawn, Michigan: D. H. Enterprises, 1979. A listing of every known show recording by year, including differences between various issues of the same recording, history of the show recording, information about bootleg records, etc. $12.00. Address: D. H. Enterprises, P.O. Box 201, Grawn, Michigan 49637.

Collector's Price Guide to 45 R.P.M. Picture Sleeves. By Lloyd, Ron, and Marvin Davis. Medford, Oregon: Winema Publications, 1979. Lists hundreds of picture sleeves with price range, record label, and number. Covers over 200 recording artists. $7.95. Address: Winema Publications, P.O. Box 172, Medford, Oregon 97501.

Early Rock 45's Records Checklist: 1952–1959. Jacksonville, Illinois: Ladd Publications, Inc., 1978. Pocket-size book lists over 500 singles with specific rock & roll titles issued between 1952 and 1959. $3.00. Address: Ladd Publications, Inc., P.O. Box 137, Jacksonville, Illinois 62651.

Edison Cylinder Records: 1889–1912. By Allen Koenigsberg. Brooklyn, New York: Antique Phonograph Publications, 1979. Chronicles the history of the Edison phonograph from the first tinfoil models to 1912 and catalogs all the cylinders made by the Edison Company in America. The 8,000 selections are arranged chronologically, numerically, and alphabetically by both title and artist. Also contains an illustrated history of the phonograph. $14.95. Address: Antique Phonograph Publications, 650 Ocean Avenue, Brooklyn, New York 11226.

55 Years of Recorded Country/Western Music. By Jerry Osborne and Bruce Hamilton. Phoenix, Arizona: O'Sullivan Woodside & Company, 1978. Traces the history of country/western music from its early days into the revolutionary rockabilly explosion of the early 1950s on to the current scene. Documents the values of these thousands of records. $7.70. Address: O'Sullivan Woodside & Co., 2218 East Magnolia, Phoenix, Arizona 85034.

The 45 R.P.M. Handbook of Oldies. Los Angeles, California: Record Rack Publishers, 1976. A complete guide of over 14,000 hit singles of the past listed alphabetically by artist and song title, record label and number. $7.95. Address: Record Rack Publishers, 1532 South Berendo Street, Los Angeles, California 90006.

A Guide to Record Collecting. By Jerry Osborne and Bruce Hamilton. Phoenix, Arizona: O'Sullivan Woodside & Company, 1978. The complete introduction to collecting records. Tells how to start collecting records, where to buy the records in demand, and who will pay top dollars for old records. Listed are the most collectable recordings in the fields of popular music, rock, movie sound tracks, big band music, country & western, disco, and rhythm & blues. $6.70. Address: O'Sullivan Woodside & Company, 2218 East Magnolia, Phoenix, Arizona 85034

The Illustrated Discography of Surf Music, 1959–1965. By John Blair, Ed. Riverside, California: J. Bee Productions, 1978. The first comprehensive catalog of surf music alphabetically lists over 800 45s and LPs by artist. Also contains over 100 artist, label, and LP cover photographs. $4.00. Address: J. Bee Productions, P.O. Box 1584, Department A, Riverside, California 92502

The Illustrated Encyclopedia of Classical Music. By Lionel Salter. London, England: Salamander Books, Ltd., 1978. Comprehensive listing of over 130 entries arranged by composer and a recommended discography for the definitive collector of classical music. $7.95. Address: Salamander Books, Ltd., 27 Old Gloucester Street, London, England WC1N 3AF.

The Illustrated Encyclopedia of Country Music. By Fred Dellar, Roy Thompson, and Douglas B. Green. London, England: Salamander Books, Ltd., 1977. Comprehensive listing of over 450 of today's superstars in the country field. Also contains selective discographies, over 150 photographs, and over 300 record jackets pictured. $7.95. Address: Salamander Books, Ltd., 27 Old Gloucester Street, London, England WC1N 3AF.

The Illustrated Encyclopedia of Jazz. By Brian Case and Stan Britt. London, England: Salamander Books, Ltd., 1978. Comprehensive listing of over 400 of today's modernists and the traditional pioneers of jazz music. Also contains selective discographies, over 150 photographs, and nearly 300 record jackets pictured. $7.95. Address: Salamander Books, Ltd., 27 Old Gloucester Street, London, England WC1N 3AF.

The Illustrated Encyclopedia of Rock. By Nick Logan and Bob Woffinden. London, England: Salamander Books, Ltd., 1976. Comprehensive listing of over 600 alphabetically arranged entries accompanied by 350 full-color and 90 often rare and/or historical black-and-white photographs. $7.95. Address: Salamander Books, Ltd., 27 Old Gloucester Street, London, England WC1N 3AF.

Casey Kasem's American Top 40 Yearbook. New York, New York: Grosset & Dunlap, Inc., 1979. By Jay Goldsworthy, Ed. The official publication of the worldwide syndicated radio program "American Top 40." Special features include biographies and photographs of every recording act to make the Top 40 charts during the survey year 1978, the weekly *Billboard* magazine Top 40 charts for the survey year, and the final rankings for the top pop, soul, country, disco, and jazz hits, as well as the top album rankings. $4.95. Address: Grosset & Dunlap, Inc., 51 Madison Avenue, New York, New York 10010.

The Official Price Guide to Collectible Rock Records. By Randal C. Hill. Orlando, Florida: House of Collectibles, 1979. Lists over 25,000 current buying and selling prices of the most collectable singles, extended play records, and albums. Also includes a comprehensive listing of over 12,000 memorable song titles recorded by more than 500 artists as well as over 100 rare photographs and biographies of the most famous recording artists in the history of rock & roll. Contains complete Sun discography. $8.95. Address: House of Collectibles, 773 Kirkman Road, No. 120, Orlando, Florida 32811.

Olde Records Price Guide: Classical and Popular 78 R.P.M.'s, 1900–1947. By Peter Soderbergh. Des Moines, Iowa: Wallace-Homestead Books, Inc., 1979. Contains current market prices for swing, big band, dance orchestra, and classical 78's made by over 575 artists 1900–1947. Numerous essays also included. $7.95. Address: Wallace-Homestead Books, Inc., 1912 Grand Avenue, Des Moines, Iowa 50305.

Original Record Collectors Price Guide for Blues, Rhythm & Blues, and Soul. By Jerry Osborne and Bruce Hamilton. Scottsdale, Arizona: Jellyroll Productions, 1979. Comprehensive listing of nearly every important rhythm & blues record and postwar blues record. Contains a chronology of black music from blues to rhythm & blues to soul with latest pricing values. $10.95. Address: Jellyroll Productions, Department 123, P.O. Box 3017, Scottsdale, Arizona 85257.

Pop Annual: 1955–1977. By Joel Whitburn. Menomonee Falls, Wisconsin: Record Research, Inc., 1978. Complete listing of top pop records from 1955 to 1977 including accurate information on record label and number. $50.00. Address: Record Research, Inc., P.O. Box 200, Menomonee Falls, Wisconsin 53051.

Popular & Rock Records 1948–1978, 2nd Edition. By Jerry Osborne and Bruce Hamilton. Phoenix, Arizona: O'Sullivan Woodside & Company, 1979. Spans the entire history of rock music including current collector prices as well as year of release on over 30,000 45's and selected 78's. Special notations are made on prized collectable picture sleeves. $8.70. Address: O'Sullivan Woodside & Company, 2218 East Magnolia, Phoenix, Arizona 85034.

Record Albums 1948–1978. 2nd Edition. By Jerry Osborne and Bruce Hamilton. Phoenix, Arizona: O'Sullivan Woodside & Company, 1978. Contains over 28,000 listings that chronicle the values on popular, rock, country/western, rockabilly, rhythm & blues as well as original cast and movie sound track records. $8.70. Address: O'Sullivan Woodside & Company, 2218 East Magnolia, Phoenix, Arizona 85034.

The Rolling Stone Record Guide. By Dave Marsh and John Swenson, Eds. New York, New York: Random House/Rolling Stone Press, 1979. Reviews 10,000 albums currently available, assigning a rating to each on a scale from indispensable to worthless. Categories include rock, pop, soul, country, blues, jazz, and gospel music. $8.95. Address:

Random House, Inc., 201 East 50th Street, New York, New York 10022.

60 Years of Recorded Jazz. By Walter Bruyninckx. Mechelen, Belgium: Bruyninckx Publishers, 1980. Comprehensive discography consisting of four parts, each containing full information on all recorded artists in the history of jazz. $40.00 per part. Limited Edition: Address: Bruyninckx Publishers, Lange Niewstraat 121, 2800 Mechelen, Belgium.

Top Country Singles: 1949–1971. By Joel Whitburn. Menomonee Falls, Wisconsin: Record Research, Inc., 1979. Complete listing of top country singles from 1949 to 1971, including accurate information on record label and number. $25.00. Address: Record Research, Inc., P.O. Box 200, Menomonee Falls, Wisconsin 53051.

Top Easy Listening Singles: 1961–1974. By Joel Whitburn. Menomonee Falls, Wisconsin: Record Research, Inc., 1979. Complete listing of top easy listening singles from 1961 to 1974, including accurate information on record label and number. $25.00. Address: Record Research, Inc., P.O. Box 200, Menomonee Falls, Wisconsin 53051.

Top LP's: 1945–1972. By Joel Whitburn. Menomonee Falls, Wisconsin: Record Research, Inc., 1979. Complete listing of top albums during this 1945–1972 period, including accurate information on record label and number. $30.00. Address: Record Research, Inc., P.O. Box 200, Menomonee Falls, Wisconsin 53051.

Top Pop Artists & Singles: 1955–1978. By Joel Whitburn. Menomonee Falls, Wisconsin: Record Research, Inc., 1979. Complete listing of all top pop artists and their singles from 1955 to 1978, including accurate information on record label and number. $50.00. Address: Record Research, Inc., P.O. Box 200, Menomonee Falls, Wisconsin 53051.

Top Soul Singles: 1945–1971. By Joel Whitburn. Menomonee Falls, Wisconsin: Record Research, Inc., 1979. Complete listing of all top soul singles from 1945 to 1971, including accurate information on record label and number. $25.00. Address: Record Research, Inc., P.O. Box 200, Menomonee Falls, Wisconsin 53051.

INDEX OF RECORD DEALERS
LISTED BY CATEGORY
OF RECORDING

For dealers who carry all major categories of recordings, see the index entry "All Major Categories."

INDEX OF RECORD DEALERS
LISTED ALPHABETICALLY

CANADIAN RECORD DEALERS